VICTORY CELEBRATIONS

PRISONERS

THE LOVE-GIRL AND
THE INNOCENT

VICTORY CELEBRATIONS

PRISONERS

THE LOVE-GIRL AND THE INNOCENT

Three Plays
by

ALEXANDER
SOLZHENITSYN

Farrar, Straus and Giroux
New York

CONTENTS

PUBLISHER'S NOTE

This volume contains a trilogy of plays conceived by the author in the years 1952–3 while under sentence of hard labour in the Gulag, and they appear in order of composition. *The Love-Girl and the Innocent* reached dress-rehearsal stage in Moscow, but was banned by the authorities at the last moment. In 1981 it was produced by the Royal Shakespeare Company. The other two plays have never been publicly performed.

VICTORY CELEBRATIONS

A Comedy

Translated from the Russian
by Helen Rapp and Nancy Thomas

DRAMATIS PERSONAE

Lieutenant-Colonel BERBENCHUK, Divisional Commander,
Special Army Artillery Reconnaissance

Major VANIN, Divisional Deputy Commander, Political
Branch

Captain DOBROKHOTOV-MAIKOV, Staff Captain

Captain NERZHIN, Commander, Radio-Intelligence Unit

Captain LIKHARYOV, Commander, Topographical
Intelligence Unit

Lieutenant GRIDNEV, accredited officer of Counter-
Intelligence, SMERSH

Captain ANECHKA, Divisional Medical Officer, Vanin's
wartime "wife"

GLAFIRA, Berbenchuk's wife

GALINA

Lieutenant PROKOPOVICH, technician

Divisional PARTY ORGANISER, "liberated"

Divisional CHIEF CHEMIST

Lieutenant YACHMENNIKOV, Platoon Commander in
Nerzhin's unit

KATYA ⎱
OLYA ⎰ , girls from the neighbouring unit

SALIY   ⎱ indistinguishable pair of Tartar Red Army
ZAMALIY ⎰ , soldiers

The divisional COOK

DYAGILEV, soldier

Radio Operator

Staff Sergeants and soldiers

The action takes place on 25 January 1945, in East Prussia.

11

PUBLISHER'S NOTE

This play, in the original Russian, is in iambic verse.
The translators' notes are printed on pages 94–5.

The set for the four acts remains the same throughout. It is the hall of an ancient castle. On the right, there are several curtained windows. In front of them, there is a grand piano, a small round table and some armchairs. At the back, tall double doors, flanked by ordinary ones. All around the hall is a portrait gallery of military ancestors, and above that a musicians' gallery. To the left, there is a small table with a radio transmitter, and odd bits of furniture. Downstage a radiogram, and downstage of that a staircase leading up. From above there hangs a grand but unlit chandelier. When the current is on, a few bright bulbs fixed up temporarily in the chandelier emit a strong light.

ACT ONE

The stage is in complete darkness, apart from the red glow of the transmitter light. From the back one can hear the ringing tones of:

MAIKOV: Hold on, hold on, don't drop it, chaps. You, up there with the rope.

A VOICE (*from above at the back*): The rope is holding, sir.

MAIKOV: Careful now. Saliy, some lights in here, whatever you can find. (*Quietly.*) No questions? Gently now. We'll edge it down. You, Zamaliy, where are you?

A VOICE: Here, sir.

MAIKOV: Get the technician. At the double!

A variety of flickering lights appear simultaneously through the doors at the back, on the gallery, on the stairs. They are torches, lighted candelabra, candles, oil lamps and flares. They are all in motion. What gradually emerges from the darkness is an enormous wall mirror, several metres high, which reflects the lights on to the audience as it is slowly

13

*lowered sideways. It is being held up by soldiers with batons
and bare hands from below and by ropes from above. In
front, at the little table on the right, two female figures are
revealed.*

MAIKOV: Come on, light bearers! The torches, the candles!
All right, up there?

A VOICE (*from the gallery*): O.K. up here.

MAIKOV: Gently now. Hold it up, hold it. With your
shoulder. Catch it, catch it. Hold on!

*The mirror slips more and more on its side and finally reaches
the floor with its shiny side facing the audience. It is stood on
its edge. A pause. The ropes are being untied.*

MAIKOV: That's army discipline, that is! Right. Let's lift it.
On to the stools.

*The mirror is propped up against the stools which are there,
ready waiting.*

GALINA: What's the mirror for?

MAIKOV: Well, it's Columbus's egg. A very simple idea.
But I must confess, a bit of swank on my part. There is
to be a celebration in our unit, a big dinner, a big show,
and not a table in the hall. Got nicked, I suppose.

*A bright electric light blazes up in the chandelier, after which
all the other lights are put out and taken away, apart from
two or three forgotten candles. Some fifteen soldiers can be
seen moving around arranging things. They eventually leave.
DOBROKHOTOV-MAIKOV is a slim officer of medium
height with a blond moustache and a military bearing. He
wears many medals. Now and again he unnecessarily clanks
his spurs. At the table on the right sit diminutive ANECHKA
in military uniform, and GALINA, soberly dressed, mainly in
black. The RADIO OPERATOR is bent over the transmitter.
The mirror sparkles at the audience.*

MAIKOV (*measuring*): Not too low? (*He leans elegantly on the
carved legs of the mirror support which are now sticking
forward. To* GALINA) An inspiration, dear lady. You, as
a pianist, will know that it is not subject to logic. (*He
gestures to the soldiers who return from off stage to lift the*

14

mirror on to the stools, shiny side upwards.) Over here,
right under the chandelier. It overwhelms us,
unexpectedly, menacingly! The way Surikov[1] envisaged
Lady Morozova[2] as a crow on the snow, one wing aloft.
Come, Dyagilev, off with these mirror legs.
He moves away, giving orders. DYAGILEV, *an elderly man,
strokes the mirror legs affectionately, having been told to
break them off.*

ANECHKA: You see, I am younger than he is by twelve
years.

DYAGILEV: Got to use your head . . .

ANECHKA: Perhaps this difference is for the best?

DYAGILEV: They're pinned as well as glued . . .

RADIO OPERATOR: I'm receiving. I'm receiving.

MAIKOV (*to* DYAGILEV): Stop thinking about it. Chop
them off.

A sergeant enters quickly, and pointedly salutes MAIKOV.
PROKOPOVICH *is behind him; he assumes an excessively
unmilitary and gloomy pose, standing for a long time at the
back, as if unnoticed by* MAIKOV.

MAIKOV: Well, Sergeant?

SERGEANT: It's about the table cloth . . .

MAIKOV: A concert grand . . . And Gothic gloom . . . And a
white table cloth. No, all wrong. No table cloth. Tell them to
unload the fifth Studebaker. The whole on to this mirror.
The sergeant salutes.

GALINA: My school friend and I used to devour romantic
novels. But, when all's said and done, it's nothing but a
sad tale of men's love withering away . . .

DYAGILEV (*continuing timidly to examine the mirror legs*): Did
you say chop them off, Comrade Captain?

MAIKOV: I said off with them.

DYAGILEV *taps gently with the haft of his axe.*

ANECHKA: Well?

GALINA: Well, if that's inevitable, there's nothing more
reassuring than an elderly husband. He'll never let you
down, not ever.

MAIKOV (*moving* DYAGILEV *aside*): Come on, Burlov,
give it a bash.

*Another soldier spits into his palms, and, taking the axe,
knocks the mirror support off in two blows.* ANECHKA
blocks up her ears. The soldiers, under the direction of
MAIKOV *and of the* SERGEANT, *begin bringing in a vast
amount of refreshments from the corridor and arranging them
on plates, dishes, in decanters, in glass jars and in tins. They
carry in lots of crockery, china, silver and crystal glasses, as
well as flowers. The enormous "table" is covered completely
with food and wine. The soldiers are trained to a T and
operate with the precision of circus performers.* MAIKOV'S
conducting gestures are theatrical.

MAIKOV: I'm interested to know, Prokopovich, are you an
officer or a vicar's son. What have you come for?

PROKOPOVICH (*about to leave*): Excuse me, I was told you
seemed to want me.

MAIKOV: "Seemed" nothing. I did want you. But you
stand there like a sack of potatoes. What happened?
There wasn't any light. A fault? A fuse?

PROKOPOVICH (*woefully*): A fuse . . .

MAIKOV: The men can't work in the dark. Bear that in
mind. The light isn't to go out tonight for a second. Is
that clear?

PROKOPOVICH (*shuffling*): My function, formally
speaking . . .

MAIKOV (*in a theatrical whisper*): What did you say?
Answering back? That's bad. What about your thousand
a month? What about the extra ration? In Civvy Street
you'd get it in the neck for that extra butter. Where do
you think you are, at war, or on holiday? And who's to
repair the arm of my radiogram? And who, forgive the
crude image, is to keep the bloody show on the road? An
Abyssinian prince, perhaps?

GALINA: But Anechka, all this fruit, this wine. Is it usual?

ANECHKA: Oh, no. We're celebrating today.

MAIKOV: I've been too soft on you as it is. Get down to

16

work and start on the radiogram.

Thereafter PROKOPOVICH *examines the fault, comes and goes carrying a screwdriver, a soldering iron, radio components, and settles down to his repairs. Things are still being brought in to put on the mirror, but less frequently.*

ANECHKA: You will, of course, join us at table. You've already met the divisional commander and his wife. As for me, you're probably thinking there's nothing in that head of hers: the way she pours her heart out the moment she enters the room.

GALINA: No, don't say that!

ANECHKA: I hardly ever get the chance. I'm always among men, a bivouac existence. I've been missing feminine company. You *will* come?

GALINA: It's a bit awkward . . .

ANECHKA: Not another word.

MAIKOV (*still making arrangements, but overhearing snatches of their conversation*): And you will be the princess of the Staff ball. I'd have said you'd be the queen, but you know the size of the division . . .

ANECHKA: Go away. You have this terrible habit of interfering in women's talk.

MAIKOV: I'm going.

ANECHKA: That's almost all there'll be. No need to bother about the Head of the Chemical Unit, or the sound technician. You'll also meet the Party Organiser – not much joy there; a couple of battery commanders, but they're nice enough chaps. Here's one now.

LIKHARYOV (*entering from the corridor, with a touch of foxtrot in his step, walks towards the radiogram. He too is wearing spurs, and has an excellent military bearing. He hums*):

Es geht alles vorüber, es geht alles vorbei,

Und nach jedem Dezember kommt wieder ein Mai . . .

MAIKOV: You're on the slippery slope, old son.

LIKHARYOV: Shall I choose a few records while there's time? (*Choosing.*)

MAIKOV: You've forgotten your native land, your native Provence.

LIKHARYOV: I get along, while there's still a chance.

MAIKOV: Oh, Ivan, was it you
            Who all these years of war
            Was sweaty, torn and footsore?

LIKHARYOV (*straightening his coat*): Is my jacket all right, Comrade Captain? Not too tight in the shoulder? (*He selects some records, and carries away a batch, dancing and glancing at* GALINA):
            Es geht alles vorüber, es geht alles vorbei
            Und nach jedem Dezember . . .

ANECHKA: As for me, I'm a bit shy about dressing up. Even a tiny touch of colour seems vulgar with my kind of clothes. It's sad. I'd try things on and end up wearing a military shirt. Even before the war, at college, I used to dress like a school girl. It's a pity I can't do it now.

GALINA: There're lots of things to wear, anything you like. The owner's wardrobe is . . . Come to my room.

ANECHKA: Thank you, love, I'll come. But will there be something . . .

GALINA: I'm sure there will. I used to be like you, but those Viennese taught me a thing or two.

RADIO OPERATOR: Ryazan calling. That's how it works. Kostroma calling. I'm receiving loud and clear.

MAIKOV: When are you going to change your call signal, you fool.

RADIO OPERATOR (*waving a bit of paper*): I've got them here. I just can't get used to these foreign names.

MAIKOV: "We are Scythians, we are Asiatics"[3] and yet we shovelled out the French. When the Germans barged in, we shoved them out. Hey, Prokopovich, what's your view of the Slavs?

PROKOPOVICH: I'm busy, Comrade Captain, can't you see?

MAIKOV: Oh, hell. No one to talk to.

ANECHKA: I'd like to warn you, don't call me Anechka.

Address me formally. This is the army and I'm an
officer . . .

GALINA: Yes, of course. Must abide by the rules.

RADIO OPERATOR: Comrade Captain, the second battery,
BZR, is leaving the battlefield and Nerzhin will be here
in an hour.

PROKOPOVICH *gets the radiogram working. Music.*

MAIKOV: It took you two hours to transmit the order. Get
your stuff out of here.

RADIO OPERATOR *removes his transmitter. Galina is
trying to hide her excitement.*

GALINA: Excuse me. I . . . I can't have heard it right.
What name did he say, what name?

ANECHKA: Which? Nerzhin?

GALINA: Yes.

ANECHKA: Do you know him?

GALINA: No. That is . . . I used to know someone . . .
And BZR?

ANECHKA: I would decipher it for you, but I mustn't. Our
divisional operations are secret.

GALINA: Where's he from?

ANECHKA: Who?

GALINA: Nerzhin.

ANECHKA: From Rostov.

GALINA: Can't be him then.

ANECHKA: Aren't you from his district? Didn't you
mention . . .

GALINA: You must have misheard . . .

ANECHKA: Really? Well, maybe. (*Impulsively.*) Can I be of
help? You seem worried. I've been watching you all
evening – something is oppressing you, some fear, some
anguish . . .

GALINA: You have a kind heart. Thank you for that. But
in this no one can help me.

The table is ready, although MAIKOV *is still moving things
around. The soldiers have stopped going backwards and
forwards.* PROKOPOVICH *is still working on the radiogram.*

19

The music is cut short. GLAFIRA *comes in quickly; she is
rather portly; her hands are full with a gleaming kettle and
something wrapped up in a cloth.*

GLAFIRA: Who's here? Oh, it's you, you poor suffering
thing! You've been saved, but how many are there still
awaiting liberation, wretched slaves. I took you to my
heart – close, so close. I'm all a-tremble.

ANECHKA: Are you ill?

GLAFIRA: How I hate them. Just let me get hold of some
damned Fritz: I'll scratch his eyes out. To seize this
wonderful girl! Nazis! A slave market!

PROKOPOVICH: Up – to get radio stations: down – for
records.

GLAFIRA: Staff Captain! Tell him off ! Why do the lights
fail all the time?

MAIKOV *dismisses* PROKOPOVICH *with a gesture.*

GLAFIRA: I've been wandering about here and there, and
went to investigate the kitchen. Just look, on a shelf,
these twenty-nine little white china jars. (*She tips them
out of the cloth and arranges them on a small round table.*)
The tops are perforated and there's something written on
them. Of course I don't speak foreign languages, but I
licked each one – that's pepper, poppy, mustard, fennel;
this is dill, vanilla, ground nuts, carraway, cinnamon.
Well, of course, I grabbed the lot. They'll do fine. But I
mustn't go on like this. Maikov, what am I to do with all
my things? And then, just look, a lovely little pair of
false teeth.

ANECHKA: You poor thing. I didn't know you hadn't any
teeth . . .

GLAFIRA: Of course I've got teeth. But you never know
what might happen. If not for myself, then I can always
flog them. Hundreds of people ask for them in towns.
And now look. I've discovered quite by chance that this
isn't at all an ordinary kettle. Oh, Frau! That monster
Hitler looks after his own. Put this kettle on the stove,
and there's no need to watch it. All on its own, as soon

as it starts to boil, it starts to whistle. Boy, does it
whistle! As soon as I heard it whistle I said to myself –
that's just what we need. But I mustn't go on like this.
What am I to do with all my things? Where am I to stow
my luggage? A most intricate kettle: I wouldn't mind a
dozen of them. Staff Captain!

MAIKOV: Madam, with due respect to you and your family,
I can't allocate more than three pairs of cart horses and
two motor cars for your transport.

GLAFIRA: If the divisional commander orders you to, you'll
do it. What does he give me? Three pairs of cart horses.
Am I to lie down and die in this land of our enemies?

ANECHKA: You know, Glafira, you're a bit odd. You
shouldn't attack the commander and the unit like this.

GALINA: I think Comrade Doctor, I'll go up to my room.
I'll wait for you there. (*Moves towards the staircase.*)

GLAFIRA: Why? What's the matter?

ANECHKA: Nothing, nothing.

GALINA: To try on some clothes . . .

GLAFIRA: Who is trying on clothes? She is? There's no
point, Galina. Her tiny size, her chest . . . Let her stay
in her uniform. The major won't mind. But, have you a
large selection?

SALIY – *or is it* ZAMALIY? – *one cannot tell them apart –
comes running in through the door on the right, leaving it
ajar. He is out of breath.*

SALIY: It's the divisional commander! A major with him,
and some fat lady lieutenant! (*He nods towards the door
through which one now can see in the distance another large
room.*)

MAIKOV (*in a rush*): Come on, my fairy princess! Remove
your loot!

GLAFIRA *rapidly collects the jars into her cloth, and picks
up the kettle.* SALIY *disappears.* GALINA *comes to a halt
on the first step of the staircase.* MAIKOV *issues his
commands as if on the parade ground, but with a touch of
humour.*

21

Att-en-tion! To the right, dress! (*Marches off with a military step towards the piano, opens it.*) Musicians, quick march! (*Plays, while standing, Mozart's "Turkish Rondo".*) *There enter, to the strains of music, from the depths of the second large room a tall imposing Lieutenant-Colonel* BERBENCHUK, *adorned with many medals, a ruby-cheeked, thickset Major* VANIN, *and a very young Lieutenant* GRIDNEV, *whose prematurely puffy face is cherubic.* MAIKOV *stops playing, and with a sternness of voice suitable for the parade ground, but with the same touch of theatricality, announces:*

Comrade Colonel! Permit me to report! Everything is ready for the celebratory dinner!

BERBENCHUK *pompously acknowledges the report, makes a gesture of "dismiss", moves forward and examines the mirror.*

BERBENCHUK: A sumptuous spread. (*With emphasis.*) No slaughtering of livestock?

MAIKOV: I let them live.

BERBENCHUK: And no harm to the civilians?

MAIKOV: Didn't find any.

BERBENCHUK (*looking at* GRIDNEV): In which case, I suppose we deserve this treat.

GRIDNEV: As Suvorov[4] used to say, what's won on the field of battle is sacred.

BERBENCHUK: Well said. And to the point. I must confess it would be a pity not to avail oneself of what's been won on the battlefield. May I present the accredited representative of Counter-Intelligence SMERSH, and Staff Captain.

MAIKOV: Maikov.

GRIDNEV: Gridnev.

They shake hands. MAIKOV *pulls him along downstage, walking between* ANECHKA *and* GLAFIRA, *who has frozen, still holding the cloth and the kettle.*

MAIKOV: De-lighted. Delight-ed!

GRIDNEV: What are you delighted about?

MAIKOV: That our establishment is complete. Don't laugh at me, but I hate holes in establishments, as well as in trousers. No establishment is complete without its own SMERSH agent. So why not us? And here you are, sent to us. I love the SMERSH lot. We must establish close friendship and have a drink to start with. Now I would like to introduce our Medical Officer, the Divisional Doctor Grigoryeva.

GRIDNEV: Delighted. What do they say – a snake around the goblet?

ANECHKA: That's a witty beginning, but I'm at a loss – what snakes, which goblet?
She moves over to VANIN, *her heels clicking firmly, and introduces him to* GALINA *at the foot of the stairs.*

MAIKOV (*nudging* GRIDNEV *in the ribs*): What's your first name then?

GRIDNEV: Vladimir.

MAIKOV: Vlad? Well, I'm Alex . . .

GRIDNEV: I don't quite follow . . .

MAIKOV: Stop being so fierce. You'll follow all right. That's the way I am, see? We're generous – there! (*Slaps him on the shoulder.*) Couldn't be better . . . Everything will go swimmingly!

BERBENCHUK: Hmm, yes . . . This . . . actually . . . this is my wife. I've got Army permission for her to come with me.

GLAFIRA (*freeing one hand which she stretches out like a stick*): Glafira Berbenchuk.

GRIDNEV (*greets* GLAFIRA *reservedly, addresses* BERBENCHUK): You've got Army permission, did you say?

BERBENCHUK: Yes, yes. I filed a special application. After all, I've been in the Army for twenty years, training, campaigns, let's face it.

GRIDNEV: I see. However, there are three women here. On our way here I thought you mentioned two . . .

BERBENCHUK: This third one . . . is . . .

GLAFIRA: A slave. Snatched from Hitler's claws . . .

MAIKOV: Hey, look at you! Taking quite an interest in skirts, I see . . .

GRIDNEV: Now, look here. You're getting a bit too familiar.

MAIKOV: Sorry, old chap. I'm a simple man. I want to have fun, to share my experiences, to open my heart, I hope you don't stick by the rules, Yes sir! No sir! May I be permitted to report, sir!

GALINA (*to* VANIN): No, no, just call me Galina.

GLAFIRA (*summoning* BERBENCHUK *who is moving towards the group of people by the staircase*): Eugene, it's time to dress for dinner. (*Taking hold of him, she leads him to one of the doors.*)

GRIDNEV: Our work is such that we are allowed to by-pass army regulations.

MAIKOV: Not another word . . .

BERBENCHUK (*on his way out*): Captain Maikov.

MAIKOV: Here.

BERBENCHUK: Make arrangements for our guest.

MAIKOV: Certainly, sir.

BERBENCHUK: Supper in an hour?

MAIKOV: As you say, sir. An hour.

Exeunt GLAFIRA *and* BERBENCHUK.

MAIKOV (*to* GRIDNEV): I must dash to the kitchen, but just let me say one thing: you've touched a sore spot. A combat soldier knows how to get out of bed at night; he knows how to rattle off double quick both the field and the unwritten code by heart; he's part of the garrison; he's all discipline. Isn't that so?

GRIDNEV: I suppose so . . .

MAIKOV: Come on, say it. Isn't that so?

GRIDNEV: Yes, it is.

MAIKOV: Well, I'm doing you a favour, you idiot. I'm doing my best for you.

He leaves quickly, after VANIN *and* ANECHKA.

GRIDNEV: Miss!

24

GALINA *continues upstairs.*

Miss!

GALINA *slows down.*

GRIDNEV: One moment!

GALINA *stops at the top of the staircase;* GRIDNEV *is in the centre of the stage at the foot. During the rest of the act the electric light steadily fades, the stage growing darker and darker.*

GRIDNEV: Come down here for a second.

GALINA: I'm in a hurry.

GRIDNEV: What are you in a hurry about?

GALINA: What is it you want?

GRIDNEV: I have this little business to discuss with you.

GALINA: I'm listening.

GRIDNEV: No, it's me who's going to do the listening. You'll be *telling.*

GALINA: What?

GRIDNEV: Come on down.

GALINA: I can hear you from here.

GRIDNEV: I don't want to shout.

GALINA: Shout? What right have you to shout?

GRIDNEV: This little purple book . . . (*pulls out his credentials*) do you know its power? (*He turns over the pages.*) Whoever presents this has a right . . . to detain civilians . . . to investigate . . . Do you know the limits of my rights? Come on then. Come down!

GALINA *descends a few steps.*

More.

GALINA *descends a bit more.*

More!

GALINA *is almost down.*

Come here. I see you're nervous . . .

GALINA: The way you're behaving . . . (*She can hardly stand up, and leans on the mirror.*)

GRIDNEV: That's neither here nor there. Let's be precise. There's always a reason for being nervous. He whose conscience is clear before his Country isn't . . . Have you got some certificate, some German *pass?*

GALINA: No.

GRIDNEV: No? Why not? The Germans used to issue passes to our people. That's no secret.

GALINA: Not to us.

GRIDNEV: Who's us?

GALINA: Slave labour from the East.

GRIDNEV: Did they give you something instead?

GALINA: Oh, yes, a badge.

GRIDNEV: Yes, I know. I'm just having a little joke. You've unpicked your little badge very neatly: not a trace, no tell-tale mark, Miss er . . .

GALINA: Pavlova.

GRIDNEV: Wonderful, wonderful! Do you know, there was a philosopher in England, an agnostic, Hume. He used to say – don't trust your eyes.

GALINA: Can I go?

GRIDNEV: Yes, of course you can go.

GALINA *hurriedly ascends the first steps.*

GRIDNEV: Let me ask you one more question.

GALINA *stops.*

GRIDNEV: Where are you from?

GALINA: From Kharkov.

GRIDNEV: You don't say! So am I. I know every bit of Kharkov by heart. Even the houses and their numbers. Come on, give us a smile. It would be nice to remember our younger days . . . The chances of war . . . When were you liberated?

GALINA: When was I what?

GRIDNEV: I'm saying, when did they set you free?

GALINA: Oh, I see, *liberated*. Last night.

GRIDNEV: Where?

GALINA (*coming down*): Here.

GRIDNEV: So, you lived here?

GALINA: I did.

GRIDNEV: How long for?

GALINA: About a year. I can't remember exactly.

GRIDNEV: What were you doing here?

GALINA: I was a servant.

GRIDNEV: What kind? A cook? A milk-maid?

GALINA: No, a chambermaid.

GRIDNEV: But in Kursk, what did you do?

GALINA: In *Kharkov* I was a student.

GRIDNEV: A nice little place to spend the war in. One is
tempted to say . . . A starched apron, a lace collar. The
master of the house – some grinning S.S. Officer, so
gentle in the family circle . . .

GALINA: You know perfectly well, we were taken by force.

GRIDNEV: But it is *you* they chose. After all, you're not
unique. Who was it you managed to please? The Nazis,
or just men?

GALINA: But what was I to do?

GRIDNEV: You could have joined the army, the partisans.
You could have been a Zoya Kosmodemyanskaya.[5] But
not you, my little bird. You worked it all out perfectly.
What you've forgotten is that we were going to come,
that we *have* come! Just look out of the window. (*He
goes to the window and pulls back the curtains.*)
*Shimmering blue light floods the ball-room, where the light of
the electric bulbs is already dim.*
Have a look! The night is blue. Look how many
headlights over the three autobahns! That's your death
rolling in! That's fate delivering its avenging blow!
GALINA *has turned towards the window. She makes a
momentary gesture of despair behind* GRIDNEV's *back.*

GRIDNEV: And look at all those fires – one, two three! (*He
hits his chest with his fist.*) We risked our lives in front of
the tanks. We sacrificed ourselves for our beloved Leader
and our country. While you stayed here, curled up on a
couch, book in hand. Have a look – the artillery, the
motorised infantry, the cavalry! And do you imagine the
glorious Intelligence of the Cheka will put on kid gloves
for you? You thought you could sneak in under the
protection of Stalin's sacred flag at the moment of

victory. Didn't Mayakovsky[6] say: he who is not with us
is against us? (*Advances on* GALINA. *She moves away,
and, tripping over a chair, sits down.*) Your entire life,
your friends, your meetings, where you are from and
why you stayed behind here all by yourself, our
Intelligence network knows all about you in detail. We
can see right through you! Come on, cards on the table.
Your mask is off! (*He bangs on the table.*) You've lost!
GALINA *droops. A pause.*

One thing could remove half your guilt in the eyes of the
people: if you say you're sorry and make a clean breast
of it. Who gave you secret instructions? What was your
assignment here?

At the last words GALINA *lifts her head in surprise, and a
faint smile lights up her face.*

GALINA: Oh, Lord! Such pitiless words, said in such
threatening tones. Do you like chocolates? I've always
had a sweet tooth. (*Rising.*) Let's pinch some while
nobody's looking. (*She takes a handful out of a dish and
offers them to* GRIDNEV.) Do have some with me. Don't
worry, they're not poisoned! Ha, you look terrified. Did
you think I was left behind to offer poison to Soviet
officers? Never fear, these chocolates are delicious: they
melt in the mouth. (*She eats one.*) Well, I'll eat it on my
own, and like a faithful dog will die in agonies, crawling
towards the door. Won't you be sorry? Or would you be
pleased that your prognosis was perfectly correct?

GRIDNEV: Are you having me on?

GALINA: Oh, no, you're quite right. Everything you've said
is true. I am a woman born to be happy! I don't care
what country it's in, and under what idiotic government.
I can't stand uniforms. I prefer to wear a dress. I
wouldn't exchange fashionable shoes for an aircraft
gunner's boots, nor my silk stockings for a soldier's
socks. Where did you get the idea that I wanted to be
free? I can be a slave if I want to. I want a home and
family. How could such brilliant minds imagine that I

want to drive a tractor? Maybe I was destined to be a
butterfly. Perhaps I was born to be a Geisha girl. You
can talk about equality for a hundred years, but you can
have it as far as I'm concerned. We used to have quite a
good time without it. What's all this rubbish – as if I
owed something to somebody all the time . . . I never
took anything from you . . . I've eaten three chocolates,
and I'm still alive. Do try one.

GRIDNEV *hesitates*.

Shame on you. Turning a lady down. And in any case
what's all this stuff in aid of? Why all this melodrama?
You yourself don't believe a word of it. People in smart
uniforms like yours don't throw themselves in front of
tanks. Suppose, through some chance of war, you'd
found yourself in Crete, I bet you'd have said: To hell
with it all, and fallen in love with a Greek girl . . .
Where am I from? From Kharkov? From Rovno? Did I
lead a blameless life? Well, not quite. But am I guilty
before the Soviet people just because I'm good-looking?
Why, when you're so young as to be barely out of the
spotty stage, are you so keen to become a spy? The way
you talk – trumpets, oaths, corpses – one day you'll be
ashamed of all this nonsense!

GRIDNEV: Miss Pavlova, I hope I didn't . . .

GALINA (*walking round the table*): Didn't, kidn't,
fidn't . . .

GRIDNEV (*following her*): Let's make friends.

GALINA (*offering her little finger*): My bones ache.

GRIDNEV: You're quite right of course, and I'm wrong.
But I'm sorry, and being sorry . . .

GALINA: Removes half the guilt.

GRIDNEV: You must forgive me. In the line of duty I had
to . . .

GALINA: You didn't have to anything. Don't you
understand that?

GRIDNEV (*pursuing her*): Miss Pavlova: Which is your
room?

29

GALINA: So that's it! All leading to that.

GRIDNEV: Yes, that's it. I'll not let you go . . . I love you.

GALINA: Don't use that word!

GRIDNEV: Galina, my darling, my sweetheart (*embracing her*).

GALINA (*tearing herself free*): Let go!

GRIDNEV: Only till morning.

GALINA: And after that?

GRIDNEV: After that I'll let you go behind the lines. I'll get you a pass, some papers. Or else, if you like, you can stay here, with me. You can travel with me. How about it?

GALINA: I don't see how . . .

GRIDNEV: We'll think of something. My secretary, say. Come on, Galina, my sweet, look at me. In wartime you can get away with anything. Who'll know?

Attempts to kiss her. GALINA *tears herself away.*

GALINA (*raising her voice*): I'll scream.

GRIDNEV (*rooted to the spot*): All right then. Go on, scream. As one great Humanist put it – if the enemy does not submit, destroy it.

A pause. They stand apart.

Scream! Scream! As loud as you can. When your defenders come running . . . You must have been away from the Soviet Union for a long time. You don't know the meaning of this blue stripe. Let them come running. I only have to say: I have a-rres-ted her! That's all. After that you'll find yourself deserted. You'll be locked up in the cellar. Five days, no food, no sleep!

GALINA (*slumps*): So. A woman has only two choices: to be locked up in a cell, or to be a tart.

GRIDNEV (*approaching slowly*): Don't be so stubborn. You've nothing to lose. Just this one night. After that we'll go our separate ways. You can do what you like.

The bulbs are quite dim. The blue light through the windows grows ever more purple from the reflection of the fires. As it grows dark, the light from the forgotten candles become more

noticeable. SALIY *comes running in and stands to attention.*
What do you want?

SALIY (*saluting*): Private Saliy, sir. I am to conduct you to
your quarters.

GRIDNEV (*hesitating. To* GALINA): I'll see you in your room
. . . Just remember, there are guards at every exit and
entrance.

He and SALIY *go out.* GALINA *walks over to the staircase,
mounts a few steps, but comes down again. She wanders
listlessly about the stage. She draws the curtains together, one
after another. She sits at the piano, her head bent. Then she
begins to play. While she is playing she doesn't notice that
Captain* NERZHIN *has entered. He isn't wearing his
greatcoat. He stops and listens, and then sits down silently.
When* GALINA *stops playing:*

NERZHIN: Darf ich Sie bitten, gnädiges Fräulein, ein
bisschen noch?

GALINA jumps up. NERZHIN *rises too. They look
searchingly at each other.*

GALINA: Sergei!!

NERZHIN: Galina!

*They kiss briefly; touch hands rapidly; talk, interrupting each
other. The candle light is dim.*

I . . .

GALINA: I, too . . .

NERZHIN: Did you retreat with the Germans?

GALINA: Oh, dear. That's a long story . . . I don't
recognise you. In your uniform! A captain! I went to
study at the Vienna Conservatoire. To learn the piano.

NERZHIN: How do you mean – in Vienna?

GALINA: In Vienna, yes, which is haunted by the ghosts of
Mozart, Haydn! But what about Liussia? I met her in
the bomb shelter, just before the surrender of Rostov.
She was as white as a sheet . . .

NERZHIN: She fled to the Caucasus. And then, further and
further into the mountains, under fire, along goat tracks.
She got to Kazakhstan, half dead. But do explain . . .

GALINA: Oh, Lord, there's so much to tell you, Sergei. (*Walking about restlessly.*) Where can we go? Come to my room . . . No, you can't do that.

NERZHIN: Why, what's the matter? What are you afraid of?

GALINA: You must be careful, too, if you have anything to do with me.

NERZHIN (*undoing the holster of his pistol*): Why, any Germans here?

GALINA: If that was all. Some half-baked Cheka type is prowling around.

NERZHIN: You must be dreaming. This is Staff H.Q. of our Unit.

GALINA: Aren't you afraid?

NERZHIN: Afraid? What of?

GALINA: Am I glad you're here. As soon as you go – where are you going? You will take me with you? Please say you can – I beg of you!

NERZHIN: I don't understand . . .

GALINA: You'll understand soon enough.

NERZHIN: Of course I'll take you, but I'm going to the front . . .

GALINA: Which front?

NERZHIN: Does it matter to you?

GALINA: It's terribly important to me which front. Just give me a lift. I'll get off at some point and try to get there myself. Oh, Igor, Igor! This miracle proves you are right: God does exist, somewhere in Heaven.

NERZHIN (*looking around*): Who are you talking to? Who's Igor?

GALINA: My fiancé.

NERZHIN: Is he here?

GALINA: No, luckily not: he's not one of you.

NERZHIN: So he's with them?

GALINA: Yes, he's with us.

NERZHIN: I can't understand a word you're saying. Sit down and tell me all, in the proper order. You're getting married?

GALINA: Yes, I am. Wait a bit, I'll tell you everything.
Look, I'm still shaking. He was interrogating me
here . . .

NERZHIN: Who was?

GALINA: That Cheka type.

NERZHIN: What type?

GALINA: The type with horns.

NERZHIN: Calm down. You're with me now. What's more,
here, close to the front, they've not got much power over
us.

GALINA: You used to be such a weedy student, but look at
you now – you're taller, harder. Your voice, your
gestures, are so mature. They say the battle front is
horrible, and yet it regenerates men, the way
motherhood regenerates women. When are you leaving?
Soon, I hope. I must escape, I must get away.

NERZHIN: What's the hurry? You're not among wild
beasts.

GALINA: Almost.

NERZHIN: What's going on here. Has the mirror fallen
down?

GALINA: They're having a celebration.

NERZHIN: But why are *you* here? How did you get to this
place?

GALINA: Not all at once, Comrade Captain. I hate the
words "Comrade", "Citizen" . . . "Sir" or "Madam" are
much more civilised. As for me, I'm a slave labourer, a
servant, liberated yesterday, with the arrival of your
army.

NERZHIN: Don't say that. How on earth did you get here
from Vienna? Who's your fiancé? Why so silent, eh?

GALINA (*in some difficulty*): Your lot would think it a
betrayal. He's your enemy. He's an officer in the Russian
Liberation Army.[7]

NERZHIN: Not necessarily.

GALINA: What?

NERZHIN: An enemy.

GALINA: Sergei, my love. Can it be that you do understand? Then, why do you work for them? Are you one of us?

NERZHIN: Hold on: "one of us". Not to be an enemy doesn't mean being a friend.

GALINA: Well, tell me. There's a commissar here, Vanin. Is he a good man?

NERZHIN: None better.

GALINA: What about the political instructor?

NERZHIN: Not just him. They're all a splendid lot.

GALINA: If that's so, then tell me, how is it, by what chemistry, by what power, are you all made to serve these *Morlochs*, these enemies of our people?

NERZHIN: Serve whom?

GALINA: The *Morlochs*.

NERZHIN: Are they something out of H. G. Wells?

GALINA: No, out of Moscow. And their leader is from Gori.[8]

NERZHIN: *Morlochs!* I like that.

GALINA: Don't laugh. We've laughed our youth away, alas.

NERZHIN: "Alas", Galina. You're quite right. Your words remind me of how once, when I was a school-boy I was running along, carefree and whistling. An old man stopped me and said fiercely: "How dare you whistle, you puppy. We've whistled Russia away, with all this piping."

GALINA: That's not it, that's not it. You're still joking. I don't like it. You talk about all this as if it were someone else's tragedy. But look around you, just stop to think – do you know what sort of a place you're living in? We have an agreement, Igor and I, look. (*She pulls out something which hangs on a chain around her neck.*) This is a phial; it's instant poison, so that if he and I fail to meet, or if, God forbid, I fall into your hands, I would rather die than find myself in one of those prisons.

NERZHIN: Galina, are you quite mad?

GALINA: I've no wish to rot in prison; to choke on copper

dust in Dzhezkazgan, or to bleed to death from scurvy in
Zapolyariye; to search for food in dustbins, or to sell
myself to the Ruler of Siberia!

NERZHIN: You're talking rubbish, Galina.

GALINA: That was our agreement. Don't talk me out of it;
don't waste your breath. He'll shoot himself. No one will
take him alive. The U.S.S.R.! It's impenetrable forest! A
forest. It has no laws. All it has is power – power to
arrest and torture, with or without laws. Denunciations,
spies, filling in of forms, banquets and prizewinners,
Magnitogorsk[9] and birch-bark shoes. A land of miracles!
A land of worn-out, frightened, bedraggled people, while
all those leaders on their rostrums . . . each one's a hog.
The foreign tourists who see nothing but well organised
collective farms, Potyomkin[10] style. The school-children
who denounce their parents, like that boy Morozov.
Behind black leather doors there are traps rather than
rooms. Along the rivers Vychegda and Kama there are
camps five times the size of France. Wherever you look
you see epaulettes with that poisonous blue stripe; you
see widows, whose husbands are still alive, who
surreptitiously wipe away their tears; and you see all
those invented *Matrosovs* and silly *Zoyas* who fulfil their
plans one hundred per cent. Applause! For a land of
miracles, where hymns and odes are sung to hunger and
misfortune. For the miracles of Communism when whole
peoples are transported into the depths of Siberia
overnight. And Rokossovsky.[11] Wasn't it only yesterday
that he was in a labour camp, a slave, not a man at all,
felling trees in Siberia, loading them on to barges, but
who, today, is summoned, he is needed, he's made a
Marshal. But tomorrow, perhaps he'll be back in Siberia.
Oh, I can't bear it . . .

NERZHIN: Galina, my dear, you frighten me. It's you, and
yet it's not you. Your face shines with a new light.
You're possessed. Your eyes burn. Who inspired all this?
Where does it come from?

GALINA: As your komsomol girls would say: I've been forged anew. You'd think they were talking about horseshoes, not people. But they're not so wide of the mark: like pack horses, we're forced to pull till we drop – no other way out. Yes, he's forged us all, that blacksmith – executioner, forged us all on one and the same black anvil.

NERZHIN: I do agree with a lot of what you say. Most of it is true. But nothing is all black in nature.

GALINA: Don't argue. I don't know. All I do know is that I shall be dead tomorrow unless you take me away today!

NERZHIN *is bemused by all he has heard.*

Tell me, how am I to behave among the Soviet people? Is there some special way? Can you advise me?

NERZHIN: You'll manage. We're a rough lot, of course. All you have to do is to laugh, to sparkle, to slow foxtrot around!

GALINA: And are we supposed to know each other?

NERZHIN: N-no . . . Let us pretend I fell in love with you. So who's your fiancé? A White Russian?

GALINA: No, he's like you and me – he was a Soviet, a lieutenant. He was taken prisoner.

NERZHIN: And in the German army . . .

GALINA: No, it's the Russian army now; you're out of date. They have Russian divisions and Air Force as well.

NERZHIN: So I've been told.

GALINA: You have been told?

NERZHIN: That they established a committee in Prague.

GALINA: He told me. He was there. Oh, it will be splendid.

NERZHIN: Galina, darling, it's too late.

GALINA: It's a bit too late.

NERZHIN: Not just a bit, Galina . . .

GALINA: You always were so obsessively logical. But life isn't the same as mathematics, you know. We must have our dreams. There's a need for tenderness, Sergei, my dear . . . After all, I've only one road ahead of me.

When you write to Liussia, tell her that quite by chance you were the one to lead her friend to the altar. The candles were burning; Scriabin's music played; but the bride wore black, and it seemed oddly in keeping. Tell her you weren't destined to meet the groom: that you never entered the church where the wedding was to take place. But Sergei, I may be hardhearted, fickle, bad, but do wish me joy . . . (*sobbing*).

NERZHIN: Galina, dearest. What now? I told you I would take you away. In a day or two you'll . . .

GALINA: I've stopped. I cried because my heart was so full. You arrived like a descending angel and will disappear again, perhaps forever . . . I was so close to him! But the tanks! Your tanks got in the way. I must tell you that Europe trembled that terrible morning of January 13th when the last gates of Warsaw fell to the hammer blows of Ivan the Mighty. A Walpurgis night of confusion: a witches' sabbath. Some were stunned; some sneaked away; some ran; while I – I made a dash here in the hope of getting to Rastenburg where his legion is stationed; where he is; where my life is either to end or to start again.

NERZHIN: So that's where he is! I should have guessed.

GALINA: Why, what do you know?

NERZHIN: I . . . I don't know anything.

GALINA: But you just said . . .

NERZHIN: I understand now how you ended up here. Come on, my love, tell me more.

GALINA: That's all. It took me ten days from Vienna. There were fires, bombs, always changing trains, complete confusion. And now that I'm almost there, when I could have got there on foot, your lot turn up, God knows from where. They're like menacing lava, these armies, these endless armies . . . You look worried – what is it?

NERZHIN: It's that we've got Prussia in a pincer

movement, and that any minute now, the pincers will close.

GALINA: And he's there!

NERZHIN: Yes, he's there.

GALINA: The Germans were talking about it, but I refused to believe it. But it's written on every face I've seen. Well, let it be . . . so long as I can be with him and we can die together.

NERZHIN: Galina, darling, hold your head up high. You'll never win if you let your spirits droop. If you're to face being surrounded, march under a steadfast banner. I don't know the man you've chosen, but if he's worthy of your love, tell him I've no fears for the fate of Russia while there are women like you. No matter that for the time being we wear different brands on our foreheads, that we sport different uniforms. I give you my word that in a couple of days you'll be over the other side, whatever my marching orders – West, North, or East.

GALINA: Shake!

NERZHIN: Shake!

GALINA: What a weight off my shoulders. And again. (*They clasp hands, crosswise.*) There's no turning back. Hurrah! Would you mind if I kissed you once more?

NERZHIN: I would not.

GALINA: God forgive me my sins.
    They kiss. Suddenly the lights go up. They gasp and jump apart.

GALINA: What did I tell you – a land of miracles! (*She runs happily to the piano and starts playing.*)

38

ACT TWO

The same scene, the same actors, in the same position. Enter
BERBENCHUK, *unnoticed by the other two. He walks slowly
towards them, listening.*

BERBENCHUK: So you're responsible for the music!

GALINA (*rising shyly*): Comrade Colonel . . .

NERZHIN: Comrade Colonel. I came at your request . . .
    BERBENCHUK *makes a friendly gesture, as if to say — we
    are off duty. Throughout this scene he is very gracious, his
    bass voice vibrant.*

BERBENCHUK: I too, I also used to play. (*Sits down at the
    piano and executes a few bars of Chopsticks.*) Well, what
    do you think of my battery commander? He's not a
    lady's man, a bit out of touch with all these . . . niceties.
    Compared to other officers, he's a bit eccentric, a
    theoriser. But don't imagine it's easy to be a commander.
    Ah well. It's not just courage. You need to be clever as
    well. (*He sits down with* GALINA *at the little round table.*
    NERZHIN *is a little further off.*) They sit around bored
    over at Staff HQ – but watch out! First lull in the
    fighting and they send some commission over to check
    up on Berbenchuk. Sometimes you can lay on a meal for
    them with the assistant quartermaster's help and all's
    well. But sometimes it's "Drive us out to one of the
    units; must get to the front, come what may." So I have
    to consider where to send them. After all, there are only
    three batteries. But I'm not easily rattled. I take the bull
    by the horns. I ask – what is your special interest? Well,
    this and that. Fine. You want to look at the technical
    side? You're interested in pushing paper around? Secret
    papers? Fine. We'll send you to Makarov. He's a
    perfectionist. Army stores? Every last cable-reel is
    labelled: "Responsibility of Private So-and-So". If you're
    interested in the stores records – here they are for you to

39

read, neatly written out in copper-plate – four files. As to our operational maps, well, each one's an ikon. A hundred transparent sheets, so fine one daren't touch them. Makarov is a stern taskmaster. Yes, we regular soldiers deserve respect. Now, that other fellow, Likharyov, he's a bit flighty. Loves dancing. He's here today. He's one of those who never wait to hear the end of an order. Yes, sir, certainly sir, and he's off, straight into a minefield. But out he comes, unscathed. In an ordinary field of potatoes he comes a cropper. (*Roars with laughter:* GALINA *smiles politely.*) He rushes into battle; likes his drink, and is quite hot on girls, if I may say so. His men would follow him anywhere; plunge over ditches; squeeze through minute crevices – if there's a granary in sight! Their stores are full to bursting, the whitest of white flour. Or else they'll kill a pig, out of sheer pity, seeing as how the poor thing was hurt by a splinter on the battlefield. (*Laughs.*)

GALINA (*innocently*): With a gun?

BERBENCHUK: Mmm, yes. But once it's skinned, how can you prove anything? Let me finish. Any inspection of his set up I do myself. I wouldn't dream of allowing inspectors anywhere near it. Ye-es. But whenever a bespectacled intellectual arrives from Moscow, to find out if our technical reconnaissance is at a high scientific level, he's directed to Nerzhin. Need to correct for humidity? Hygrometric gradient? No-o-o problem! We're not country bumpkins. And what's the other thing? Temperature? . . .

NERZHIN: Inversion?

BERBENCHUK: So the fellow's as pleased as punch. (BERBENCHUK *kisses his fingers.*) But when an instructor from the Political Section arrives, I see at once that something's up. A denunciation! Trouble! So he, too, is despatched to Nerzhin. And he'll be so blinded by science there, he won't know if he's coming or going. In Nerzhin's section even a nit-wit can manage to look

40

down his nose and pontificate on lease-lend, or on
Churchill, or what have you. He (*nodding towards*
NERZHIN) is hardly human. When everybodys drunk,
he isn't. When everyone's asleep, he's awake. He's
reached the rank of Captain, and he still looks down on
the way we do things here. He's softened up a bit lately,
though, I'm glad to see. He's married, and is
scrupulously faithful to his wife. Faithful beyond
measure.

GALINA: Is there a measure to faithfulness?

BERBENCHUK: Well, you know, where an officer is
concerned . . . Having arrived at Headquarters for his
instruction, he . . . and you . . . should have . . .

NERZHIN: Listened to music?

BERBENCHUK: That's fine, my dear chap, but war doesn't
wait. Out there, there is bloodshed, casualties every
second . . .
(*Having noticed* SALIY/ZAMALIY *who enters, carrying a
bowl.*)
This way Saliy!

NERZHIN (*gets up with determination and unfastens his
mapcase.*): Can I have your instructions, sir?

BERBENCHUK (*to* GALINA): Californian raisins. Spoils of
war. Have some.

NERZHIN (*advancing*): Instructions, please, sir.

BERBENCHUK: Wait!

GALINA (*taking some raisins*): You're having a very cosy war.

NERZHIN: I request . . .

BERBENCHUK: Don't pester!

GALINA: But where did you get . . . ?

BERBENCHUK: There were some Red Cross stores around
here. I was able to discover precisely where, and we
pounced . . . Do you smoke? (*Getting a packet of
cigarettes from one of his pockets.*) These are Chesterfields,
and these (*getting them out of another*) are Camels.
(*Lighting one.*) Miss Pavlova, how would you react to the
idea of being made a member of my Division?

GALINA: Can it be done?

BERBENCHUK: You name it: I can do it. The Division is mine, so is the rubber stamp. I can order a new uniform; or have a fashionable skirt run up in no time. Just think how patriotic that is: an extra uniform to defend us. And *personally* I would be very pleased . . .

GALINA: But in what way can I be useful to you?

BERBENCHUK: Not to me, not to me, Miss Pavlova, but to the *country*. You just watch: I issue an order, and you are enlisted forthwith. Simple as that.

MAIKOV enters swiftly, accompanied by two soldiers.

MAIKOV: Where's the milk? American milk?

The under-cook points to it on the table.

And the German?

The cook points.

Dried? Condensed? (*Admiring the table.*) Hell's teeth!

BERBENCHUK (*good-humouredly*): Hey, Maikov.

MAIKOV (*absently*): Yes. (*To the under-cook.*) And what's this?

BERBENCHUK: Hey . . .

MAIKOV: What are these peasant mugs doing here?

BERBENCHUK (*irritated*): Staff Captain!

MAIKOV: Yes . . . (*To the under-cook and soldier.*) Take them away, you idiots. (*It is only at this point that he bumps into* NERZHIN *and greets him casually as he walks on.*)

BERBENCHUK (*thunderously*): Staff Captain!

MAIKOV: Yes sir. (*In an undertone to the soldiers.*) Crystal glasses, thin ones, the ones that ring! (*Exit cook, quickly.*)

BERBENCHUK (*beside himself*): Staff Captain!

MAIKOV (*freezing to "attention"*): I'm all ears, sir.

BERBENCHUK: Do I have to repeat myself?

A pause. MAIKOV's *attitude, as if forever frozen into complete submission, disperses the Colonel's doubts. He is mollified.*

Would you make this lady citizen – I don't know if she is a Miss or a Mrs – a soldier of our Division, as of this date. She has agreed.

42

NERZHIN (*rising, formally*): Comrade Colonel, I . . .

GALINA: Agreed? When?

BERBENCHUK: Is that clear?

MAIKOV: Yes sir.

BERBENCHUK: Do it then!

MAIKOV (*resignedly*): I can't.

BERBENCHUK: You can't?

MAIKOV: We have no right. And, alas, even *you* . . .

BERBENCHUK: What's that? If she's taken in at my command . . . Do what is necessary; make it formal. After all, who am I? I'm the Supreme Commander.
MAIKOV *looks meaningfully at* BERBENCHUK, *who wilts.*
But if that's my wish . . . If you . . . If I . . . You know better how to tackle this.

MAIKOV (*rattling it off*): Instruction zero-zero-one hundred and eighty-nine, Order four hundred and fifteen states that without the clearance of the Regional Army Committee, or the certificate of the Medical Committee . . .

BERBENCHUK: But what are you here for? Aren't you the Staff Captain? Well, do it somehow or other.

NERZHIN: Comrade Colonel, I must insist on my instructions . . .

MAIKOV (*approaching* BERBENCHUK, *quietly*): Especially now that we have this fellow from SMERSH . . .

BERBENCHUK (*to* NERZHIN): Ah, yes, your instructions. Come over here. (*Moves away with him.*)
GALINA, *trying to move away unnoticed, goes past and ascends the staircase.* NERZHIN *has opened his mapcase and is holding his map spread out in front of* BERBENCHUK.
Where's the map? Ah, here . . . The enemy have retreated to the East. They are entrenched, entrenched . . . Where the hell is Liebstadt? Where is it? Eh? It was here . . . Or is it to the side? Well, anyway, the enemy have retreated; we are advancing; there are battles going on (*he makes sweeping gestures over the map*) here somewhere . . . or perhaps here . . . I will even venture

a guess that we've reached *this* sector by now.

NERZHIN: I would like to be precisely sure. You showed me first . . .

BERBENCHUK *is not looking at the map, but over it at* GALINA, *who is leaving.* NERZHIN *falls silent. A sergeant comes running through the door on the right. He is in winter clothes, with a sprinkling of snow on his coat.*

SERGEANT: Comrade Captain, our cook, who is in the Opel . . .

MAIKOV: What about him?

SERGEANT: He's stuck.

MAIKOV: Not with the cake?

SERGEANT: He can't get out: he's holding the cake in both hands.

GALINA *has gone.* BERBENCHUK *hurriedly returns to the map.*

BERBENCHUK: So . . . that's the situation – in general.

MAIKOV: Get a detachment to pull him out! What the hell!

SERGEANT: Who shall I get, sir?

MAIKOV: Telephonists, signalmen, scribblers, topographers, photographers, radio-operators!

The SERGEANT *runs off.*

NERZHIN: I didn't quite get it . . .

BERBENCHUK: You'll sort it out. You're clever enough. Captain Maikov will give it to you in detail.

He dismisses NERZHIN *by touching the peak of his cap, and hastens after* GALINA. NERZHIN, *still holding the mapcase, follows* BERBENCHUK *with his eyes.*

MAIKOV (*looking at* NERZHIN, *sings*): As, poring over tattered charts, his daring course he traces . . . (*He puts his arm around* NERZHIN's *shoulders and turns him towards the mirror.*) Not bad, eh? What do you think? After all, we're bound to remember a day like this! King Arthur used to entertain at the round table, but who had a meal on a mirror? Such a celebration will be remembered a long time.

NERZHIN: But what's the occasion for it?

MAIKOV: Two: the Major's birthday, and . . .

NERZHIN: And?

MAIKOV: Oh, I'll think of something.

NERZHIN: Look, while you're still sober, give me my
instructions.

NERZHIN *moves the little table forward, spreads the map
over it; they both sit down,* MAIKOV *cross-legged.*

MAIKOV: Now, then. The situation. As usual, nobody
knows what the situation is. You hear a rifle shot, and
you pull over on to the verge. Then you get out and
check. Seems O.K. Liebstadt. The Passarge. Over the
bridge to the right shore, and – nach Osten!

NERZHIN: To the East! But wait! (*Jumping up.*) That
means Prussia is . . .? (*An excited handshake.*)

MAIKOV: Encircled! Our tank corps has finally closed the
pincers today: cut through the Germans at Elbing, and
broken out to the Baltic!

NERZHIN (*in great excitement*): That's what Samsonov[12]
always dreamt of!

MAIKOV: And that's the second reason for our celebrations.
N. brigade will fix up a telephone-line for you. You're to
do your reconnaissance in this (*he marks it up on the map*)
sector. Pass on any targets by radio, or you can let the
brigade hit some of them. Your job is to find them. You
must be ready by 0400 hours. Where's your battery?

NERZHIN: When I was leaving, they were still disman-
tling . . .

MAIKOV: Good. So you can stay with us an hour or two.
You'll be able to appreciate our elaborate repast and
entertainment. I'd be very hurt if a connoisseur like you,
Sergei, didn't . . . Everything was going so well – a
happy birthday, the war coming to an end, the
appearance of this charming girl – but then in crawled
this reptile from SMERSH.

NERZHIN: Who's that?

MAIKOV: Haven't you met him? Sent by Army H.Q.

NERZHIN: Seconded to our Division?

MAIKOV: U-huh.

NERZHIN: Not a front-line soldier?

MAIKOV: Well, what do you think? A pink piglet, stuffed full of the rubbish of the N.K.V.D. school. The whole world begins and ends with his school: how were you dressed; what did you eat; how to sniff people out with tracker dogs . . . I must go. Just cook up some report and sketch out a plan. Mark it 4 a.m.

NERZHIN: But where is the front; where am I to go, Alex? I've no idea.

MAIKOV: Just write something. As Vanin says, it's the paper that counts. You give it to me; I pass it on to the Army Command; Army send it on up to Group HQ. That way you can stay the night. No need to go anywhere. Write some nonsense – who's to know? They've hundreds and thousands of bits of paper like that. If I find out something new in the morning, I'll add a correction or two. If not, I'll send it as it is. That's no problem!

NERZHIN: No, but it's silly.

MAIKOV (*drawing himself up*): Is that so? Then may I add, Comrade Captain, that I shall be expecting the messenger with your report and plan by 5 a.m.

NERZHIN: Where shall I send him? Here?

MAIKOV: Of course.

NERZHIN: That's sillier still. It'll take him till 6 to get as far as Liebstadt, let alone back here.

MAIKOV: That's your problem. You're not a baby any more. You're an officer, and it's high time you understood why they call military reconnaissance "the eyes and ears of the army" – and artillery reconnaissance most of all. (*As* MAIKOV *proceeds to wax lyrical,* NERZHIN *looks at him with amused admiration.*) Now that we're in the land of the enemy, in the midst of a hostile nation each document demands of us the utmost rigour and precision, now, as never before . . .

NERZHIN (*hums*):

> Having discovered rebellion on board
> He pulled a gun from his belt
> (*together*)
> Scattering golden flakes
> From his lace-embroidered cuffs.

MAIKOV: Just write something! (*Exit.*)

NERZHIN, *alone, sketches, writes and talks to himself the while.*

NERZHIN: Who'd have believed, innocent and trusting as I was in 1940, I would now be sitting down meekly falsifying historical evidence, and concocting this sort of rubbish . . . ?

VANIN *enters, smoking a pipe. Every time he appears he smokes something different – a foreign cigarette, or a Russian one, or a home-rolled cigarette of incredible proportions.*

NERZHIN *doesn't notice him.*

NERZHIN: When we were young, did we imagine this war to defend the Revolution would turn out like this – labels and tags and bits of paper to deceive our superiors? Heroic sacrifices – they're all pie in the sky. Everything we read is so far removed from reality.

VANIN: What a surprise! Education doesn't improve the mind. You should read little and write even less.

NERZHIN (*jumping up*): Comrade Major, they tell me that today . . . Congratulations! Many happy returns, with all my heart. (*They shake hands.*)

VANIN: Many thanks, old chap. But I'm getting old. It's time I retired.

NERZHIN: But how old are you?

VANIN: Thirty-six.

NERZHIN: Is that all? I'm nearly that. But all the same, my muscles, my arteries . . .

VANIN: How old are *you*?

NERZHIN: Twenty-seven.

VANIN: Ha! Wait till you get to my age.

NERZHIN: Nine years' difference is nothing.

VANIN: The point is it's my fourth decade. I'm aware that

life's been wasted; that there're no curly-headed kids
under my feet.

NERZHIN: Kids?

VANIN: Yes, kids: happy, healthy kids. We bachelors, who
eat in state canteens and sleep any-old-where, don't
realise there's something missing.

NERZHIN: Ah yes, the old canteens. They always remind
me of my childhood, the menu scribbled with chalk on a
scratched blackboard. And it was always the same:
cabbage and tapioca pudding. But look at you: well
built, rosy cheeked: perhaps not too much military
bearing, but still an army gloss. No, you're not too
old.

VANIN: To look at, perhaps, but I feel old. When I came to
town from my village during the heady days of the New
Economic Policy I was only a boy. And ever since then
I've been in a whirl . . . ever since. Those were the
days!

NERZHIN: Yes, I remember!

VANIN: You? Remember? Bread, threepence a loaf, and
cinema hoardings the size of a house. But we tightened
our belts and went into battle, thinking that we were
storming the sun itself: that the smell of meadows would
permeate the towns; that villages would glisten with
shining glass laboratories; that four hours of dedicated
work would be enough to achieve equality; that we
would become masters over life, over nature, over
history. After our voluntary Saturday shifts we took part
in debates; after our cell meetings, we worked in clubs;
after workers' classes we went to university. All duly
authorised of course. Amidst all this activity, dear boy, I
failed to notice that my life was passing by. And now
that I'm almost forty, with a scar from a wound at
Khortitsa, a scar that's more jagged than Chkalov's
flight . . .

NERZHIN: As yes, the New Economic Policy – we'll never
see the likes of it again! It flourished under our own

skies. And it was you who . . . (*He pretends to throttle himself.*)

VANIN *goes towards the radiogram and switches it on absentmindedly. We hear: "The news about the latest, grandiose victories of the Red Army stirred a flood of enthusiasm and unprecedented patriotism among the women textile workers in Ivanov. At their numerous shop-floor meetings the women workers applauded the wise strategist of genius, the leader, father, teacher and best friend of the textile workers, Comrade Stalin. The women spinners of Molomonov and Natyagushin stayed by their forty looms for 72 hours, fulfilling the plan for as far ahead as 1969 . . ."* VANIN *switches the radio off.*

VANIN: Ah, well. We know that our sleigh is wonky. But the disgruntled mare goes on pulling it up and down hill all the same.

NERZHIN: All that's happened, Major, could have been a bit gentler – without executions, without the terror. Ever since that last decisive quarrel between Bukharin[13] and Stalin . . .

VANIN: But there was no quarrel. The first was writing innumerable memos; the second was placing his supporters in key positions.

NERZHIN: So that's how it was.

VANIN: Yes, that's how it was.

NERZHIN: So much the worse! Since historical truth is hidden, and since it's being further obscured, the opposition from the right . . .

VANIN: What opposition? From the left, from the right – all that, you know, is just words, my dear fellow. What are you trying to find out from me? You know what I think. All Bukharin wanted was that Russia should have enough food. He was right, therefore.

NERZHIN: That's just what I think. He was right. I feel sometimes that the very core of the Revolution, its very structure had a fatal flaw. But where and in what way? I scratch about for the truth, like a pig digging for truffles.

VANIN: So did I. But now, I fear, things are much simpler.

NERZHIN: Tell me how?

VANIN: Why do you want to know?

NERZHIN: It's of the utmost importance to me!

VANIN: I said "simpler": I should have said "more complicated". It would take too long, and this isn't the place. You would want statistics, graphs, diagrams, and I'm not versed in these things. You've clever, of course, but can you make a distinction between words and facts?

NERZHIN: Er . . . in what way?

VANIN: Oh, dear! Just go away and die! You've answered it already: you don't know the distinction. No amount of books will make you understand. Imagine a collective farm so prosperous that even our book illustrators couldn't portray it: where great lorries, and not your miserable hand carts, overflow with the daily harvest of grain; where there are electric milking machines, motorised ploughs, electric grain driers; where everything is strictly planned; where – don't laugh – not a penny of the communal money finds it way into private pockets; where there are orchards, bee-hives and vegetable gardens; where the hostel is a colonnaded house, and where some old codger sits issuing coupons for everything from apples to apartments. There's discipline, naturally, and time-keeping – after all, the enterprise is worth millions, orders must prevail. In the office the schedule is being worked out for the following day: who goes where; who does what. Now then, would you say a peasant would want to join this collective farm paradise?

NERZHIN: I would say, yes.

VANIN: Well, let me tell you, he would not. Imagine being told that someone was coming into your study to break down the wall between you and the next door study, because in there are other thinkers like yourself, and intellectual efforts must be pooled. The District Committee would be issuing the topics for research, and

your timetable would be worked out so as to insulate you
from distractions like visitors or parties! Would you
accept that?

NERZHIN: Of course not. To lose the freedom of ideas . . .

VANIN: There you are then. Is a peasant a cow? How does
he spend his years, months, days? Thinking of his
stomach? He dreams of his harvest, working in the sun-
drenched fields. He loves his little apple tree, not only
because it provides him with fruit. Do you see my point?
Points such as these make up the whole of life my friend:
millions of them. Otherwise you're welcome to sit down
and reel off laws on the subject of class struggle. Just as
the distinguishing features in a police dossier can't
provide a convincing photofit, so a Marxist method can't
explain or evaluate or improve society. Marx, of course,
was right in many things, but to start a world explosion,
to hold this live wire in bare hands . . . ! You could, I
suppose, imagine that the grizzly bear is a bone-setter,
and self-taught at that.

NERZHIN: Good God! Stop heaping coals upon my head. I
expected all sorts of things, but not a blow below the
belt. Tell me, though, how come you carry your rank
and your duties as a commissar so easily, so
lightly?

VANIN: Me? Oh, I'm guided by some vague precepts. I let
myself be carried along by the current. The main thing
is, I can't see, and I don't know, anything better. I am a
bell which summons people to church, but stays outside
it . . .

NERZHIN (*walks about agitated*): But how's one to live?
What's one to think?

VANIN: Thinking is the last thing you want to do. There is
authority. There are orders. No one grows fat from
thinking. You'll get your fingers burnt from thinking.
The less you know, the better you sleep. When ordered
to turn the steering wheel, you turn it. Suppose
tomorrow they tell you the earth is square? Well? What

do you do? You know the situation is awkward, but you go to a party meeting and declare: "Comrades, the earth is square." Do you know the story about a political adviser who is asked by the soldiers: "How come we must respect the Church again?" And he says: "Well, lads, I was all wrong. I used to say: there is no God, but, blow me, now there is . . . (*They both laugh.*)

MAIKOV *enters quickly.* SALIY *and* ZAMALIY *follow him carrying a huge cake. A tall dark* COOK *overtakes them, mincing fussily along. He wears a white cap and a crumpled, unbuttoned army coat over his white apron.*

MAIKOV: I'll lock you up in a dungeon, you freak. Squashing a cake like that . . . Put it there. (*Showing where.* SALIY *and* ZAMALIY *put it ceremoniously on the table.*)

COOK: Comrade Major!

MAIKOV: I've been a captain for two years, and nobody has promoted me to major yet. Where did you steal those ten skirts? Why were you late? Why are you always drunk? Shame on you! Into the dungeon with you, you ruffian. Any questions? Straw and water.

COOK: Many years of devoted service. How can you, Comrade Captain!

MAIKOV: If I had time, I swear by all that's sacred, I would go into the dungeon myself, out of sheer curiosity. Oh, ancient stones of medieval prisons, where so many noble hearts beat . . .

COOK (*tearfully*): I defended my country with my very blood . . .

MAIKOV: You mean the blood of all those pigs you shot, and all those butchered sheep. Arrest him!

SALIY *and* ZAMALIY *throw themselves on the* COOK.

COOK (*fighting to free himself*): Stop it, you louts. Go easy.

MAIKOV: I'll get a woman cook tomorrow – young and neat . . . Ugh, you swine! One cook died in a bombing raid; another stumbled on a mine; the third drowned; good people never survive. And look at you – you were

52

poisoned, burnt, you fell off a cliff; and you are still alive.

COOK: O.K. lock me up, but I shall die innocent.

MAIKOV (*to* SALIY *and* ZAMALIY): Don't make a mistake, mind. There's a wine cellar next to it.

VANIN (*stopping them. To the* COOK): It was because of you that we were investigated four times by the political department. And you are still in one piece.

MAIKOV: Our C.O. had a row with the Commander of 35 Corps because of you. And you are still alive.

COOK (*freeing himself, insolently*): Because of me? You've got to prove it, thanks very much (*takes off his cap*). It's not my fault that I happened to tame a colt which looked very much like one the Corps Commander lost . . . Anyway, today I've baked a cake so light that nobody in the whole Army could do it better. I'm proud of it. May I (*looking at* VANIN) go? VANIN *waves his hand. The* COOK, *free now, departs with* SALIY *and* ZAMALIY.

MAIKOV: I'd have punished him.

VANIN: Ah, to hell. So far as looting goes, he's not as flagrant as some. But, joking apart: a top secret order to the Front, Number 007 (*as if reading*): "It has been observed that when units of the Second Byelorussian Front crossed into Prussia, they were responsible, with the connivance of officers, for the, so far occasional, incidents of arson, killing, rape, theft and pillage both in villages and along the roads. It is the duty – more, the right – of all those in command to stop these acts forthwith in their own units, as well as in any others without distinction, by any means, including execution, in order to maintain the honour of the Soviet Army."

NERZHIN (*whistles*): That's rough! But what are we to do about the instruction of the Political Section about "our sacred revenge"? What about those *parcels* home? What about those pamphlets entitled "Russian Reckoning with the Enemy"?

MAIKOV: F-friends, do tell me for God's sake, does that mean I can get rid of Glafira's transport?

NERZHIN: No, but really it's a bit much. They tempted poor old Ivan, promised him the earth, egged him on, just as long as they needed him to slog his way to the Baltic . . .

MAIKOV: Are you telling me that we're not to drink liqueurs; have pastry without vanilla; eat dried potatoes? No, something's wrong here. It will surely all be explained . . .

NERZHIN: You promise him half the world as you're preparing for the leap.

MAIKOV: I'm a gourmet, not some Tolstoyan ascetic.

NERZHIN: And the moment everything's within his grasp, it's "Now, now! No fooling about!"

MAIKOV: A victory without a celebration – that's too much.

NERZHIN: Are we just rosy innocents, wearing epaulettes and singing hymns?

MAIKOV (*draws the blind, looking out of the window where the light is no longer blue but crimson*): Just look at those magnificent fireworks! (*He closes the blind.*) Rape, yes, rape is terrible, but if the little German girl is, as they say, *willing* . . .

NERZHIN: That soldier, who cowered with me in the marshes of Lake Ilmen when the Stuka was strafing us, am I to execute him? Just because he pinched a "Moser" watch? Or, even dragged a girl into a bunker? Lying there with him in the Russian cornfields, and saying good-bye to life in the middle of scorching smells and smoke, holding him down and saying "Don't move, this one isn't for us" – am I to raise my hand against him now? Before our offensive, didn't you read out an order which was the exact opposite, and didn't you justify that too?

VANIN: What if I did?

NERZHIN: Where's the truth then, where are the lies? You used to say that however much the soldier suffers, at the

end of the road there will be prizes . . . And now, am I
to shoot him?

VANIN: Just you try! I'd have you court-martialled at once.

NERZHIN: So what about the order?

VANIN: What's an order? (*He blows.*) A piece of paper.
When a thing like that begins to move, there's no
stopping it. Do you think, O lowly insect, you can
control events? As to the order, comply within reason,
but don't go executing people or upsetting them. Learn
to be less rigid. Our little lives are overrun with great
and dirty politics. (*Embracing both* MAIKOV *and*
NERZHIN.) We do, dear friends, torture ourselves far
too much with doubts and decisions. But regardless of
us, everything is for the best.

NERZHIN: The Major is fond of saying: "All's for the
best"; "Too much learning will not improve the mind";
"Fear not the beginning, fear the end". I can't get to the
bottom of these sayings.

MAIKOV: What the devil do you mean, it's for the best?
There we were living quietly, peacefully, as if under the
protection of our guardian angel, and blow me, if that
fat, pink piglet from SMERSH doesn't burst in to
disturb our peace.

NERZHIN: There he goes, torturing a nice girl . . .

VANIN: What, already?

MAIKOV: He interferes in everything; gets in the way . . .

VANIN: He won't get far here. He came, and he'll go again.

MAIKOV: What makes you say that? Everywhere else, these
plenipotentiaries get entrenched like a bloody carbuncle.
Do you think we're so special that he'll just stay a week
or a month and then be off and leave us in peace?

NERZHIN: According to Gauss[14] (*shrugs*) some elliptic
function: an exception to the rule.

VANIN: Gauss, my foot. I knew how to get rid of those
carbuncles.

NERZHIN: MAIKOV (*together*): You did? How?

NERZHIN: What did you do?

VANIN: I would quietly collect evidence against them.
There he would sit, the wretched creature, behind locked
doors, writing away. (*Furiously.*) Vermin, and so young
too. I can see right through them, for all their uniforms.
Little fleas serve bigger fleas, but they can all feel
threatened by a piece of paper.

MAIKOV: But what did you put on it?

VANIN: Oh, anything, whatever came into my head. The
main thing was to be ahead of them; to prevent them
getting a head start. This one let on about a secret
installation, in his cups; another one gave false
information when filling in his form; the third expressed
doubts about our victory; the fourth was sympathetic to
the enemy – anyway I can't remember it all. But once
you've put it down the whole thing snowballs. They
devour each other like rats. They're both vigilant and
suspicious. Some bald-headed investigator will look into
the doings of a curly-headed colleague and will find him
guilty of this, if not of that. After all, everyone is guilty
if you look closely enough. In 1937, for five months, I
could not go to bed properly because of *them*, listening
for footsteps on the stairs, for the knock. Late at night,
when everybody had locked their doors, my old mother
would say: "What's going to happen, Arseniy? What do
they want? To lock everybody up, so that only *they*
remain?" She would wander about making the sign of
the cross over all the shutters and doors with her feeble,
wrinkled hand . . . Not a night would go by without
some arrest being made, Black Marias darting in and
out. They arrested all the big-wigs and their children,
party leaders, trade-union leaders, the bourgeoisie and
the proletariat, big and small, but there I was, intact,
shivering on my leather couch. All that remained in town
was the Chief of the G.P.U. and me, Arseniy Vanin. I
was all prepared to tell them everything and sign
anything, like a lamb led to slaughter, about who my
connections were from my very childhood. I tidied up

my affairs, but, there, they never took me – I survived!

MAIKOV: As for me, being an artist, the favourite of Muses, I was nearly done for. (*The eyes of the other two are turned towards him.* MAIKOV *sits, relaxed, on the edge of the mirror, dangling his legs.*) Some clever dick once suggested that in the design of posters, note books, exercise books, in paintings, in sculpture, in everything that's been touched by a brush, a chisel or a pencil, there lurk agitation, subversion, sabotage. He started a trend which became an epidemic, a pestilence. Searching, detecting, endlessly till they dropped, they espied Trotsky's goatee beard among oak leaves; an inscription "Down with the CP(b)" on Prince Oleg's shield. Nowadays, of course, I'm an Impressionist, but I belonged to the narrow-minded realist school. At the end of my studies, for my final diploma, I presented a carving entitled "The Kiss of Psyche and Eros". It was rather realistic and somewhat lacking in modesty. Between ourselves, when people gather roses, they assume certain poses. (*He jumps down and tries to represent his sculpture, becoming either Psyche or Eros.*) She's leaning back, one arm hanging down: he is holding her by her waist, leaning over her like that! Well, some dolt of a Komsomol detected a Swastika in it. No diploma, naturally, and I was dragged here and there to the Party Committee. All the gymnastics of detection were applied to my miserable creation – learned experts, a commission – to determine if it was indeed a Swastika. They have several juries. Had I known I wouldn't have touched mythology – to Hades with it! On one occasion the Director himself crouched before Psyche and Eros in various positions, staring. I couldn't restrain myself any longer I was so furious, and shouted from the hall, "Why don't you get under the table, you might get a better view of it." So they decided at once that a Swastika it was and that my sculpted pair should be examined by the N.K.V.D.

VANIN: Hey-ho, that was a cheerful year. One story after
another. A friend of mine, a vet, got arrested. They said:
"You've been unmasked; you're an enemy of the people;
confess that you were poisoning livestock." But, says he,
sitting on the edge of his chair, trembling: "There's been
no cattle plague recently." "Ah-ha, you would have liked
there to have been?" And they knocked his teeth out.
They locked him up in a cellar for a week under a lamp
so big (*he demonstrates with both hands the size of the
globe*); three-hundred grammes of bread was all he was
given; not allowed to sleep – as soon as he fell asleep,
they'd wake him up: "Write down, I poisoned . . ."
"The collective farm camel." "Insolent, are you? Making
fun of the Cheka?" They gave him a beating. "Go on,
confess, you rat. Otherwise we'll send you to that famous
place where ninety-nine men weep, while one man
laughs." He became so weak that he confessed.
However, still having his wits about him, he stated that
he used to inject cattle against glanders. So they
increased his bread and soup ration, but condemned him
to the North for fifteen years; his accomplice got ten.
Well, when the days of Yezhov[15] were over, someone
came across his forgotten file. It pays, sometimes, to
invent a clever lie. Horses suffer from glanders, not
cattle. Yes, they got the message in the end. He shared
his cell with an old codger, a simple peasant in an old
caftan and birch-bark shoes – good old Russia. He never
lived to see his trial. To get some peace, the poor old
thing testified that he was plotting a rebellion on his
farm; that he had a tank, eleven hand-grenades and a
number of shot-guns; that he had planned to attack
Leningrad, raping the Komsomol girls all the way . . .
In those days the Military College of the Supreme Court
churned out two hundred sentences a day. It happened
like this: two guards would come running in. "Are you
Petrov?" "I am." (Or Petushkov – they muddled things
up a bit). All would remain standing: no time to sit

down. All done ship-shape and naval fashion, Whistle
and lift, Loading, Heave-ho, ten-twenty. Or else, it
would happen like this. A load of unsentenced deportees
would arrive North from Chelyabinsk. They would be
chased into the yard to hear their verdicts. An officer
would come out, wearing elegant boots, followed by
sergeants with case-files of Mishkins, Mandrykins,
Gromovs, all this in the middle of a cruel winter. They
would stand, huddled, stamping their feet. The sun had
a frosty halo. In this temperature it's impossible to turn
the pages over with bare hands. So, not to torture
himself and all the others, the officer would announce:
"You've been sentenced (in absentia) by a Special
Commission. Everyone got ten years, except for a few
who got eight. Understood. Dismiss." And off they
would go, to their bunks. – (*A pause.*) Well, Maikov,
why are you silent? Cheer us up. Fetch your guitar.
Exit MAIKOV. NERZHIN *is rigid with tension.*

NERZHIN: Then what they used to say is true? About
tortures, torments?

VANIN: What . . . ?

NERZHIN: That they used to beat, harass, starve, chase
people out to the bathhouse naked through the snow;
that they squeezed a dozen people into a single cell.

VANIN: There was a time when . . . when, at dawn, they
would push people into the cells who had been
imprisoned under the Tsar. The events were so
confusing for them, their plight so miserable that they
would rush towards any newcomer asking: "Whose
revolution now? Who is in power? Tell us quick,
comrades!"

Re-enter MAIKOV.

MAIKOV (*singing and strumming on his guitar*):
> The golden rims of the Alpujarras
> Are growing dark and dim.
> At the sound of my guitar
> Come out, my love, be seen.

VANIN: I don't think that's a very cheerful song: there are better ones . . .

MAIKOV: Which one would you like?

VANIN: Well, Alex, the one about the steppe beyond the Volga, about the steppe . . .

They sit down at the round table, MAIKOV *with his guitar, and sing.*

> Far, far beyond the Volga the wide steppes spread,
> Where freedom grew and flourished like a tree.
> Think how bitter was the life men in those days led,
> For a man to leave his hearth,
> His native village and his wife,
> And go beyond the Volga to be free.

The accompaniment has stopped, but VANIN *goes on singing, with a sob in his voice:*

> . . . For a man to leave his hearth,
> His native village and his wife,
> And go beyond the Volga to be free.

ACT THREE

The same scene, the same actors, in the same positions.
GLAFIRA, *dressed for dinner, descends the staircase.*

GLAFIRA: Staff Captain! Captain! The Commander said one
hour, but two have gone by . . . (*Noticing* VANIN, *lowers
her voice.*) Excuse me, Major.

    VANIN *and* NERZHIN *continue to sit motionless.* MAIKOV,
*irritated, bangs the guitar strings, rises, thinks for a moment,
then claps his hands three times.*

MAIKOV: Saliy and Zamaliy!

    SALIY *and* ZAMALIY *rush in simultaneously, one from the
left, the other from the right.*

SALIY AND ZAMALIY: Yes, sir!

MAIKOV (*indicating the banqueting table*): Let's mount an
assault on this redoubtable spread. Summon the guests!
(*Gives* GLAFIRA *a nudge with the guitar.*) Have fun, my
girl! And the roast piglet is to be here in five minutes;
after that, in seven minutes, let's have the meat-ball
conserve. (*He claps his hands again;* SALIY *and*
ZAMALIY *dance around the stage as if in a ballet. To*
GLAFIRA.)
What are the views of this member of the Military
Council?

GLAFIRA (*imitating a somewhat vulgar gypsy style of dancing,
stamping her feet, playing the guitar and singing in a fast
tempo*):

        Play, my guitar, play and ring out,
        Sing, gypsy, sing me such a song
        That will obliterate my poisoned days,
        Days without peace or love.

    SALIY *and* ZAMALIY *are gone. As soon as* GLAFIRA's *last
note dies down,* MAIKOV *puts a foxtrot on the radiogram,
turns up the volume, and leads* GLAFIRA. *She hugs him,
holding the guitar behind him. From the corridor*

LIKHARYOV *and two girls in military uniform rush in, performing a complicated dance in a threesome. They are* KATYA, *who is tall, free-and-easy, the high collar of her tunic unfastened to reveal the sparkling whiteness of the lining and* OLYA, *a shy blonde. In comes the* CHIEF CHEMIST *who circles rhythmically around the dancing threesome; he is bald, elderly and portly.* LIKHARYOV *offers him* KATYA, *so that there are now three pairs of dancers, whirling about wildly to compensate for the small number dancing. In the meantime,* VANIN *has pulled himself together; he walks slowly over to the radiogram and switches off the music. They all stop.* GLAFIRA *examines the girls; they look at her.* NERZHIN *continues sitting in the same place.*

VANIN (*to* NERZHIN): You understand, don't you. I gave permission for a small supper, a sort of family affair, but look at this – a regular ball.

MAIKOV (*looking around*): And non-political, as well.

GLAFIRA: Who gave Likharyov permission . . .

LIKHARYOV: Forgive me, Comrade Major. I knew there was a shortage of girls, and if I couldn't find them . . .

MAIKOV: Nobody could!

LIKHARYOV: I couldn't invite the German girls.

MAIKOV: No patriot could!

LIKHARYOV: So I rush off in search, and what do I see? A familiar Chevrolet. And there is the Staff Captain of a unit I know. By frontline reckoning we are brothers, in a sense. We have a sister in common.

VANIN: He's your brother? Well, get him!

MAIKOV: What a pig you are!

LIKHARYOV: No, you don't understand. We have a nursing sister in common.

KATYA: You are a wretch, Arkadiy.

LIKHARYOV: So I rush up to him: Help, Comrade! Now, he's not one to leave a friend in the lurch. Katya, the typist (*he introduces her to* VANIN) is rented out for twenty-four hours, the same way they rent out a cine

film. "Take her you're welcome." "What? Only one?
You must be joking I need three, minimum two." "I
don't have any more." But I spot a pair of blue eyes.
"What about this one?" "Well . . . she's undergoing
sniping training." "On a course?" "No, one-to-one."
"Well, I give my word as an officer: all she'll be doing is
drinking tea: no wine, no waltzes, upon my word."

GLAFIRA: How can you make such promises in advance, on
a woman's behalf?

VANIN: What's more, you danced.

LIKHARYOV: Permission to speak – a foxtrot. I talked him
into it: Olya shall come for an hour, no more. (*He
introduces her to* VANIN.) She has to go beddy-byes early.

VANIN: Where're you from?

OLYA: From Vologda.

VANIN: Called up?

OLYA: No, I volunteered. I'm a Komsomol.

VANIN: My dear child, did you think we couldn't manage
without you? You should be spending your time day-
dreaming over books, or walking in the park. Oh,
carefree youth, where art thou gone?

MAIKOV: And how many Germans have you killed?

OLYA: Oh, dear. No. I've not taken any part in battles yet.
The CHIEF CHEMIST *greedily examines the table and tries
to engage* NERZHIN *in conversation.*

CHIEF CHEMIST: How much longer are we going to
damage our health by abstaining?

PARTY ORGANISER (*enters with* GRIDNEV): National in
form, and Socialist in content. Isn't that so?

GRIDNEV (*constrained*): I suppose so.

PARTY ORGANISER: So that our duty to the Party . . .
They cross the stage. BERBENCHUK *enters from the left. He
wears his ceremonial uniform and is beaming.* MAIKOV
attempts to begin his report, in a rather affected manner.

MAIKOV: Comrade Colonel . . .

BERBENCHUK (*stops him good-humouredly*): My first
question is, where do these girls come from?

LIKHARYOV (*pushing* KATYA *forward*): Due to an emergency (*pushing* OLYA) from the rear reserves.
They shake hands. SALIY *and* ZAMALIY *enter carrying roast suckling pig on large dishes. Thereafter they serve at table.* MAIKOV, *from time to time, gives orders to both of them and to other soldiers.*

PARTY ORGANISER: All this will be discussed by the Party Committee.
GALINA *appears at the very top of the staircase; she wears an evening dress.* ANECHKA *is quite transformed by a pretty dress and new hair style.* GRIDNEV *is the first to notice them and rushes forward to greet* GALINA.

GRIDNEV: Yes, yes, we'll discuss it later, Secretary.

KATYA (*to* BERBENCHUK): I've heard that one before, Colonel!

CHIEF CHEMIST: Well, Nerzhin, do you think we'll ever start to eat?

PARTY ORGANISER: This dish, is it real silver?

GLAFIRA: What are we waiting for, Eugene? We're all here.

BERBENCHUK (*having also spotted* GALINA *and edging his way towards her slowly*): What do you mean, *all*? Look at them coming down, so lovely in their party dresses!

GLAFIRA (*rushing to overtake him*): Oh, Anechka, what a ludicrous bow!
BERBENCHUK, *being held back by her, is slow in reaching* GALINA, *who is approached by* GRIDNEV.

GRIDNEV (*familiarly*): Where've you been? I went up to see you.

GALINA (*with dignity*): Comrade Lieutenant? . . .

GRIDNEV: Did you forget?
He attempts to take her arm. They are separated by NERZHIN, *who squeezes himself between them.*

NERZHIN: Excuse me. (*Offers* GALINA *his arm.*) May I?
GALINA *takes his arm.* GRIDNEV *stands in the way.*

GRIDNEV: Who are *you*?

NERZHIN: And who are *you*?

GRIDNEV: No, *you?*

NERZHIN: I'm a battery commander, and *you?*

In the meantime, BERBENCHUK *reaches* GALINA *and stealthily leads her away. Upstage there is some pre-banquet animation.* GRIDNEV *and* NERZHIN *are downstage.*

GRIDNEV (*attempting to reach* GALINA): Hullo, there. Where're you going?

NERZHIN (*standing in his way*): All right then, who *are* you?

GRIDNEV (*trying to get round him*): None of your business.

NERZHIN: Oh isn't it? Well, the girl is none of your business either.

GRIDNEV: Trying to be clever, are we?

NERZHIN: Not clever, and not daft, either.

GRIDNEV: A sight to familiar.

NERZHIN: I give as good as I get.

GRIDNEV (*fixing him with his eyes, emphatically*): So, what sort of a person are you, Comrade Captain?

NERZHIN: A battery commander, as I said.

GRIDNEV: I'm talking about your *social origins.*

NERZHIN: I beg your pardon?

GRIDNEV: I repeat, your origins.

NERZHIN: You were asking . . .

GRIDNEV: I was asking who your parents, and your grandparents, were, and you gave me a rather shifty look.

NERZHIN: Well, no one's asked a question like that for a good ten years, and if one never expected to hear it again, how is one to react?

GRIDNEV: So you've heard the question before?

NERZHIN: Who hasn't? At every turn. But it's gone out of fashion. We're just Russians, just patriots.

GRIDNEV: You seem to be aware of this new formula.

BERBENCHUK: Comrades, please don't stand on ceremony: make yourselves at home. Come and sit down, sit down!

LIKHARYOV: Olya, darling, over here!

OLYA: I'm superstitious; I don't want to sit on a corner.

65

They arrange themselves around the mirror. MAIKOV *walks towards* GRIDNEV *and* NERZHIN.

GRIDNEV: Yes, things change. They move along. We're all just Russians again now, but with a difference. When you were applying for officer training, didn't you notice such a question in your application form?

NERZHIN: I did. I just thought it was an out-of-date form.

GRIDNEV: Special Departments don't have out-dated forms.

MAIKOV leads them to the table and settles them down: GRIDNEV *is placed next to* GLAFIRA, NERZHIN *next to* MAIKOV *himself.* PROKOPOVICH *arrives at the last minute and squeezes himself on to an end, without a companion to talk to. We can hear the noise of eating and general conversation:*

May I?

Please do!

A piece of ham?

What on earth is this?

No rank pulling.

This is Prussian pork, with good old Russian horseradish.

OLYA: I don't understand. When do you people fight? Ever since I arrived you've been doing nothing but eat, while back at home they're thinking of you, grieving over you, listening to the latest news.

When you get married, tell your husband . . .

Pour me some more . . .

Yes, but don't give me any fat . . .

So who will start?

The commander, who else?

Attention!

Silence!

BERBENCHUK (*rising*): I've been in command of this Division now for three years. Perhaps it's changed a bit since I took over, but we swept aside the enemy artillery fire. Perhaps the guns weren't always ours, but we have a

right to claim that it was due to our counter-intelligence
that we made this advance, this great advance . . . from
Holy Moscow, and even from Rzhev . . . like a, like a
flood . . . like some awesome lava, carrying our noble
Soviet ideals . . . knowing no rest . . . always in the
forefront of battle . . . under the same leadership – I've
been here from the start, my deputy came later – at
Staraya Russa, at Oryol, Bobruisk, Byelostok. And so,
today, to sum it up, we're active participants, not on the
side lines. Today, is the Major's birthday, my deputy.
He's not a regular soldier; he's not a combatant, but he
knows where he belongs. And, what is more, even
Prussia is down the drain . . . so it's appropriate . . . I'm
a simple soldier, unaccustomed to . . . In short, I
propose a toast . . . Ye-es, a toast, to the Army . . . to
us . . . to . . .

GRIDNEV: Funny. There is a long established Soviet
tradition which demands that the first toast is proposed
to Him, who . . .

VANIN (*interrupting, holding up his glass*): . . . Who
illuminates our path by the light of the red stars of the
Kremlin. What do we mean when we say "the Army"?
We mean the Supreme Commander! The Colonel is
proposing a toast to Stalin!

PARTY ORGANISER *applauds loudly.*

BERBENCHUK (*with a hiccup*): Y-e-s, yes. Naturally. Yes!
All rise, clink glasses, rhubarb, rhubarb . . .

MAIKOV: We did have some liqueur somewhere. Bring it
here, Saliy. (*To* GRIDNEV.) Drink, like a man! In
tumblers, Russian fashion, with or without *zakuski*. (*He
fills* GRIDNEV'S *and* NERZHIN'S *glasses.*) Now the three
of us are faithful friends.
He and GRIDNEV *drink;* NERZHIN *hardly touches it.*
MAIKOV *walks away.*

GRIDNEV: So, what was your answer?

NERZHIN: Answer?

GRIDNEV: On your application form.

NERZHIN: Oh, that. A clerk's son.

GRIDNEV: Meaning?

NERZHIN: Meaning that my mother worked as a clerk in an office.

GRIDNEV: Not a complete answer. It doesn't give me a full picture of you. And, then, who was her father? And your father? And finally, your father's father?

NERZHIN: Well, my father was killed six months before I was born. So what am I to say about my origins?

GRIDNEV: I'll help find the right pigeon-hole for you. Who killed him? Whose bullet? Whose shrapnel?

NERZHIN: German.

GRIDNEV: In the Army?

NERZHIN: Yes, the Russian Army.

GRIDNEV: The Tsar's Army.

NERZHIN: No, the Russian Army.

GRIDNEV: Shall we simply say a butcher's army?

BERBENCHUK (*animated, talking to* GALINA): A huge crowd, you see, shouting, carrying things. So he rolls back a bit and then runs his tank straight into the store! (*Roars with laughter.*)

GRIDNEV: So what was he? The unknown soldier? I doubt it. His rank? Could your memory dredge up . . .

NERZHIN: It could. A simple ensign.

GRIDNEV: Ah-ha. An en-sign. How come?

NERZHIN: Easy. He'd been a student.

GRIDNEV: Ah, a student. One moment. (*Lights a cigarette, importantly.*) He was the son of . . .

NERZHIN: A peasant.

GRIDNEV: A Lomonosov?[16] You see traps are laid by those little insignificant questions. I see it all clearly now. Your grandfather was never a peasant. Where did your father get his money for studying? An income from a wooden plough? (NERZHIN *is upset.*) Ha, ha, ha. I'm only joking, Captain. You can breathe freely – for the time being.

BERBENCHUK: The tank is stuck; the engine is roaring;

68

and out there a hospital is on fire. So he thinks the mob will loot the lot. He jumps up on to the tank turret and shouts: Hey, you infantry, leave something for me!

GALINA *laughs with* BERBENCHUK. GLAFIRA *is getting nervous.* MAIKOV *returns.*

MAIKOV (*to* GRIDNEV): When did you start smoking? Recently?

GRIDNEV: No, long ago.

MAIKOV: Come on, stop pretending.

GRIDNEV: Let me tell you. It was when I was at college. I got drunk, and was after a girl, and suddenly there was that patrol. But they didn't arrest me.

LIKHARYOV (*to* OLYA): I wonder what kind of sniper you'll make. Just imagine what it's like to have a gun pointing at you.

GLAFIRA (*to* GRIDNEV, *pointing at* GALINA): See that bit of skirt over there (*whispering into his ear*). She may have been a chambermaid, but she's a tart. Once I'd discovered that, I wasn't surprised that she . . . (*Whisper.*)

GRIDNEV: You don't say!

GLAFIRA: Slept with the Nazis. Not surprising.

GRIDNEV: Such a lovely girl – and tainted.

GLAFIRA: Aren't you an innocent.

CHIEF CHEMIST (*to* KATYA): How can one know? When I said good-bye to peace, I thought that that would be the end of my film-making. But the war's nearly over. I'm about to go back, and here (*he points to his chest*) I have a star; (*to his shoulder*) and here three more; while here (*pointing to his breast pocket*) a Party card.

ZAMALIY (*comes running in*): Sir . . .

MAIKOV: Bring them in, bring them in! (ZAMALIY *runs off.*)

CHIEF CHEMIST: I must say, once you have a medal, you breathe more freely.

GRIDNEV: Do you know, I almost went to bed . . .

GLAFIRA: God forbid! It's the pretty ones that pass it on.

CHIEF CHEMIST: The next thing is to exchange a forty-year old wife for two of twenty, da-de-da, and life would be fine.

KATYA: Would *I* suit?

CHIEF CHEMIST: Tut-tut! A wife ought not to be thrown about: after all, she's not a ball. Would you like a little of this?

LIKHARYOV: I remember meeting five girls: they were as young as you. They marched with a proud step, wearing medals. The medals of four of them were battle honours, but the fifth one was for "outstanding courage". "How did you earn this highest award?" I asked. She lifted up her pretty head and said: "I stood up to them."

SALIY *and* ZAMALIY *remove glass jars quickly out of buckets of boiling water and empty the meatballs on to plates.*

GRIDNEV: Those bloody Germans have learned how to make home preserves?

CHIEF CHEMIST: First you fry them properly . . .

GLAFIRA: And while they're still hot, you seal them in jars and store them in the cellar . . .

MAIKOV: And leaving all this behind, the peaceable population has to flee . . .

LIKHARYOV: In come the barbarous Slavs . . .

ANECHKA: Who throw these jars into boiling water . . .

KATYA: They then remove the rubber rings, and . . .

NERZHIN: Here they are sizzling, as if straight from a frying pan.

MAIKOV: We'll have some frothing champagne . . .

PARTY ORGANISER: Or else ordinary Russian vodka . . .

GALINA: To quench our thirst
            We still demand
            A goblet full
            Of sparkling wine.

MAIKOV (*clinking glasses with* GRIDNEV *and*
NERZHIN): No questions asked!

CHIEF CHEMIST: *I* want to ask a question: why are there no more speeches?

BERBENCHUK: Captain: that's an oversight.

NERZHIN (*rising*): Comrades, to maintain the tradition . . .
But, being a soldier, I'll be brief.
Silence reigns.
When this commotion is over, when we have parted and
gone our various ways, those of us who survive will long
remember Major Vanin's special gift of combining gaiety
with sadness and with firmness of purpose. We will
remember that he was wiser than any of us, that he
was . . .

PARTY ORGANISER: Devoted to the ideals of Lenin.

NERZHIN: That he distinguished between the dead letter
and the living spirit . . .

PARTY ORGANISER: That he adhered to the directives of
the Political Wing.

NERZHIN: That he adhered and acted upon them with zeal.
That he was both a politician and a man. Comrades,
raise your glasses. Let's wish him a long life and a better
one!
*They all rise and drink. Rhubarb, rhubarb . . . To convey
the next stage of general inebriation, the remarks that follow
are spoken in a sing-song.*

BERBENCHUK: Whom shall we appoint to be in charge of
radio?
Arkadiy
Arkadiy
Who can compete with him?

LIKHARYOV (*dances his way to the radiogram*): The Russian
soldier will now engage in battle with gramophone
records (*he switches on*): foxtrot for the blondes, tango for
the brunettes.
*Soft dance music continues throughout the next scene. The
following remarks are spoken, as if inwardly.*

GALINA: I love to see the kaleidoscope of fate.

NERZHIN: I love to see the flow of unbridled festivities.

CHIEF CHEMIST: I love to hear the tinkle of crystal
glass.

MAIKOV: Although your wings are tired, you still want to fly upwards.

ANECHKA: When in the midst of drunken stupor, you still have faith, you still believe . . .

VANIN: . . . that wasted lives will change for the better. *Thereafter in ordinary conversational manner.*

KATYA: I see no point in worrying about difficult problems.

PARTY ORGANISER (*stretches his arm in the direction of* GRIDNEV, *his index finger pointing, like a figure on a poster*): Are your denunciations to the Party in order?

GRIDNEV (*grumbling, half-audibly*): Mind who you put your questions to. God, what fools they send us.

OLYA: All right, if it's Tokay, just a sip.

MAIKOV (*to* GRIDNEV): We've so far had five Party Organisers, each one dafter than the last.

GLAFIRA (*to* OLYA): I sent my mother a trunk-full from Homel.

CHIEF CHEMIST: Could you pass that bottle, old chap?

GLAFIRA: I send one parcel after another: this way we've collected a trousseau for my daughter.

MAIKOV: Hey, let's sing a drunken song.

GRIDNEV: Ho-ho!

LIKHARYOV: Ha-ha!

BERBENCHUK: Well, Maikov?

MAIKOV: What?

BERBENCHUK: Say something . . .
    A Toast.
    A Story.
    A Funny Story.

MAIKOV (*rising heavily. As he begins to speak, the music slows down as on a run-down gramophone, and finally it stops*): Since it's my turn, I'll try and say something suitable for the occasion.
Silence.
I'm in a funny mood today. You're expecting some

lighthearted after-dinner speech, some jokes. But, dear
friends, it is today that I suddenly realised what these
four years of fighting mean to me. Victory is here – give
me your hand. I feel its soft touch: it's fragrant and
gentle. But the hand that held us down in the trenches –
how hard it was! Whoever forgets 1941, I'll scratch one
of his eyes out!!
Everyone shudders.
And he who speaks evil of it – I'll scratch out the other.
I speak these burning words for all those who've been
forgotten, whose names are lost . . . When
Messerschmitts flew over the fields of rye stubble,
chasing every car, every soldier, we scrabbled in the dry
dust of our roads, our lips parched. I see our Russia
through tears, through flaming hay ricks, through fallen
bridges, through smoke . . . Do you know what I'm
proud of? Not that I'm among the victors, but that I was
among those who retreated. When we were surrounded,
we saved our guns, dragging them with ropes a few yards
at a time, our muscles bulging with the strain. Of all the
medals I'm proudest of it's this (*he touches his chest*)
early, simple one. I'd give the entire collection for this
little one (*he touches it*). I'm also proud of the fact that
one of my forefathers fought against the Pretender. We
were taught history from Pokrovsky, but in the most
abridged version of specially selected extracts, where a
roll-call of saints consisted of the Razins, Khalturins,
Bakunins and Dombrovskys; where Suvorov was
described as an executioner, Kutuzov a lackey and
Nakhimov a pirate. It seems funny now. But which of
us, when filling in our forms, shunned our officer origins
like the plague, and said that in our youth we were
miners; that our fathers and grandfathers were peasants,
and our great-grandfathers shepherds? I'm proud of the
fact that the Dobrokhotovs fought at Poltava; that one of
them was executed for treachery by Biron; that we
fought at Rymnik and Preussische-Elau; that my great-

grandfather Maikov is buried at Balaklava; that my grandfather took Plevna; that my father was wounded at Muckden . . .

He is still speaking as the curtain comes down.

ACT FOUR

*The same scene; the same actors. There are now a samovar and
tea-cups on the table. Some time has passed, so that a number of
people have left the table and are dancing.* NERZHIN *is
dancing with* GALINA; *the* PARTY ORGANISER *with*
ANECHKA; BERBENCHUK *with* OLYA; LIKHARYOV *with*
KATYA, *and the* CHIEF CHEMIST *is dancing with* GLAFIRA.
General inebriation is in the air. PROKOPOVICH *is alone, with
a bottle for company.* BERBENCHUK, *still in ceremonial
uniform, has a shiny black top-hat on his head. The radiogram
plays a waltz loudly. To the right, at the little round table, sits*
VANIN. *At the back, behind the mirror, more or less centrally, is*
GRIDNEV. *Whenever a pair of dancers approaches* VANIN, *he
takes the opportunity of teasing them.*

VANIN: Sergei, look out! I'll be writing to your wife. Look
out, Sergei.

NERZHIN: Don't single me out, Comrade Major.
Everybody else is dancing. Why pick on me? Ah, well.
There's nothing for it: go on, write away.

VANIN: Arkadiy! You cheat! What are your promises
worth? Look, just look, Olya is dancing a waltz!

LIKHARYOV: It wasn't me. It's the Colonel. What can I do
in front of a superior officer?

In the meantime, MAIKOV, *unobserved by the dancing
couples, smuggles in under the piano two photographers, who
crawl out, the first setting his camera, the second carrying a
flash.* MAIKOV *walks over to the radiogram and switches
over from the music to the newscast. The music stops, and
simultaneously there is the flash of the bulb. All are frozen as
if in a dumb show, and listen in amazement to the
announcer's voice: . . .* "The leader of the whole of
progressive humanity, the greatest of all thinkers who ever
lived, the genius and the wisest of men, powerfully per . . ."
MAIKOV *switches back to music, just as unexpectedly.*

Everyone starts dancing again, laughing at this prank.
GRIDNEV *is gloomy. The waltz speeds up towards the end and stops.* BERBENCHUK, *waving his top-hat, dances with abandon, a hopak across the stage.*

BERBENCHUK: Having eaten
Cherry cakes
(*repeats*)

Laughter, applause. The dancing pairs walk about the stage.

LIKHARYOV (*approaches* NERZHIN): Excuse me, Signor, time's up. The lady promised me the next dance. (*Takes* GALINA *away to choose another record.*)

NERZHIN, *left alone, wanders off to join* VANIN *and sits down next to him.* MAIKOV *sits down next to* GRIDNEV.

CHIEF CHEMIST (*walking past with* GLAFIRA): This (*pointing to his medal*) I have. And this (*pointing to his epaulette*) I have; and this, what's more (*pulling out his Party card from his pocket*). What's more, I have something in my savings book, and a few expensive coats stashed away in my suitcase.

BERBENCHUK: Saliy, over here!

VANIN: That's not Saliy, that's Zamaliy.

BERBENCHUK: Oh, hell. They've been here three years, and I still can't tell the devils apart.

ZAMALIY *comes running, carrying a bonbonniere.*

BERBENCHUK *offers sweetmeats to* OLYA.

PARTY ORGANISER (*walks past with* ANECHKA): That's the way it was, Doctor. But now, no sooner do I eat something than I have a cramp, here, and here, like this . . .

ANECHKA: You *are* a cheerful partner. Come and see me later, and I'll give you some tablets.

MAIKOV (*to* GRIDNEV): So you took me seriously, did you? Don't worry. I'm a shy little man. My father, it's true, used to peddle pastries, but all the others looked after sheep.

NERZHIN (*to* GRIDNEV): Where did you get this idea that "education doesn't improve the mind"?

VANIN: My friend, he who understands this needs no explanation, but he who doesn't will never see.

MAIKOV: To tell the truth, I'm a proletarian through and through – the illegitimate son of a servant girl. You did learn at school about the gentry, about how, if a girl got caught in the hay-loft . . . That damned feudalism. Le droit de Seigneur!

GRIDNEV: I see, but still, you're half noble by blood.

MAIKOV: Don't pay attention to blood. Look deeper. Deep down I'm a peasant, a worker. Yes, I'm proud of my rough origins: we, the Dobrokhotovs – that means "well wishers" – we wished well, but to whom? To the people, of course!

A tango. GALINA *and* LIKHARYOV *are dancing. The music gradually dies down.*

VANIN (*to* NERZHIN): I feel I'm responsible for everything. It was my fault entirely. Just consider: it was I who surrendered Lutsk, and Lvov. It was I who surrendered Novograd. At Kovel, I almost died, but no sooner was I better, than I surrendered Korosten. It was also I who surrendered Zhitomir. And later on, when no one was looking, during the general exodus, it was the two of us – Vlasov[17] and I – who gave in at Kiev.

MAIKOV (*to* GRIDNEV): But you did study the practical side of things?

GRIDNEV: Of course, both theory and practice. You must know how to proceed when making an arrest. There are millions of ways of doing it. It has to be done quietly. So that no one should know. You can disguise yourself as a pilot, an electrician, a chauffeur, a postman . . . For example, how do you arrest an archimandrite? Well, you ask permission to spend the night in his monastery.

VANIN: I surrendered Poltava, and Lubny and Khorol. As to all those Piryatins and Byela Tserkovs . . . It's a good thing that our lot never got as far as the Volga, otherwise we might have surrendered Stalingrad itself. As we started to fall back, no amount of rearguard defence, or of official order No. 227 or whatever, could stop us. People would be saying: "Friends, isn't Moscow behind us?" While I – while all of us – felt "To hell with it".

ANECHKA *approaches* VANIN *and* NERZHIN, *who soon moves away, looks behind the curtains through the windows, opens his folder of maps, wandering about nervously.*

GALINA, *having finished dancing with* LIKHARYOV, *talks to him and to* BERBENCHUK, *while watching* NERZHIN *anxiously.* NERZHIN *goes out through the door on the right.*

GRIDNEV: The archimandrite, of course, is only too happy to take in Christian pilgrims. The Cheka agents sit there, talking of the Last Judgment, and of Paradise. When the monks have gone to bed, the agents stand up and say: "You're under arrest, you vermin." Will I ever forget? . . .

GLAFIRA (*among a group of people on the left of the stage, sings to her guitar*):
You can forget me, gypsies,
I'm leaving the encampment.
I am singing my very last song.

CHIEF CHEMIST (*very drunk, leaning over the bannister of the staircase, recites either to* KATYA, *who is close by, or to no one in particular*):
And I dreamt that my heart aches no more,
That it's a china bell in golden Cathay . . .

KATYA: What's all this?

CHIEF CHEMIST: That's by Vertinsky,[18] Katya. Did you ever hear him sing?

KATYA: That old stuff. It's old . . .: it's cloying.
She moves away. The CHIEF CHEMIST *remains standing for a while, then comes down to the first step of the stairs. The music is quiet, as if from behind glass.*

ANECHKA: Did you enjoy the party?

VANIN: I did.

ANECHKA: Why look so sad, then?

VANIN: Which of us can control his feelings? When the war
ends, let's go somewhere far away, far from visitors,
books, newspapers, news, from meetings and duties.
Somewhere where the peasants are, beyond Tambov,
Ryazan . . . You can be a doctor there, so long as you
don't inflict too much damage. I'll be looking after an
orchard, and seeing to the beehives. In the morning a
chill will rise from the river. Geese, flocks, silence.

ANECHKA: What fantasies! You'd be the first to get
restless.

BERBENCHUK *takes* GALINA *by the arm and leads her
downstage, away from her group of people.*

BERBENCHUK: Miss Pavlova, I'm bewitched. I'm charmed.
I'm not that old!

GRIDNEV (*watching him; to* MAIKOV): So one can be
arrested when one least expects it, least knows. Now
that's a first-class arrest! When he's hurrying to an
assignation, or off on holiday, or some new assignment
. . . When he's away from his usual surroundings, his
friends . . .

MAIKOV (*filling* GRIDNEV's *and his own glasses*): Oh, wine!
Who is that nameless genius, lost in the mists of
history . . .

GLAFIRA: Eugene!

Watching BERBENCHUK *anxiously, she has left her group.*
BERBENCHUK's *talk with* GALINA *is animated. They have
moved closer to* VANIN. ANECHKA *has walked over to the
dancing couples.*

MAIKOV: . . . who trod the grapes for the first time with
his bare feet . . .

GLAFIRA (*from a distance*): Eugene, come over here.

BERBENCHUK: Well what is it now? (*To* GALINA.) Excuse
me. I'm sorry.

LIKHARYOV: I used to love picnics, with all those pretty
birds, colourful and slim.

GALINA, *left alone, looks uncertainly around.*

VANIN: You look pale, Galina.

GALINA: Not used to such festivities. (*She obeys his gesture and sits next to him.*)

BERBENCHUK: All right, Glafira, my love . . . I'll do my best . . .

GLAFIRA: Anybody else, but not her!

GRIDNEV: Are you trying to get me drunk? The thing is, the more I drink, the soberer I get.

GLAFIRA: You can sniff around those two (*nodding at* KATYA *and* OLYA.) I have a sixth sense, being a Soviet citizen. Do you know who she is? Have you examined her papers? (*She leads him to a group of people on the left.*)

MAIKOV: I was hoping to make friends with you. What a rotter you are.

GRIDNEV: Captain Maikov. It's late. Can you enlighten me? Are there guards at all the exits?

MAIKOV: At all the entrances.

GRIDNEV: No, I mean exits.

MAIKOV: This isn't a prison. It's a unit.

GRIDNEV: Is that so? (*Pointing to* GALINA.) Just remember, if you let this girl escape, you'll get it in the neck.

MAIKOV (*rising, coldly*): Your papers?

GRIDNEV: Which?

MAIKOV: That little chit.

GRIDNEV: Er . . . mm . . . Counter-intelligence, you see, don't like to leave too many traces behind.

MAIKOV: In that case, I don't propose to be answerable for every passing girl.

GRIDNEV: You needn't be afraid. We never make a mistake. If someone is arrested, it's for a good reason.

MAIKOV: Never mind that. I'm an official and I need a signature and a rubber stamp. (*He rises. Furiously.*) You . . . a-a-a-h . . . You've ruined the party: spoiled all the fun. You've killed it, snuffed it out like a moth.

GRIDNEV: Since you're going, could you send the Commander to me.

Act Four

MAIKOV: As far as I can see, you've only one stripe on your shoulder. (*He walks over to the window on the right.*)

GALINA (*to* VANIN): I met a lot of emigrés, I must confess. They were well-off, well fed, their houses comfortable. What were they missing? Why did they leave it all? What attracts them to our unkind, evil country? You enter a richly furnished sitting room, and what do you see – a country landscape with a ravine, a birch tree, a barn – and a wooden fence. I once met an old landowner. Do you know what he did when he arrived in Smolensk? He knelt down to kiss the cobbles in front of the cathedral. This love of one's country! It can't be understood, or cured, or justified. Some will be hanged here; some will be imprisoned, but they keep flying into the candle flame.

GRIDNEV (*beckons the* PARTY ORGANISER): An *operational* request, Party Organiser. Send me the Divisional Commander, at once.

The PARTY ORGANISER *goes off to do so.*

GALINA: As to the young people, they've taken their university degrees there; they speak several European languages, but marry their own kind. And they don't think for a minute that they'll go on living abroad. For them – it's all for the time being, for the time being . . .

MAIKOV *summons* VANIN *to come over to the right.*

OLYA (*taking part in a game, which has started up on the left of the stage*): Forfeit! You must pay a forfeit for that.

BERBENCHUK (*approaching and bending over* GRIDNEV): You wanted me, Comrade Lieutenant?

GRIDNEV: I did. Well, how are things? The state of affairs . . . ?

BERBENCHUK: Not too bad, on the whole . . .

GRIDNEV: How's the Division?

BERBENCHUK: On full alert, as you can see.

GRIDNEV: And how's Galina?

BERBENCHUK: Miss Pavlova? She's got what it takes, don't you think?

GRIDNEV: She's a spy.

BERBENCHUK (*flabbergasted*): She's what?!

GRIDNEV: So you never spotted it?

> GALINA *shrinks from the glances on all sides. She turns nervously first to* GRIDNEV *and* BERBENCHUK, *then to* VANIN *and* MAIKOV.

GRIDNEV: You think you're good-natured. But to my mind you're simply short-sighted. The girl just flicks her skirt, and you . . .

BERBENCHUK: Out of sheer boredom, don't you know. But I . . . Oh, dear . . .

GRIDNEV: You're spineless, that's what. Wherever you are, in the U.S.S.R., or abroad, you must perceive the enemy under any guise. Whoever you meet, man or woman, you must always think this might be an enemy. You must always be on the *qui vive*.

> MAIKOV *goes quickly out into the corridor.* VANIN *returns thoughtfully to* GALINA. *A kind of line has been formed through* GRIDNEV *which separates* GALINA *and* VANIN *from the rest of the company. The* CHIEF CHEMIST *who has been sitting all this time on the bottom step, with his face in his hands, lifts his head and starts to recite:*

CHIEF CHEMIST:

> Are you a prophet, or just a deceiver,
> Who constantly speaks of a new paradise?
> Stop your music, you mad organ grinder!
> I want to forget your song! Otherwise . . .
>
> *He lowers his head once again.* BERBENCHUK, *utterly beside himself, moves away from* GRIDNEV.

VANIN (*to* GALINA): I'm very much afraid that these miles you have to cover on your way home will not be easy for you. You won't be received in a brotherly fashion: there'll be bayonets at the frontier. Let me give you a bit of advice. Get rid of all this jewelry and finery. When speaking of home, say 'ome. Use your fingers to blow your nose. Attach yourself to a party of peasant women, who are being herded home, frightened at being pushed around. Tie a scarf round your head, and put on an old country coat. Don't have a suitcase; carry a bag. Don't be squeamish about suet. Have some sausages with you, and some tobacco. There's no better friend than that, even if it doesn't last long. Whether it's the frontier guards, or the railway patrols, who don't want to let you in to the *Sovietische Union*, "Have a smoke" you say and generously fill their palms with it. They'd roll their cigarettes and ask: "Where are you from, girl?" "From Orlov," you'd say. They would chuck you under the chin and say "Off you go, you cow, we don't need your pass." You must forget everything you've seen – the forms of government, the customs, the differences, new ideas, dresses, even light and air – and when you get there, change your address; and if they ask if you've been under the occupation – the answer is, No.

BERBENCHUK, *as if afraid to cross the invisible line, stays downstage, and in a hoarse, theatrical whisper, tries to attract* VANIN's *attention.*

BERBENCHUK: Major! Hey, Major!

VANIN: Eh?

BERBENCHUK: Vanin!

VANIN: What?

BERBENCHUK: Major!

VANIN: Well, what is it?

BERBENCHUK *is making signs.*

VANIN: You come over here.

BERBENCHUK *refuses, desperately.*

VANIN: Can't you? Oh, misery! I can hardly move my legs I've drunk so much.

Rising heavily, VANIN *crosses the invisible line and leaves* GALINA *finally alone. People on the left have imperceptibly disappeared –* ANECHKA, GLAFIRA, *the* PARTY ORGANISER, PROKOPOVICH *are gone.* GALINA *has shrunk into herself.* GRIDNEV *keeps his eyes on her the whole time. The electric light grows dim.* VANIN *and* BERBENCHUK *are downstage.*

VANIN: What is it?

BERBENCHUK: Oh, my God, she's a spy.

VANIN: Who is?

BERBENCHUK: Shush, not so loud! We're lost!

VANIN: But, who?

BERBENCHUK: We! You and I. After all you're my
dep . . .

VANIN: Who's dep.? What's dep.? They'll start with you:
you're the chief. (BERBENCHUK *is shattered.* VANIN *in a
businesslike manner*). Did the plenipotentiary say so?

BERBENCHUK: Yes.

VANIN: Has he got a warrant for her arrest?

BERBENCHUK: Seeing that he talks like that, maybe he
has.

VANIN: You think he has. But coming here, he knew
nothing about her.

BERBENCHUK: That's true. You're right.

VANIN: Go to bed. I'll wake you tomorrow.

BERBENCHUK (*in a weak voice*): Captain Maikov.

VANIN: I'll tell him. You go to bed. Take your wife with
you.

BERBENCHUK: With my darling Glafira! (*Is about to leave,
but immediately turns back again.*)

VANIN: If you're not going, you'll have to deal with it
yourself.

BERBENCHUK: Suppose I go to sleep, what sort of dreams
shall I have? Still, I have some hope . . . You're good
chaps, you two. (*Departing.*) The Division, it's lost (*He
meets* KATYA *at the back of the stage and returns, holding
her by an outstretched arm.*) You'll sort it out, Arseniy?

VANIN: Of course I will.

BERBENCHUK: You've got me out of trouble. You're a
good friend. But should anything . . . you know, don't
knock on Glafira's door . . . She'll start looking for me
. . . I'll be, so to speak, I'll be with Katya.

He departs with KATYA. LIKHARYOV *and* OLYA *are also
gone. The light is ever growing dimmer.*

84

GALINA (*fingering the phial round her neck*): I can hardly
breathe. God, I'm terrified! Sergei is gone. All the
friends have gone.

She steps back. GRIDNEV *rises and advances upon her
slowly.* VANIN *remains motionless downstage, in the centre.
Suddenly, at the very top of the stairs there are loud
footsteps, and almost immediately afterwards there is a pistol
shot and the sound of broken glass. There is running about
on the staircase –* MAIKOV, *his head bandaged with a
bloodstained cloth, waves an unsheathed sword, the* PARTY
ORGANISER *behind him in his underclothes, getting dressed
as he runs, and* SALIY *is holding a pistol above his head.
They rush around the stage, infecting both* VANIN *and*
GRIDNEV *with their panicky movements.* VANIN *minces
around in a ludicrous manner. Some look through the
windows.*

MAIKOV (*shouting in snatches as he runs around the
stage*): They've got through! The machine guns! I'm
wounded. We're surrounded. There's only one escape
route that isn't cut off!

In a kind of chain, all five, VANIN *and* GRIDNEV
included, run off to the left. SALIY, *being the last to go,
shoots into the air once more.* GALINA *rushes around,
anxious, but relieved, and runs upstairs. The* CHIEF
CHEMIST *lifts his head and looks around in amazement.
The light is dim.* NERZHIN *enters from the right. He wears
his greatcoat and a fur hat. His slow gait is out of tune with
the pandemonium which has just taken place on the stage.*

NERZHIN: They've gone, I see. (*Approaching the piano, he
absent-mindedly plays a few notes.*)

CHIEF CHEMIST: Who was shooting here?

NERZHIN: You must have imagined it, you soak. (*The same
depressing chords.*) Oh, chemist, chemist, where's your
anti-gas? (*The same chord.*) A typically Russian
celebration. It started sideways and ended sadly.

CHIEF CHEMIST: Well, tell me something funny.

NERZHIN: Such as? . . . It was only today that I stood

among the ruins (*we can hear music, which emanates from some unknown source*) of German glory . . . I think it was by chance that our army avoided going across the field which had a wooden sign, saying "Mines". I found not too far from Hohenstein newly blackened ruins, already sprinkled with snow.

NERZHIN *is so taken up with his story that he fails to notice the departure of the* CHIEF CHEMIST, *or* SALIY's *arrival and stealthy movements. He puts something under the corners of the carpet. Towards the end of his speech the light is so dim that the arc lights themselves become visible.*

A memorial has been put up at the very edge, the very point the Russian Army had reached and was surrounded thirty years ago. Seven gloomy towers, to denote the number of Wilhelm's divisions, linked by a wall with images of soldiers set into it like saints, arrogant and still . . . Flag poles for raising standards; a ceremonial arena; an altar at which gloomy Teutonic oaths and speeches were made. The mob used to come here to see their rulers. And suddenly it's all blown up, the cold granite and uncaring marble are blackened by the smoke of the explosion. There is a yawning gap in the ring of wall, some towers flattened, others still standing like skeletons . . . Having had one victorious moment, they thought, in their madness, they would last forever. There I stood, by Hindenburg's vault, an enemy soldier, neither proud nor happy, with a tired smile on my lips, thinking how absurd human vanity is, how disgusting . . . in the midst of the countryside. The branches of trees, momentarily shaken by the blast, are again covered with star-like flakes of snow. You may have been a glorious Commander, you may have received all the honours, but what are your diamond, star-studded and brilliant medals compared to this silent and reconciling snow.

Lieutenant YACHMENNIKOV *appears in the right hand door. He wears his greatcoat, with a leather belt and a fur hat. He is slender and young; all white from the snow. At*

first he stands in the doorway, then enters quietly.
A tangle of eternal injuries! You triumph, then you
weep, then triumph again. If only we could learn the
lesson of this generous earth of how to *forget* . . . Oh,
you inglorious enemy of my people, how can I get
through to you against that wall of incomprehension?
Look, Germany, what your evil triumphs have led to.
Today it is we who rejoice, like Balthasar. But what
retribution, what wrath are we sowing for our children?
Oh, innocent Russia, demented Russia . . .
Yachmennikov! Ooo, you're all covered with snow!

YACHMENNIKOV (*officially*): Comrade Captain, the engines
are still running. The whole battery has arrived. What
are your orders?

NERZHIN: Sit down. Where are the men?

YACHMENNIKOV: I've brought them into the house.

NERZHIN: Soon we'll be off: to fight.

YACHMENNIKOV: What's all this? On that mirror?

NERZHIN: Ever read the Bible?

YACHMENNIKOV: My mother used to. And father read it
on Holy Days. As for us, we spent our time studying the
Shorter Manual.

NERZHIN: Should you live, do read it. Today it's the
Major's birthday.

YACHMENNIKOV: Is that so? Well, he's a good man. One
could wish such a . . .

NERZHIN: Let's drink to him.

YACHMENNIKOV: Shouldn't I switch the engines off?

NERZHIN: Let them tick over quietly: we're not that poor.
Apart from the Baku oilwells, we possess Ploesti[19] now.
What will you drink? There's some nice Corsican wine
here, such as we've never tasted, you and I.
YACHMENNIKOV *looks at himself in the mirror.*
What are you looking at?

YACHMENNIKOV: I'm just checking if they'll know me at
home.

NERZHIN: Your parents will. But I doubt if the girl friends

will. As I remember you from your student days, you've become a man. And what, Victor, are you going to tell them at your village council in Godunov, and your friends of the Vladimir district? Will you tell them how we followed in Rokossovsky's footsteps, how we ate our dinner off a mirror – will they ever believe it?

YACHMENNIKOV: It wouldn't do to talk about such things in our village.

NERZHIN: So what shall we drink to, you conqueror? If you live, you'll get home, and get married, and propagate the tribe – who doesn't do that? Let's think of something special, something original. What is your special wish?

YACHMENNIKOV: Special, special? . . . That somehow or other they would disband the collective farms.

NERZHIN: Abandon the collective farms! I must say! You're no fool. But since that's the toast you want, raise your glass.
They drink.
But you know, Marx did write that it would be best not to disturb the successful peasants. For them Communism is unknown territory, a sort of Mars. Disband the collective farms! It's all talk, Victor, it's palliatives. They babble on to persuade you to face those iron tanks.

YACHMENNIKOV: I look at it that way, too. Those collective farms are useful to the State, not to us. Without them the State wouldn't get a grain out of us peasants. They wouldn't be able to do a thing.

NERZHIN: Well, you old castle. Did you hear our toast? Up with the Russians! I'll pour you some of this vintage wine: the bottle is all dusty . . . And I'll tell you what *my* dreams are: that in Russia you could say out loud whatever you think. That's not going to happen soon, eh?

YACHMENNIKOV: Not too soon, I expect.

NERZHIN: What if it does?
They clink their glasses and drink.

Now you drink to any Major you like. I've had enough,
even before these two glasses. But help yourself. Fill
your pockets!

(*Shoving food towards him.* YACHMENNIKOV *declines.*)

YACHMENNIKOV: Comrade Captain, our cars are
chock-a-block!

NERZHIN: Oh, hell, I forgot. I come from a starving
district. Will we ever get rid of this greed? Well,
brother, let's roll on further across Europe. Don't put
my Blitz-Opel in front. I'm taking a girl with me. Don't
. . . don't look at me like that.

YACHMENNIKOV: How do you mean, like that? I'm not
looking like that.

NERZHIN: But thinking?

YACHMENNIKOV: I'm thinking that there're three front
seats . . .

NERZHIN: I bet you're thinking the Battery Commander is
at it at last. But, no, old friend, she's engaged to
someone else.

YACHMENNIKOV *stands to attention, salutes and turning in
a military manner, leaves.* NERZHIN *moves slowly towards
the staircase, but on hearing a noise from above, runs
upstairs. There enter quickly, and in a preoccupied manner,*
VANIN *with grenades and a cartridge belt;* GRIDNEV
*carrying an automatic weapon (he doesn't know how to carry
it or sling it and is in constant danger of either killing himself
or his companions); the* PARTY ORGANISER *who carries a
rifle with a bayonet. Behind him,* MAIKOV *in ceremonial
uniform, still with a bandage round his head as before. He's
pulling a heavy machine gun by a rope with one hand, while
in the other he carries a sword. This whole scene is uneasy,
under moving searchlights.*

VANIN (*smoking a pipe*): No panic. Stay calm. We are
unbeatable. Captain Maikov, you must maintain radio
contact with us.

MAIKOV: Everybody down!

He, GRIDNEV *and the* PARTY ORGANISER *throw*

themselves down. VANIN *imperturbably continues to stand, smoking. A sizzling fire-cracker explodes upwards from underneath the carpet.*

VANIN: Well, well, the infernal machine hasn't exploded yet.

All three rise. Thereafter, GRIDNEV *and the* PARTY ORGANISER *move with great caution.* MAIKOV, *having unsheathed his sword, waves it around.*

MAIKOV: Boy, what a sword! Party Organiser, shall we chop them down Cossack fashion? Want to take it? (*He ties the sword to the* PARTY ORGANISER'*s belt.*) Vlad, you dare-devil! Take the machine gun at least! (*He shoves the rope of the machine gun into* GRIDNEV'*s hand.*)

GRIDNEV (*pushing it away*): What am I to do with it? I've . . . no idea.

MAIKOV: Then let me give you a Maxim gun and three hundred bullets.

VANIN: Calm yourself, Lieutenant. Remember what Chapayev[20] used to say. What should a Communist do at a moment like this?

PARTY ORGANISER: Enough of this demagogy! We are the leaders. Our lives are precious to the people.

VANIN: That's just what I'm saying. Into the car, I say! Be off with you!

They move towards the exit. MAIKOV, *stretching out his arms, stops them leaving.*

MAIKOV: You'll get lost! To be on the safe side, take a map at least.

GRIDNEV (*pushing it away*): I don't know how to read a map.

MAIKOV: So what did they teach you?

GRIDNEV: The principles of Leninism. Spy-ology. The history of the Party . . .

With an awkward movement, he steps on another fire-cracker: it sizzles and goes off.

MAIKOV: Oh, dear, how careless. But I'm glad you've survived your baptism by fire!

VANIN: Party Organiser! Don't panic! Who shall stay here to maintain the Party rule?

MAIKOV: When you return, you'll have to bury our corpses.

VANIN: No panic. I open the conference of the Party Group. (*He climbs on a chair, puts one foot on the mirror, and leans on one knee.*) GRIDNEV *and the* PARTY ORGANISER *approach* VANIN. MAIKOV *moves away.* Comrades! Just one question: which of the three of us shall stay behind in the Division, as Party link? I suggest Gridnev.

Everybody looks at GRIDNEV.

GRIDNEV (*animatedly*): Comrade Deputy Commander. Considering . . . (*He searches his pockets.*) Here's my medical certificate . . . My health is poor . . .

VANIN: Who, then?

GRIDNEV: Party Organiser, you wouldn't mind . . .

PARTY ORGANISER: Hey, no! I can't either. I would suggest Likharyov.

VANIN: But where is he?

MAIKOV: With a girl, somewhere.

PARTY ORGANISER: In that . . . case – the Staff Captain.

GRIDNEV (*shifting his automatic awkwardly*): Stop squabbling, for goodness sake. We shall all be taken prisoner.

MAIKOV (*rushes towards him and moves the barrel down*): For God's sake, keep it down!

VANIN (*in the same position, completely cool*): He (*nods at* MAIKOV) can't be left. He's not a *member*. He's only a candidate.

MAIKOV *guiltily lowers his head.*

Or shall we trust him? Maikov!

MAIKOV *raises his head. He grows in stature noticeably with each phrase.*

PARTY ORGANISER: The Party!

GRIDNEV: Over to you!

VANIN: Completely!

PARTY ORGANISER: Great trust!

GRIDNEV: A big responsibility!

VANIN: You'll lead the fighters . . .

PARTY ORGANISER: In the sacred cause of Comrade Stalin!

GRIDNEV: You'll be in charge of the Commander's Units.

PARTY ORGANISER: And you must see to it that the organisation should grow. New recruits!

VANIN (*getting off his pedestal*): Where the hell's my pipe? I'm too old to go off travelling in the middle of the night . . .

SALIY AND ZAMALIY (*come running in together*): The car is ready!

> GRIDNEV *and the* PARTY ORGANISER *both start rushing.* VANIN *pushes them along.*

VANIN: Go, go! For Stalin! For Mother Russia!

> *They go out left.* ZAMALIY, *at a sign from* MAIKOV, *noisily pushes out the machine gun in the same direction.* MAIKOV *is alone. His cheerful excitement evaporates. He stands pensively, then pulls off his bandage, moves over to the piano, leans despondently on it.* NERZHIN *appears at the top of the staircase with an elegant ladies' suitcase in his hand.* MAIKOV *sees him.*

MAIKOV: Et tu Brute! Looting! It's a nightmare . . .

NERZHIN: I'm off, Alex.

MAIKOV: Be off, then.

NERZHIN: So long!

MAIKOV: Au revoir!

> NERZHIN *stands more than halfway up the staircase.*
> GALINA *in a fur coat, joins him silently.* MAIKOV *can now see her as well. He whistles, then leaning on the music stand, with his back to it, he smiles and sings:*

Having climbed his rickety bridge,

He remembers the port he has left . . .

> NERZHIN *and* GALINA, *arm in arm, descend the stairs, the spotlights following them:*

Act Four

ALL THREE: And flicks off the foam of the sea
From his naval and elegant boots!
Exeunt right, waving to MAIKOV, *who waves back.*

CURTAIN

1951
Ekibastuz
Composed orally while on gang labour.

TRANSLATORS' NOTES

1. Vassily Surikov, 19th-century painter.
2. Theodossiya Morozova, member of the Old Believers Sect: starved to death for her beliefs in 1672. Subject of Surikov's dramatic picture.
3. A line from a poem by Alexander Blok (1880–1921).
4. Alexander Suvorov, famous Russian General (1729–1800).
5. Zoya Kosmodemyanskaya (1923–41), Heroine of the USSR, executed by the Germans.
6. V. V. Mayakovsky (1894–1930), Futurist poet.
7. Russian Liberation Army, set up under the aegis of the Wehrmacht, headed by General A. Vlasov and consisting of the Soviet prisoners of war and White émigrés, in the hope of liberating Russia from Bolshevik rule.
8. Gori, a town in Georgia, north-west of Tbilisi, Stalin's birthplace.
9. Magnitogorsk, a town in the Urals.
10. Potyomkin, a reference to fictional villages created by Prince Potyomkin (1739–91) to impress Catherine the Great.
11. K. K. Rokossovsky (1896–1968), Marshal. Twice Hero of the USSR. Deputy Minister of Defence and Chief Inspector of the Armed Forces.
12. General A. V. Samsonov (1859–1914), Commander of the Second Army on the Eastern Front in the First World War.
13. N. I. Bukharin (1888–1938), leading Bolshevik, purged and executed.
14. K. F. Gauss (1777–1855), German mathematician.
15. N. I. Yezhov (1895–1938), Commissar of Internal Affairs.
16. M. V. Lomonosov (1711–65), a peasant's son, Professor of Chemistry and Physics, member of the Academy of Sciences.
17. A. A. Vlasov, General in the Red Army, taken prisoner in

1942. Head of the Russian Liberation Army. Arrested by the Soviets in 1945, executed the following year.
18. A. Vertinsky, émigré "diseur", returned to the USSR after the war.
19. Ploesti, Roumanian oil-field.
20. V. I. Chapayev (1887–1919), Bolshevik Hero of the Civil War.

PRISONERS

A Tragedy

Translated from the Russian
by Helen Rapp and Nancy Thomas

DRAMATIS PERSONAE

KLIMOV, Peter, former prisoner of war, Sergeant in the Red Army, now Private in the American Army, 25 years of age

KULYBYSHEV, Kuzma, former prisoner of war, Private in a unit of conscripted prisoners, over 40

BOLOSNIN, Igor, former Lieutenant in the Red Army, now Ensign in the Russian Liberation Army, 28

PRYANCHIKOV, Valentin, former prisoner of war, former officer in the Red Army, 28

PECHKUROV, Ivan, former prisoner of war, Private, 23

YELESHEV, Anatoliy, former prisoner of war, formerly officer in the Red Army, 40

MEDNIKOV, Vasiliy (Vasya), former prisoner of war, 23

VOROTYNTSEV, George, Colonel in the Russian Imperial Army, 69

RUBIN, Leo, Major in the Political Section of the Red Army, 33

KHOLUDENEV, Andrew, Captain in the Red Army, 26

GAI, Paul, Sergeant in the Red Army, 24

TEMIROV, Captain in the Russian Imperial Army, Captain in the Royal Yugoslav Army, about 60

DIVNICH, Eugene, under 40

MOSTOVSHCHIKOV, defector, Professor of physics, over 50

PRISONER with a goatee beard

PRISONER with horn-rimmed spectacles

HALBERAU, Oberleutnant in the Wehrmacht

WRZESNIK, Leon, Second Lieutenant in the Polish Army

DAVYDOV, Major, Quartermaster in the Red Army

FIACENTE, Giovanni, Corporal in the Italian Army

PRISONER with a black eye

Prisoners

SIDOROV

PAKHOMOV

POSVYANTSEVA, Anastasiya, 28–30

POSVYANTSEV, Vsevolod, her husband, an émigré,
Subaltern in the Russian Liberation Army, 28

KOLOSOVITOV, Theodore, about 40

NEKLYUCHIMOV, Alexander, Lieutenant in the N.K.G.B.,
28

GENERAL, Head of the front-line Department of Counter-
Intelligence SMERSH, young and handsome

RUBLYOV, Prokhor, his deputy, Colonel, about 55

OKHREYANOV, Luka, second deputy, Colonel

KRIVOSHCHAP, President of the military tribunal, Colonel

MORGOSLEPOV, prosecuting Counsel, Lieutenant Colonel

KASHEVAROV, official defence lawyer

KAPUSTIN, Major in the N.K.G.B.

OGNIDA, Major in the N.K.G.B.

KAMCHUZHNAYA, Lydia, Captain in the N.K.G.B., about
30

MYMRA, Captain in the N.K.G.B.

SVERBYOZHNIKOV, Lieutenant in the N.K.G.B., a novice
investigator

LVOVA, Sophia, Head of the Medical Unit, Lieutenant
Colonel in the Medical Corps

FILIPPOV, Captain in the escort army, front-line soldier

NINEL, typist

1ST OPERATIVE

2ND OPERATIVE

GEORGE, General's orderly

1ST ASSESSOR of the tribunal

2ND ASSESSOR of the tribunal

'KHOLUDENEV's escort at the trial

Officers, Sergeants, Supervisors, escort soldiers

Prisoners

Waitresses, typists, secretaries

Prisoners

The action takes place in one of the Counter-Intelligence centres of SMERSH of the Red Army on 9 July 1945, from one midnight to the next.

(Note to Producers: A shorter version of the play can omit Scenes 6, 8 and 11.)

PUBLISHER'S NOTE

Some parts of this play are in verse
in the original Russian.
The translators' notes are printed on pages 236–7.

Scene I

A cheerless howling of dogs, resembling that of wolves, can be heard from somewhere. It dies down, as the conversation begins. The scene is the back yard of a prison, badly lit and bounded on three sides by the walls of the three-storey prison building. The only light comes from a wood fire underneath a large cauldron in the middle of the stage. Next to the cauldron a platform has been fixed up with a ladder leading to it. Two people dressed in black, in fur hats, the ear flaps raised and sticking out like horns, are fussing around the cauldron, the elder one climbing up from time to time to stir the contents with a baker's shovel. There are logs around the fire. People sit around the fire on up-turned logs, or lie on the ground. They are YELESHEV *and* KHOLUDENEV, VOROTYNTSEV *and* PECHKUROV, KULYBYSHEV, KLIMOV *and* GAI. HALBERAU *is busy twisting a thread.* FIACENTE *is either making or cleaning a cigarette holder.* DAVYDOV *is lying with his back to everybody. He has spread out some food in little bags and is eating.*

Two couples keep walking about: MOSTOVSHCHIKOV *and* DIVNICH, *and* TEMIROV *and* RUBIN. *They walk in arcs or figures-of-eight, either in front or at the back of the stage.*

All their heads are shaved and they are almost naked; one is in shorts, another has tied a towel round his midriff, RUBIN *is wrapped in a sheet.* KHOLUDENEV *and* DAVYDOV *wear officers' fur jerkins with nothing underneath.* TEMIROV *is in a Caucasian felt cloak.* MOSTOVSHCHIKOV *wears pince-nez.* VOROTYNTSEV *has a little round, grey beard, while* RUBIN's *is long and black.*

TEMIROV (*coming out accompanied by* RUBIN): I will *not* deny that your knowledge of uniforms is impeccable, but to suggest that the Life Guard Cuirassiers . . .

RUBIN: Yes, they did wear white plumes! (*They go past.*)

MOSTOVSHCHIKOV (*coming out accompanied by*
DIVNICH): Your kind of Christianity is tough. You
bring not peace, but a sword.

DIVNICH: What do you expect us to do? Do you want us to
lie down like emaciated slaves before a Juggernaut? (*They
go past.*)

KLIMOV: We'll never understand those Americans. I
suppose we're too slow-witted. There's an issue of tinned
veal, nice and pink. There are no holes in the tins, just a
dent. Never mind, they throw them out as damaged. Or
else huge boxes full of ship's biscuits. If the packing is
slightly squashed, out they go into a ditch. (*He laughs.*)

HALBERAU (*singing as he works*):
> Und warst du krank, sie pflegte dich,
> Den sie mit tiefen Schmerz geboren.
> Und gaben alle dich schon auf –
> Die Mutter gab dich nicht verloren.

PECHKUROV: I would have joined the Russian Liberation
Army, or worked for the Police. Instead, just think, four
years in a prison camp. I was never put in charge,
nobody gave me a stick to wield. I got no privileges at
someone else's expense. I just walked up and down,
emptying slop pails. If only we'd been liberated by the
Americans! But, no! It had to be our lot!

VOROTYNTSEV: *Our* lot, Ivan? That's a loaded word.
What's *ours* about them? The sound of their names? A
Russian cast of face? But after all the executions, camps,
collectivisation, that spongeful of vinegar – in what way
are they *ours*?

RUBIN (*coming out accompanied by* TEMIROV): Yes, I *am* a
Communist, an orthodox one what's more, and whatever
my personal fate . . . (*They go past.*)

GAI (*his wounded right arm in a sling*): So our Soviet General
shouts: "Soldiers, come back!" And the American
General says: "What for?" "Excuse me," says our
General, "you are guests here. Our custom is for simple
soldiers to eat at the same table as the Generals!"

KLIMOV: Well said!!

GAI: So, naturally, they rush forward for the grub.

KLIMOV: That was a lesson in democracy, no two ways about it.

TEMIROV *and* RUBIN *are by-passing* DAVYDOV, *who is chewing.* DAVYDOV *catches hold of* RUBIN'*s sheet.*

DAVYDOV: Comrade Rubin. Come and sit down, have some of this simple food my friends sent me . . . There's no one I can talk to. The only true Soviets in this prison are you and me.

RUBIN: I think, Comrade Davydov, I ought not to be in a hurry about making friends just now. (*He goes past.*)

YELESHEV (*to* KHOLUDENEV): My young friend, even though my head is crowned with silver hair – (*he lifts his hand to his hair*) oh, I forgot, it's shaved . . . But I am bound to say that I devoted my entire life to women and I have no regrets.

DIVNICH (*coming out with* MOSTOVSHCHIKOV): Yes, I grow silent before the star-studded vault of the night sky, and when I see the hues of dawn or of sunset, I grow silent at the sight of the repentant tears of a fellow human being. I love the frailty of human flesh. Our Lord decreed that we should love sinners – but when people are virtuous . . . (*They go past.*)

RUBIN (*to* TEMIROV): Do you know, they're as stubborn as mules, the way they keep quoting their book of rules. I can't stand it sometimes and answer back with a barbed retort. I'm a thorn in the flesh of the political section. And yet, what do they do themselves? They spend their time getting parcels together to send to their wives. They're looters, scroungers. Call them political workers! But who am I saying this to? You're delighted! You laugh! (*They go past.*)

DAVYDOV (*having tied up his little bags, speaking to* FIACENTE *over his shoulder*): Giovanni, have a rusk.

FIACENTE *takes it rapidly and bows.*

DAVYDOV (*after some thought*): Here! There's a bit left to go with your rusk – you can scrape off the sides and the bottom with your finger.

He hands over a small jar, which FIACENTE *takes with one hand, while pressing his other hand to his heart. He bows.*)

GAI: He used to be the Commander of our regiment. He was sensible, firm, self-controlled. He used to say: "You can see for yourself how you spent your war, who we shed our blood for." When will we learn? . . . It's a sad admission but it seems, wherever you're best off, that's where you belong. He was good at English. He pushed the four of us into a jeep – and on to the bridge!

RUBIN (*coming out with* TEMIROV): I'm an ass to have started a conversation with you!

TEMIROV: You're a destroyer of human hopes. Shame on you. Shame!

RUBIN: And you're a sad remnant of Kolchak's army. An Imperial hanger-on!

TEMIROV: But never a Communist, no, never a stinking Communist!

RUBIN: Yes, prisons are a good thing if it's people like you who're in them.

TEMIROV: At least I'm among strangers, while you are with your own kind. (*They abruptly part company.*)

GAI: I jumped off and hit him in the teeth with the butt of my gun and suddenly I saw the jeep. Hullo there! But they arrested me then.

PECHKUROV (*to* VOROTYNTSEV): The doors are shut, the keys are turned, you're surrounded by wolves in the night. We'll shoot you, we'll hang you . . . Well, I haven't got nine lives. You can write any damn thing you like in your report. I'll sign it without reading it, just leave me alone.

VOROTYNTSEV: But that's just it. That's the fatal mistake. Our weak, tattered, oppressed willpower is weighed down by this enormity, by their entire apparatus. Its sharp end is pointed right at us. During these unbearable but numbered nights, Ivan, we must, we must cling on by our fingertips. We must resist this uncontrolled gallop, this snorting, this foaming at the mouth if we're to keep some self respect.

DIVNICH (*coming out with* MOSTOVSHCHIKOV): I managed to resist the Gestapo with the help of God's strong hand, and with God's mercy I'll survive the G.P.U. (*They go past.*)

RUBIN (*putting his arms around* YELESHEV *and* KHOLUDENEV, *who are sitting down*): Well, sons of Russia! Don't let's complain about our present troubles. After all, we've always had an Eastern despotism . . . Everything that seems so hard on our little selves will pass. In the balance of History we don't count for much . . .

GAI: The anti-aircraft guns were out of ammunition. There I was on a bridge over the river and I managed to bring down a couple of Messerschmitts, fighting like a maniac for that bunch of . . . (*He wails, holding his head.*)

KULYBYSHEV: Never mind, son, it's no use crying over spilt milk. You can't make omelettes without breaking eggs. The surf is full of sand before the sea calms down. And your brain is just as addled.

RUBIN (*now with* DIVNICH): Yes, I accept Christianity. Having once adhered to a principle, I try to treasure it. But if that principle turns out to be wrong, I find solace only in Christianity. From Graeco-Roman times to the heights of German genius there's been no better teaching, and I am ready to follow the path of the Son of Man. I would drink from the cup of Gethsemane! But I have in mind the teachings of Christ, not the dogmas of the Church . . . (*They go past.*)

MOSTOVSHCHIKOV: Now, the King of Norway is a darling. He wanders about Oslo, having nothing better to do; he will drink a mug of beer in a pub with his subjects, will invite some learned foreigner to visit him, he never loses his temper, never gets ruffled, while his wife, the Queen, goes to market with her maid.

107

VOROTYNTSEV (*to* PECHKUROV): We clutch at life with convulsive intensity – that's how we get caught. We want to go on living at any, *any* price. We accept all the degrading conditions, and this way we save – not ourselves – we save the persecutor. But he who doesn't value his life is unconquerable, untouchable. There are such people! And if you become one of them, then it's not you but your persecutor who'll tremble!

YELESHEV (*to* KHOLUDENEV): I devoted all my talents, all my emotions to them! My every action was dedicated to them. As an architect, I built houses for them, I shone in society, I was the life and soul of the party – all for their sake!

KHOLUDENEV: Listening to this makes me furious! I wasted my youth poring over books! But now I'm so randy I could howl like a wolf – after any woman.
(FIACENTE *is hummimg some passionate Italian song.*)
Now, I'll be condemned to ten years . . . in some distant Arctic darkness . . . while all I want to do is run after female footprints in the sand like some wretched little dog.
KHOLUDENEV *has lowered his head.* RUBIN *is now pestering* KULYBYSHEV.

RUBIN: Yes, I did come across collective farms which were prosperous; they had cows, sheeps, pigs, goats . . .
PRYANCHIKOV *and the* IST SUPERVISOR[1] *enter quickly from the back of the stage and walk past the cauldron. The* SUPERVISOR *wears a soiled white overall on top of his uniform. The spectator cannot at first discern what is wrong with* PRYANCHIKOV's *extremely elegant suit and his awkward movements – but all the buttons of his clothes have been cut off, and are more or less held together by string.* PRYANCHIKOV's *movements are rapid but constrained, as if he is afraid of dropping something.*

PRYANCHIKOV (*still walking*): Why is it, Comrade, that you address both the military and civilians in exactly the same way: "Get going, get going!" Eh, Comrade?

1ST SUPERVISOR: Comrade my foot! Wolf, more like! Into the cauldron with those rags.

PRYANCHIKOV (*having removed a soft felt hat, lets his thick brown hair fall around his head. He lifts his right arm in a quick salute*): Heil Hitler, gentlemen! (*Thrusting his right arm forward.*) Long live Comrade Stalin! (*Waving lightly to* FIACENTE.) Viva Mussolini! (*Waving both arms.*) Živeo Mihailović! May I introduce myself? I'm Valentin Pryanchikov. I'm agitating against our return to the U.S.S.R. (YELESHEV *sidles up to him and whispers something into his ear.* PRYANCHIKOV *loudly.*) I've been warned, I know that there are stooges among us from Counter Intelligence. But being an honest man, I do not propose to hide – (*Behind his back the* SUPERVISOR *is blowing into the head-shaving razor. The conversations and movements have stopped.* PRYANCHIKOV *is the centre of attention.*) – that I am in close contact with world bourgeoisie, and almost out of touch with the world proletariat. My turnover capital is three hundred thousand francs. I own a house, a car and a wife – in Brussels. (*Sits down on a log.*)

1ST SUPERVISOR: How about lice? Got any?

PRYANCHIKOV: What did you say?

1ST SUPERVISOR: Lice.

PRYANCHIKOV (*bursts out laughing, loses his balance and would have fallen off the log, if he had not supported himself with one hand on the ground*): Ha-ha-ha! I haven't laughed like that for a long time. Where would I get them from, you cannibals, you blockheads? I've arrived from Europe, not Moscow!

1ST SUPERVISOR: Didn't I tell you to take everything off and throw it into the cauldron?

WORKMAN (*from above the cauldron*): Comrade Supervisor! There's hardly any water left.

1ST SUPERVISOR: All right. You needn't do it.

PRYANCHIKOV: Grand merci! I'm glad. In this country of ours we enjoy such simple pleasures. Oh yes. I quite forgot, gentlemen, to ask you just one question. Has the level of production not increased? Dear me! Things are still in a bad way? I judge by the fact that the Military have cut off all my buttons! I can't keep my trousers up.

KLIMOV: Were they made of metal?

PRYANCHIKOV: Certainly not. Ivory.

KLIMOV: Ever so chic, then?

PRYANCHIKOV: Naturally. Cream-coloured.

KLIMOV: That means, they took them for their *parcels*. Never you mind, friend. Everybody's buttons get cut off.

PRYANCHIKOV: But what am I to do?

KLIMOV: We'll make you some out of bread.

PRYANCHIKOV (*looking around for the first time*): But, what on earth is going on here?

TEMIROV: Bath time.

PRYANCHIKOV: Under the open sky? How peculiar!

KHOLUDENEV: What is peculiar?

PRYANCHIKOV: Where's the water, the shower, the bath-tub?

YELESHEV: The shower and the bath-tub are only half the trouble.

PECHKUROV: The trouble is . . .

KLIMOV and KULYBYSHEV (*together*): There is no water!
PRYANCHIKOV, *quite stunned, stops fidgeting and sits down on a log. At this point the* SUPERVISOR *has finished cleaning the razor and comes up from behind to start shaving his head.*

PRYANCHIKOV: Then why did they bring us out here?

KHOLUDENEV: For delousing. According to schedule.

PRYANCHIKOV (*putting his hands on the top of his head*): Hey, who's there? (*Jumps up, runs away and touches the shaven spot.*)

1ST SUPERVISOR: What's biting you? Do you want to be hand-cuffed? Locked up?

PRYANCHIKOV: Wait, I've been locked up – in a kind of coffin. Put in there, still alive. (*Touching his bald patch.*) What have you done? I shall complain!

1ST SUPERVISOR: To hell with you! Will you sit still, you fidget.

PRYANCHIKOV: What about the Atlantic Charter? You're transgressing it! . . . Aren't you? (*His last question is directed at* YELESHEV.)

YELESHEV (*in a whisper*): Give in, old chap! Everybody's been shaved. Just look around . . .

PRYANCHIKOV *turns around, examining everybody's heads. His cockiness has vanished. He sits down and the shaving begins.* RUBIN *sits down in front of* PRYANCHIKOV *on a pile of logs.*

RUBIN: So there you are, Comrade. Even though your head is not quite shaved yet, behind these walls we get to know one another quite quickly, so I can inform you that from now on you are a paid-up member of cell one hundred and twenty-five, which maintains well tried and age-old prison traditions. One of those traditions, I must tell you, is that we interview the newcomer. Get ready. Are you a citizen of the U.S.S.R.?

PRYANCHIKOV: Alas . . .

RUBIN: Right. We'll not enquire about your grandmother and grandfather, just yet. Your profession?

PRYANCHIKOV: Engineer.

RUBIN: And your age?

PRYANCHIKOV: Twenty-eight.

RUBIN: You don't look it.

PRYANCHIKOV: Merci.

RUBIN: Been a member of the Party?

PRYANCHIKOV: Heaven forbid!

RUBIN: But you belonged to the All-Union Leninist Communist Youth League.

PRYANCHIKOV: I was . . .

RUBIN: How do you mean?

PRYANCHIKOV: I mean, I was stupid enough to . . .

RUBIN: Don't let's make value judgements. That's an ideological division between us. When you left University, were you married?

PRYANCHIKOV: Oh, my Madeleine!

RUBIN: Judging by her name, you're giving me some extra
information. Then – the War?

PRYANCHIKOV: Yes, the War.

RUBIN: And a prisoner of war?

PRYANCHIKOV: And a prisoner after a bit.

RUBIN: Which camp?

PRYANCHIKOV: In Rhine-Westphalia.

RUBIN: What kind of labour?

PRYANCHIKOV: Ore mines. Most unpleasant, I might add.

RUBIN: And you've served your term?

PRYANCHIKOV: We escaped.

RUBIN: Where to, it would be interesting to know?

PRYANCHIKOV: To Belgium. To the Ardennes. Gentlemen,
this is fascinating. They have a thing there called the . . .
the Resistance. You should see those partisans! Rosy-
cheeked boys, old egg-heads, all join the underground,
north, south, east and west. They hide where they can't
be found and – do they resist! They refuse to work in
factories, or join the army . . . While the whole of
Europe is in a monstrous uproar, we've taken refuge
among trees, above us – branches and birds. And Belgian
girls bring us food. What girls! . . .

RUBIN: Madeleine?

PRYANCHIKOV: I can't deny it. The invasion and all
that . . .

RUBIN: So you grew rich, on your dowry?

PRYANCHIKOV: Yes. But in ten months I trebled it!
DAVYDOV, *clearing his throat loudly, approaches and listens
with great attention. The shaving has finished. The* 1ST
SUPERVISOR *leaves.*

RUBIN: Don't try and convince us that the economic
theories of Adam Smith or David Ricardo . . .

PRYANCHIKOV: Excuse me! And don't make such faces. I
know all about it. I know all about Marx-Engels,
Lapidus-Ostrovityanov. The point is that over there you
are not oppressed, pushed or pulled around! In one year

over there I became a businessman. I'm not joking.
Some managed to earn millions. We, the Soviet people,
don't know our own talents. Over there, let's face it,
there is no G.P.U. or finance inspectors! If you're the
proud possessor of *une tête* and an extra franc . . .

DAVYDOV: One can do business?

PRYANCHIKOV: Yes, *argent!* (*He laughs.*) It's funny,
gentlemen. We're so used to a leaden weight on our
backs, to being pushed down, to outside pressure, that
when we find ourselves in the West we're like earthlings
on the moon, leaping rather than walking. We're
bounced into success.

RUBIN: What rubbish you talk, my friend! You argue like a
shopkeeper! Somebody must pay the increased cost . . .

DIVNICH (*coming forward and gently taking Rubin by his
shoulders*): Comrade Rubin, you mustn't presume on the
rights of an interviewer. (*To* PRYANCHIKOV.) If your
arguments are so sound, what did you come back for?

PRYANCHIKOV: Who, me? I got stolen.

A VOICE: How do you mean, stolen?

PRYANCHIKOV: Just like that, in broad daylight. In
Brussels.

VOICES: Where? Whom? When? Not possible!

PRYANCHIKOV: Gentlemen, what do you take me for? Do
you think I'm subnormal or something – to come back of
my own free will?

KULYBYSHEV: There are some such . . .

YELESHEV: Who spent the whole war in the West . . .

PECHKUROV: Who suffered everything . . .

KLIMOV: Who went through fire . . .

PRYANCHIKOV: And – who returned?

KLIMOV: And who returned.

PRYANCHIKOV: They must be mad!

VOROTYNTSEV: It's difficult to say. What's more normal –
to have complete faith, or to reject faith altogether?

PRYANCHIKOV: Anyway, the war came to an end. And
Comrades arrived in their hundreds, elegantly dressed in

113

civvies and rosettes with gold inscriptions. (*Speaking
rapidly.*) Wherever there's an Ambassador and an
Embassy, in they go through every crevice, dozens of
plenipotentiaries, two hundred and twenty attachés, a
staff of three hundred and forty to round up Russian
"Ivans". Well, what could they do – it's awkward to
refuse an allied nation! The representatives of the
Repatriation scheme say: "Your mothers or your sisters
await you in devastated towns. And even if you fought
against your brother Ivan, even if you spilt the blood of
innocent babes, gun in hand, your country will forgive.
Your country calls you back!" It worked, as I observed.
They went like lambs . . .

MOSTOVSHCHIKOV: How reckless, how trusting is your
average Russian.

PRYANCHIKOV: I did what I could. Whoever I met, I'd try
and talk them out of it, beg them to avoid it like the
plague. "Are you short of cash? – Here, let me lend you
some." "Can't find any work? – Here, I'll give you a
reference." Why did I care? I was sorry for my
countrymen. And yet, I was betrayed. And who did it?
The closest friend I escaped from the camp with . . .

KHOLUDENEV (*to* MOSTOVSHCHIKOV): That's typical of
us, the Soviets . . .

PRYANCHIKOV: We met. "Need any help?" I write a
cheque for him . . . "No, no, no need," he says; "I've
decided to return." "Do you remember what it was like
on the Rhine? The way it was with the Partisans? . . .
All right. Shall we have a farewell dinner?" I book at the
most fashionable restaurant. Anybody been to Brussels?
It was there that this Judas pointed me out. I pay my
bill, I leave, and no sooner do the swing doors close
behind me than I'm hit on the head – and how! Right
across the pavement and into a car, head first!

VOICES: Passers-by? Police?

PRYANCHIKOV: I can't remember. It only took a second, it
was like lightning! Well, there I am in the Embassy,

recovering, but – I'm not going to give in, I'm going to defend myself in Belgium . . .

DAVYDOV: But who . . . who got your money?

PRYANCHIKOV: I was sort of gagged, everything went through the diplomatic bag, without inspection, to the frontier, through to Amsterdam . . .

A VOICE: But there?

PRYANCHIKOV: And from there to the airport. From London it was Soviet pilots who flew to Berlin. They'd been on a good-will mission, or a friendly mission. The Devil alone can sort that out. Those Dutch cheeseheads never opened my bags – and off into a 'plane. We landed in the Soviet zone. I hadn't understood, even then, but I did when two soldiers took charge of me. They were eating soup out of a mess tin, sitting astride a couple of logs. They offered me a spoon: "Sit down, friend, the soup is good." I tried it . . . (*He makes a gesture of throwing the spoon away, wailing.*) Oh mother Russia! Oh this country of ours!
They all droop. Silence.

DIVNICH: This country of ours, built of straw, evil-smelling, barbarous, lawless and despairing . . .

RUBIN: With slavery in our bones, slavery through to the marrow . . .

DIVNICH: Oh my motherland, you look so menacing in the dark before dawn, when the bright light of the war has grown dim. To look at you from the border, you appear half dead, speechless, smothered by the blind, unfeeling, blunt will of "Prince" Dzhugashvili . . .[2]

GAI: If they let us in from here, from Europe, we'll turn Stalin into dust and smoke!

RUBIN: You're mad! You're blind. Do you think you can turn the wheel of history back again . . .?

KHOLUDENEV: No, we'll just wait for the Security Services to give us thirty-five years!

RUBIN: But, friends, we're not the first to go back from a tidy Europe into an unwashed Russia. A hundred years

115

ago other regiments felt nauseated at the thought. But then, on the impoverished and exhausted soil a wonderful flowering took place. It produced the Muravievs, the Trubetskoys, the Pestels.[3] Now it's our turn, the turn of our generation. They did, though, crown their rebellion by reaching the Senate Square, while we're arrested on the Asian border and are prisoners of SMERSH.

VOROTYNTSEV: No, forgive me, your analogy is all wrong. If we *are* to have a rebellion, God willing, it won't be launched with the aristocratic bubbling of champagne and oysters on a silver salver, nor will it be like those borrowed dreams from distant days and far away places. It'll be done by thick-set people who will have had enough of their prison soup.

YELESHEV: Of course, your idea that we're the latter-day Decembrists is beautiful, but why be so gloomy? There's bound to be an amnesty.

PRYANCHIKOV (*animated*): Is an amnesty expected?

YELESHEV: But of course, well before we reach Siberia.

PRYANCHIKOV: And soon?

YELESHEV: Any minute now; two or three days.

PRYANCHIKOV: Does that mean they'll let us go?

KHOLUDENEV: Yes, yes, to our wives and children.

PRYANCHIKOV (*to* KHOLUDENEV): How soon?

KHOLUDENEV: After three or four five-year plans.

YELESHEV: Comrade Kholudenev, you can laugh. But the investigator was quite specific.

DAVYDOV (*approaching*): He told me that too.

KLIMOV: Don't butt in!

DAVYDOV: Why ever not?

KLIMOV (*fists clenched*): Because didn't you say you had dealings with those Nazi swine . . .?

TEMIROV (*stepping between them*): You'll be forgiven – you're just a thief. Never mind that you stole two hundred thousand – you remain socially close to the Soviet ruling class.

Scene 1

WORKMAN (*from above*): Hey, you! It's ready. Come and get it!

He starts throwing out the steaming clothes using the baker's shovel. There is a general rapid movement as they sort out their possessions. Chaos.

RUBIN: They've burnt my shirt, the buggers!

YELESHEV: Oh dear!

General hubbub and movement. FIACENTE, *who is still undressed, has brought* DAVYDOV's *things and is fussing around him.* PRYANCHIKOV, *the only one to have remained dressed, observes the scene.*

RUBIN: Anyone got some military trousers?

VOICES: Quiet! Don't shout!

RUBIN: German ones, torn.

SOMEONE: How about these?

RUBIN: The very things.

He passes them to the Oberleutnant, since they are his. The hubbub increases.

HALBERAU (*to* RUBIN): Danke sehr, danke sehr!

A VOICE: How did they make it so dirty, the pigs?

PRYANCHIKOV: I would like to know what would have happened to someone in a dinner jacket.

KHOLUDENEV: What about a dinner jacket?

KLIMOV: What do you mean, what about it? Into the cauldron!

PRYANCHIKOV: Unthinkable!

KLIMOV: Do you know what is unthinkable? Getting your *thing* into a bottle. Everything else is thinkable, my friend . . .

1ST *and* 2ND SUPERVISORS *enter.*

1ST SUPERVISOR: Line up in twos! Hands behind your backs!

The prisoners line up in a column, two by two, some still getting dressed as they walk. RUBIN *comes up with a complaint.*

RUBIN: Citizen chief, they've burned a hole in my shirt!

117

1ST SUPERVISOR: You can get it darned in your cell.
   Ma-arch!
RUBIN (*persisting*): I shall make a complaint! Who's in
   charge, who's responsible?
2ND SUPERVISOR (*pushing him into line*): March, you in
   front!
   The column disappears into the depths of the yard.

Scene 2

*A small cell. There are no bunks, the floor is covered with straw
and the prisoners are asleep on the straw, their heads to the wall,
their feet stretched into the centre. There is a door with a food
hatch and a peep-hole. Next to the door, a wooden barrel slop
bucket without a cover. The single window opening is newly
bricked up almost to the top; the bricks are unplastered and the
opening at the top is tiny and barred. The light in the cell is
dim, but it grows perceptibly lighter during the scene.*
   DIVNICH *is saying his prayers beneath the window.*
VOROTYNTSEV *and* KHOLUDENEV *are talking, lying down.*
KULYBYSHEV *and* WRZESNIK *are by the door listening to
discover what is happening in the corridor.* PRYANCHIKOV,
*being the last arrival, is asleep by the slop bucket. He is
recognisable by his hat, which covers his entire head.* KLIMOV's
*head is towards us. He is close to the audience. He is awake and
leaning on his elbows, he sings quietly in a strong, clear voice.*
KLIMOV: Where are you, where are you?
         Tell me where you are.
         Why did this war
         Send you quite so far?

         You've been going round and round
         These many wartime years,
         Tell me what encouragements,
         What medals have you found?

118

Scene 2

*The door opens with a clang and in comes a new prisoner,
with a black eye, an enormous bruise on his cheekbone. The
door shuts with an equally loud clang. All those asleep
shudder, without waking up. The newcomer's arms are
behind his back, but on finding himself in the cell, he releases
them.* KLIMOV, *as if hitting himself on the cheekbone:*

KLIMOV: The investigator?

PRISONER WITH A BLACK EYE: I value my teeth a great
deal, so, whether I had or not, I signed I'd been here,
I'd been there . . . (*He squeezes himself among the sleepers
and lies down.*) KLIMOV (*singing*):

> Are you dealing with the mines,
> Do you drive the tanks?
> Are you a pilot, rocket-launcher,
> Do you hide the partisans?
>
> Are you down with typhoid fever?
> Do you live abroad?
> Are you dead, or coming
> Back to Russia with your sword?
> Or can it be they'll lock you up
> In your country as a spy?

WRZESNIK: Take me as an example. The best thing to do
is to learn foreign languages. We're ruined for lack of
them. I could have been a spy in Great Britain. Instead,
I had to do it in the cursed U.S.S.R. No English. How-
do-you-do? If-you-please . . . What, you refuse to be
locked up in the Tower? Then go to the Bolsheviks and
eat their prison soup! Go and build Communism. Where
are we? In prison? Rotten straw, mother-fuckers! Now,
in Poland, a prison is quite different: you get two sheets,
a proper bed, books, a bed-side table. Exercise. You get
meat for dinner. White rolls for breakfast!

KLIMOV: What were you in for?

WRZESNIK: I used to be a Communist, more fool me. Once
you find yourself here, you see things more clearly . . .

DIVNICH *continues his fervent praying.* KLIMOV *is doing a*

119

*hand stand. He wears nothing but his trunks. His body is
beautifully developed.*

KLIMOV (*upside down*): And then?

WRZESNIK: And then, you can go and seek your rights! At
first, the Comrades gave us land; then they turned on the
heat. I had to serve in the Red Army. Then, suddenly,
an order from the Political Section. *Poland still lives* –
but whether you're a Catholic, holy Mother of God, or a
Party member, Leo Wrzesnik, you're now a Second
Lieutenant in the Polish Army.

KLIMOV (*lying down in his previous position, singing*):
> Your wife comes into the garden, all in vain.
> Where are you, where are you?
> Tell me where you are.
> Why did this war
> Send you quite so far?

He lowers his head and is quiet.

VOROTYNTSEV (*to* KHOLUDENEV): There was no mercy at
the altar on which we laid our heads. We didn't
recognise each other in our own country. People got
greedy, angry and hard, as if everyone had gone off his
head. As if they'd given themselves up to the Devil. It
wasn't the mistakes of the Generals; it wasn't our
principles that were wrong – nothing could have altered
the whirling course of events. They just happened,
spiralled and rushed on . . . I had the misfortune of
taking part in the Russian retreat from Mukden,
Naidenburg and from Oryol to Rostov. It was an
irresistible retreat. But I was never so bitter as during
our departure from the Crimea. I was standing there in a
motley, hysterical crowd, some weeping over their losses,
some hoping for sustenance. And I said to myself: "This
is 'us', always 'us', but what about them, those others?
Those who lord it over us, in Moscow, who fail to see
from their commanding heights?" And I thought, it
could just be that I've never known the real Russia, that
I've never loved her. But then – surely not Lenin, surely

not Trotsky? Perhaps our complaints, our moans are a
self-indulgence? After all, we have given *Russia* away as
if she were a tiny County of Mecklenburg. Can it be that
by promising government by the people, we misjudged
the true sources of renewal? . . . As I stood on the ship,
the lighthouse of Kherson glimmered once and
disappeared in the darkness. O my country, would I ever
see you again? And how, and when, and
where? . . .

KHOLUDENEV: Now you've seen it.

VOROTYNTSEV: I never thought that I would have to live
for so long so far away. The times, the people have
changed in the meantime. We did think, however, that
we would have the possibility – before we died – of
liberating Russia. But – no. Twenty-five years have
passed, and still no! And now again, no. How much
longer? And again, our allies. They let us down, they
give no support. And so our soldiers are in the hands of
the Red Army. And it's my fate to end up here, sitting
on this rotten straw, eating your undercooked gruel,
seeing what you've all become, what you've grown up
into, what you have learned. I'm grateful to my Creator
that the Bolsheviks are dead long before any of us.

KHOLUDENEV: It was Marx and Lenin who swallowed up
large chunks of our youth. Even before we fought in the
war, before we'd seen Europe, seen the rays of the sun
through these rusty bars – we were, and would have
remained, the sheep-like defenders of our country. Did
we know who we were, what we were, why they filled
our books with trunkfuls of emptiness?

DIVNICH *has moved over to the door and is talking to*
KULYBYSHEV, *who is sitting down on the straw.*

DIVNICH (*in a prophetic voice*):

It won't be long before the pious people
Will open their churches in a cloud of incense,
Before Russia will ring with church bells
And monasteries will be full again.

121

Oh my unhappy people, keep your hope,
God's grace will shine over you.
Having astounded the world with your crimes
You will astound it with your penitence.
People will make new paths to the neglected and reviled
sanctuaries,
They will follow their priests, ikons and banners in great
multitudes.

KULYBYSHEV (*picking his nose*): Yes. All that's quite true,
only I must tell you, I was one of those who closed the
churches down. (DIVNICH *staggers back in surprise*.) I
joined the twenty-five thousand. Don't worry – the
Party, the Government, Comrade Stalin personally will
do the thinking, they said, you just close down this
church and turn it into a grain-collecting centre. But, say
I, all the women will rebel. Ignorance, they said, what
do we care! And I must say, almost the entire village was
against it, while we, the activists, signed petitions in
their stead, ten times over.

DIVNICH: You too?

KULYBYSHEV: What was I to do? Do you think they could
not manage without me? The lambs join the rams.

KHOLUDENEV: How come we managed to grow up without
being aware of the presence of the Lubianka, that we
were carefree and rosy-cheeked? It's ironic that you
fought on the side of Franco, while I dreamed of joining
the Republicans.

VOROTYNTSEV: I tasted victory only once there! It was a
good battle towards the liberation of Moscow and Oryol
that we fought in Madrid and Toledo! We killed at least
a couple of hundred.

A key jangles loudly in the lock. MEDNIKOV, *pale and
shaky, enters and, as if blind, tumbles towards his place. All
those who are asleep shudder, as they did the first time, lift
their heads and put them down again.*

KHOLUDENEV: How was it, Vasiliy?

Scene 2

MEDNIKOV: Six days and nights, dear friends. God, I need some sleep!

He drops on to the straw and falls asleep at once.

DIVNICH: Well then, tell me, old man, do you believe in God?

KULYBYSHEV: What?

DIVNICH: In God, do you believe in God?

KULYBYSHEV: Who, me?

DIVNICH: Yes, you.

KULYBYSHEV: In God?

DIVNICH: In Our Lord, in Our Saviour?

KULYBYSHEV: If you're silent – you're in trouble. If you speak – trouble again. What am I to say? Maybe yes. Maybe no . . . Life is full of snares. Suppose you get stomach cramps, you roll on the floor with pain – then you pray to all the saints. But when all is going smoothly, you don't even bother to glance at those old women's ikons. Here, now, we're all traitors to our country. Cut down the raspberries – mow down the blackcurrants. But that's not what I got arrested for. I got arrested for infringing the regulations. I issued extra bread to the collective farm women. Without it, they would have died before the spring. I wasn't doing it for my own good – I had enough food at home. But this thing is choking me, I've had it up to here. This thing, I don't know what to call it – the *thing*.

It seems he is lost in thought, or dozing. VOROTYNTSEV *and* KHOLUDENEV *are also asleep. There is some music, which sounds like a prison waking up. People move about heavily in their places, struggling between sleep and wakefulness. They make remarks, as if in a delirium and drop their heads once again.*

YELESHEV: What's happening? Am I asleep or am I dreaming? It was such a lovely dream. It went too soon . . . I dreamt again of the golden head of Elsa Kroneberg! My God! To wake up in a prison is terrible.

What an oppressive moment. I've been fighting it all night.

ANOTHER VOICE: I have no will to live . . .

A THIRD VOICE: Or strength to move . . .

A FOURTH VOICE: What is the meaning of the day to come?

SOMEONE ELSE: Barely a flicker of light through the bars . . .

A loud turning of the key in the lock. Everybody shudders; they lift their heads. The door does not open and their heads fall back again.

ANOTHER VOICE: That key turning is like a dagger in your heart.

KHOLUDENEV: My life's been so short. Has it been lived – or not lived at all? Has it been lent to my country in the heat of the moment like a couple of golden sovereigns? . . .

A VOICE: And the only change you get is a worn penny.

ANOTHER: The sun will rise today, but not for us.

PECHKUROV: A German prison – and now a Soviet one . . .

ANOTHER VOICE: During the day you obediently lug your chains.

ANOTHER: You stare dumbly at the bars, at the lock.

ANOTHER: For a prisoner kindly night is a short and cruel gift.

ANOTHER: During the day one gets used to things, as if that's what it should be like. But first thing in the morning this enormous stone structure crushes the breath out of you.

OTHER VOICES: Ten years! Easily said!

Count on your fingers! . . .

No wife! . . . No mother! . . . No daughter! . . . No home! . . .

Never see it again! . . .

Never to return! . . .

And unable to lift your head from the straw! . . .

Scene 2

And unable to open your eyelids . . .
*They are all asleep again. The last bars of the dying melody
are interrupted by the grating of keys and the door opening.*

4TH SUPERVISOR (*shouting*): To the bog! At the double!

TEMIROV (*being the first to rise*): To the bog! Come on,
slop-sloppers!
With the exception of MEDNIKOV, *all rise, or jump up.
General chaos.* WRZESNIK *tries to be the first through the
door.*

4TH SUPERVISOR (*to* WRZESNIK): Sto-op! Don't push.
You with the slop bucket, go through!

KHOLUDENEV (*holding one handle of the bucket*): Leo.

VOICES: Who are you carrying it with?
With Leo.

RUBIN (*gathering things quickly, keeps forgetting some things.
His towel hangs from his neck, gets tangled in his beard, gets
in the way*): Is it my turn? Can't be. (*He quickly gets hold
of the second handle.*) A thousand pardons! Forgot all
about it!

VOICES: Don't spill it! Don't spill it! . . . Careful!
RUBIN *and* KHOLUDENEV *carry the bucket out. The
others follow. We can see everybody putting their arms
behind their backs and forming into pairs.*

KLIMOV (*standing over* MEDNIKOV): Vasiliy! Do get up, old
man. That rat will have you on your feet whether you
like it or not.

4TH SUPERVISOR (*beyond the door*): Form up in twos.
Hands behind your backs.

KLIMOV: Vasiliy!

MEDNIKOV: M-m-m . . .

4TH SUPERVISOR (*running in*): Who else is here? Up you
get! (*He kicks the soles of* MEDNIKOV's *feet with the toe of
his boot.*)

MEDNIKOV: I don't need the bog. Let me sleep.

4TH SUPERVISOR: Wha-at? Quoting regulations at me?

MEDNIKOV: Interrogations by night, interrogations by
day . . .

4TH SUPERVISOR: Order must be kept! At the double!
Everybody is gone.
March!
The column leaves. Enter the 5TH SUPERVISOR.
O.K. I do this side. You do the other. (*He indicates the
two sides of the cell and the two rows of straw.*)

5TH SUPERVISOR: Do you know, Valeriy, these searches –
I may be a fool – they cut me to the quick.

4TH SUPERVISOR: "Searches" my foot. They're the
"turnovers" here! Forget what happened in the Army.
Prisons have their own laws. The Lieutenant said – even
if you find nothing, rake it about a bit.
*They begin to stir up the straw, throw the belongings about.
Having found nothing, they leave. The prisoners return.*

VOICES: They've been at the straw again!
Another search! Up theirs!
The buggers!
Everything's been thrown about!
Can't get used to it. God, they make me furious!
*They tidy the straw, look for their belongings, spread them
out.* KLIMOV stands motionless in the middle of the cell,
arms folded.

KLIMOV: Never mind, brothers, we'll survive. We'll see
Stalin hanged yet! He will be tried himself one day!

KULYBYSHEV: You can wait for that, friend, till kingdom
come. Mice might drown a cat, but only once it's dead.
FIACENTE *comes up to* DAVYDOV.

DAVYDOV: Bed made up?

FIACENTE: Oh yes, Signor.

DAVYDOV: Now let's see to the sewing. You must learn
Russian, you know. You won't be able to manage
without it. (*They discuss the making of slippers.*)

YELESHEV (*to* KHOLUDENEV): I bet you never had to lie
next to such a filthy wall.

KHOLUDENEV: Go to hell.

YELESHEV: That's rude and silly. You're not a European.
You haven't learnt to compromise.

KHOLUDENEV: That's quite an idea – that Europe and compromise are the same. (*He moves a bit and makes room.*)

PECHKUROV (*to* KULYBYSHEV): I wonder what my dream means. It was about a church.

KULYBYSHEV: That there will be some change in our lives. Those who are free will go to prison. We shall be freed. It's a good thing to dream in prison about a church.

4TH SUPERVISOR (*opening the hatch*): Inspection!

WRZESNIK: Inspection!

TEMIROV: Everybody up!

They all line up along the cell in pairs, back to back. RUBIN *is at the end, nearest to the audience.* TEMIROV *in his Cossack cape marches along the line.*

Any questions?

RUBIN: I have one.

TEMIROV: You're a clown. How many questions can one ask? Anyone else?

PRYANCHIKOV: I've got one. Why no food? What kind of treatment is that? Why did they shave our hair off?

TEMIROV: I'm sorry, but the block Inspector will rush through like a comet. If you want to get an answer, come and stand here, right in front of the door. (*He indicates a place next to* RUBIN.)

RUBIN: Twaddle. My question is more important. I'll be speaking first.

PRYANCHIKOV *runs to change places with* TEMIROV. *The door crashes open. The block* INSPECTOR *rushes in. The* 6TH SUPERVISOR *remains by the door. The* INSPECTOR *walks past the line counting the pairs, first in one direction, then in another, amid complete silence, and is about to rush out again when first* RUBIN *and then* PRYANCHIKOV *bar his way.*

RUBIN: Citizen Inspector!

PRYANCHIKOV: Citizen! . . .

RUBIN: According to the rules, which are displayed . . .

PRYANCHIKOV: Citizen! . . .

RUBIN: The prisoners are allowed . . .

PRYANCHIKOV: But that's intolerable! . . .

RUBIN: To complain!

PRYANCHIKOV: To eat!

INSPECTOR (*unable to get away*): One at a time!

RUBIN (*raising his voice, with determination, pushing
PRYANCHIKOV aside, afraid that the INSPECTOR will
not hear him out*): I'm a victim of denunciation. I've been
arrested quite illegally.

INSPECTOR (*with surprise*): So? What do you want?

RUBIN: My case is being conducted unfairly . . .

PRYANCHIKOV: The straw is rotten. It's disgusting to sleep
on!

RUBIN: . . . I want to send a complaint to Beria . . .

PRYANCHIKOV: The slop bucket has no lid! Not hygienic!

RUBIN: Stop talking nonsense! To the Procurator General,
to the National Judiciary . . .

PRYANCHIKOV: After all, we're not barbarians. Ethiopians.
You must provide European conditions!

RUBIN: I need writing paper! I've been asking repeatedly
and can't get it.

INSPECTOR: You will not get it!

He deftly moves round them and gets out through the door.
RUBIN *runs after him.*

RUBIN: By what right? . . .

The door is slammed shut, pushing RUBIN *inwards. The key
is turned with a loud noise. The line breaks up.*

TEMIROV: Now do you understand? Why don't you send
your complaints to the Soviet Aviation Chemical Unit?

RUBIN (*attacking with clenched fists*): You and your idiotic
sarcasms! . . .

They are separated.

PRYANCHIKOV (*holding his head, in dead earnest*): What sort
of country is this? Sheer lawlessness.

KLIMOV *roars with laughter. The hatch is opened and we
can see the head of the* 6TH SUPERVISOR *and the white
overall of the dispenser.*

Scene 2

6TH SUPERVISOR: Eighteen!

Two portions of bread are pushed through the hatch at a time. They are collected and put down on a coat which is spread out on the floor.

VOICES: Rations!

Our sacred props!

TEMIROV *stands by the hatch and counts the rations. At the end he is also given sugar which he puts into a handkerchief. The hatch is banged shut.*

TEMIROV: Fritz, share out the sugar.

HALBERAU *takes the sugar, settles down comfortably, everybody brings his bits of paper, bits of cloth and, with the help of a spoon made out of a broken matchbox, he begins the ritual of sharing the sugar out. The door opens with a loud noise. An attendant in a dark overall enters carrying a wooden tub full of boiling water and a few empty one-litre tins which had contained American stew. He leaves. The door is shut.*

VOICES: Boiling water!

SOMEONE (*having tried some*): It's cool already! Swill! Some boiling water!

Almost all have settled down in their places. TEMIROV *and the* PRISONER WITH A BLACK EYE *are doling the food out.* MEDNIKOV *is asleep once again.*

PRISONER WITH A BLACK EYE: Who had the end bit yesterday?

TEMIROV: We got as far as here. (*He indicates, and starting from that place he doles out end bits of bread.*) Here you are. Here you are . . . (PRYANCHIKOV's *turn comes. He stretches out his hand.*) Just you wait, sir. (*He by-passes him.*) You'll have to miss it this time. You're a novice. (*Having come to the end of the crusty bits, he shares out the middle bits.*) That's our custom . . .

PRYANCHIKOV (*sadly*): Do I get nothing?

TEMIROV: You'll get some, but the soft bit.

He gives him the last bit of bread. They are all eating it already. One of them is sawing it with a thread, others tear

129

off tiny bits, still others bite minute mouthfuls and some have almost finished and are frenziedly chewing.

KULYBYSHEV (*muttering to himself*): A prisoner is entitled to four hundred and fifty grammes a day. Do with it what you like.

WRZESNIK: Drink your water, drink your water.

TEMIROV: According to the latest theories, a bucket of boiling water is equivalent to a hundred grammes of butter.

YELESHEV: They say a report has been sent to the Politburo. Approved at the highest level.

MOSTOVSHCHIKOV: How did they work it out?

KHOLUDENEV: It's to do with calories: after all, the water is hot, while the butter is cold.

KLIMOV: Marvellous!

DIVNICH (*standing up in the middle*): Gentlemen, I want to make a suggestion. Don't let us share out the sugar. Let's give our miserable grains to Leo for his birthday. *There is a confusion of sounds. Some come up to wish a Happy Birthday; others mutter.*

PRISONER WITH A BLACK EYE: What – give away one's only ration?

PECHKUROV: There are no such regulations.

WRZESNIK: We've hardly anything to eat ourselves.
The hatch is slid open.

6TH SUPERVISOR: Letter M-ee!

DIVNICH (*decisively*): Aren't any!

6TH SUPERVISOR (*suspiciously*): None? (*Closes the hatch slowly.*)

RUBIN (*standing up*): Comrades, I'm most grateful, very touched, but of course I wouldn't dream of taking the sugar.

YELESHEV (*to* DIVNICH): We do have M's: *M*ednikov, *M*ostovshchikov. Why do you put us into this kind of situation? It doesn't do to irritate them.

DIVNICH (*finding it difficult to get a word in edgeways*): Their psychology, you see, is slavish. If they think they're

130

Russians, let them sort the alphabet out!

MEDNIKOV (*rising, gobbling his rations*): The night
interrogator went to bed, the day-time interrogator came
to torture me . . . Dear friends, I feel I'm in for it.

DIVNICH: Gentlemen, we must rise above petty, selfish . . .
The hatch is slid open.

6TH SUPERVISOR: Who is there that starts with ee-eM?

DIVNICH (*sharply*): There's no such letter! We must be
aware that this sap, these crumbs they give us, these
eight grammes . . . (*The hatch is shut.*) will not sweeten
our existence. They've reduced us to the level of
biological needs; they don't even call us political
prisoners, which is something we could be proud of in
this prison. This title has been sanctified over centuries.
Don't let the Cheka take it away from us.
The hatch opens.

6TH SUPERVISOR: Who's here with the letter eM? E-m, I
say!

MEDNIKOV: Mednikov.

6TH SUPERVISOR: So what are you playing at? Easy,
now . . .
He shuts the hatch. MEDNIKOV *approaches the door.*
HALBERAU, *shrugging his shoulders, collects all the sugar
together and carries it on to the coat on which they shared out
the bread.*

RUBIN (*addressing everybody*): I'm most obliged. But if this
sugar is for me, (*he fills two tins with the hot water, pours
the sugar into both and stirs it with a crust of bread*) I am
stirring two goblets; one goblet is for the one who has
had no sleep for six nights (*passes it to* MEDNIKOV) and
the other is to go the rounds. (*He stirs.*)

VOICES: That's right.
That makes sense!
Bravo!

RUBIN (*taking a sip*): That's no water – it's a heavenly
drink. Nectar!

MEDNIKOV (*drinks greedily*): Well, thank you friends. It's so

gorgeously sweet I am truly restored. I feel almost
drunk!

RUBIN (*slaps him on the back*): Hold out, Vasiliy! I hope
you won't feel the beating . . .

The tin goes the rounds. The door opens with a grating noise.

6TH SUPERVISOR: Out!

MEDNIKOV, *his arms behind his back, leaves. The*
SUPERVISOR, *looking at his list*:

6TH SUPERVISOR: Anyone with the letter Y?

YELESHEV (*terrified*): Yeleshev . . .

6TH SUPERVISOR: Take your things!

YELESHEV: Me? Take my things?

The door is slammed shut.

YELESHEV: This is it. I'm finished! Quite finished!

TEMIROV (*to* PRYANCHIKOV): Every morning they take
people out of here. Some for a tribunal, some for a
Special Disc.

PRYANCHIKOV: Special what?

KHOLUDENEV: Special Discussion. If they have nothing
against you, no witnesses, no data, things are in a
muddle . . .

YELESHEV (*gathering his possessions nervously*): How many
years will they give me? I'm already an old man . . .

TEMIROV: Shame on you! You're only forty.

KHOLUDENEV: You get sentenced behind your back.

PRYANCHIKOV: Do you mean – in your absence?

KHOLUDENEV: Millions of people coming here from
Europe. To turn them round as quickly as possible, they
have created a lottery where every ticket's a winner.
Each ticket . . .

PRYANCHIKOV (*holding his head*): It's a nightmare!

KHOLUDENEV: Sign here please! Ten years. Greetings!

The door is being noisily unlocked. YELESHEV *is all ready.*
He shovels the remains of his uneaten ration into his bag
with some trepidation, embraces his companions quickly or
shakes hands with some of them.

YELESHEV: Well friends! . . . Well, brothers! . . .

Remember me kindly . . . If I upset anyone . . . hurt
somebody . . .

DIVNICH: Good luck! Let all of us who shared the prison
soup meet again in better times! (*He kisses him.*)

YELESHEV *drags his bag towards the door, which opens at
this moment. They all stand in a semi-circle to see him off,
but a newcomer enters while the* SUPERVISOR *makes a
gesture towards* YELESHEV *to remain for a while. The door
is locked again. The newcomer –* BOLOSNIN *– is tall very
thin, very pale. He is in uniform, but to start with it is not
very clear which Army it belongs to. He is holding a small
bundle, which contains all his belongings.* BOLOSNIN
*straightens up with a kind of frenzied formality and looks at
everyone.*

VOICES: A newcomer!

Where from?

Are you from outside?

YELESHEV: There's an amnesty, they say. Know anything
about it?

VOICES: He's silent.

Not a Russian, perhaps.

Sprechen Sie? . . .

Parlez-vous? . . .

Do you speak Engl? . . .

BOLOSNIN, *with a smile of exhausted bliss, leans against
the wall. He speaks slowly. His voice is weak but gains in
strength as he, obviously, enjoys the luxury of speaking.*

BOLOSNIN: No, not all . . . at once . . . I'm unused . . . to
such a brilliant gathering, my friends. Twenty days and
nights . . . twenty days and nights in a cell . . . and
another . . . sixteen . . . in a solitary . . . Anybody want
a smoke? Here – in this bundle . . .

*He extends one hand with the bundle, made up of a
handkerchief. The* PRISONER WITH A BLACK EYE *gets
hold of the bundle eagerly.* WRZESNIK *and* PECHKUROV
*join him. They start rolling cigarettes. There is a mime of
gestures in the cell as to how and who will smoke.*

BOLOSNIN: I'm thirty years old, but I never thought it would be such happiness to be with other human beings.

YELESHEV (*faintly*): Amnesty? . . . Heard anything?

SOMEONE: He's got out of a *hold*, can't you understand? Out of a cell.

    KLIMOV *is downstage, kneeling. Having torn up some wadding from a padded jacket, he has rolled it up into a taper. With an air of someone very experienced, he begins to run it up and down with a sliver of wood over the floor.* BOLOSNIN *watches him with a pensive and enchanted smile.*

BOLOSNIN: An ancient method of obtaining fire . . . Two bits of wood . . . A tinder . . .

YELESHEV: Please, please calm me down. They're waiting for me there! . . .

TEMIROV: He doesn't know, can't you see?

BOLOSNIN (*calmly*): It so happens . . . I do know.

RUBIN (*tense*): You're joking. You don't know.

BOLOSNIN (*very calmly*): That would have been a very cruel joke.

RUBIN: So there is?

YELESHEV: An amnesty?

KHOLUDENEV: I don't believe it!

DAVYDOV: Hurrah!

BOLOSNIN (*slowly*): I heard it myself on the radio while I was in the Investigator's office. (*Everybody has gathered round him, listening avidly.*) In honour of our victory over Germany an amnesty was announced yesterday – such as has never happened before.

DAVYDOV (*shaking his fists*): I told you so! Didn't I tell you?

YELESHEV: All these sentences are just to frighten us.

RUBIN: After all, it's a global victory!

BOLOSNIN: Amnesty, regardless of the length of sentence, is for thieves, speculators, swindlers, gangsters, deserters, civil and military plunderers, anyone who short-weighed, short-changed, or raped little girls. In short, the flower of the Soviet Union. The only ones not to be pardoned are former prisoners of war. (*They begin to disperse silently.*) Only those peasants who lived under the occupation, those who, under the Germans, went on working in factories, teachers who went on teaching, (BOLOSNIN *gradually raises his voice as his anger grows*) only those who were sold out on the battlefield by a bunch of Generals. Only those who were forcibly driven into Germany. Only those who have individuality, think differently, have different views. So that Stalin's merciful hands have touched everyone, if you except the whole of the Russian people.

DAVYDOV (*triumphantly*): I'm free! I've been pardoned!

KLIMOV: Oh you dregs of human society in brown tatters! Go on, jump and skip. Why don't you shout "Hop!"?

YELESHEV: O God! All is lost. I'm finished . . . (*He sinks on to his bag.*)

MOSTOVSHCHIKOV: This is, truly, unheard of . . .

KHOLUDENEV: What a typically Stalinist mocking manifesto!

GAI: And, no doubt, there's a lot of shouting and applause.

VOROTYNTSEV: Whose victory? Over whom? You mad nation! This victory is over you! . . .

Everybody is motionless. YELESHEV *alone goes out gloomily carrying his bag through the door which has been opened silently.*

VOROTYNTSEV: May I introduce myself? (*He gives a military salute.*) Vorotyntsev, Colonel in the Russian Imperial Army.

BOLOSNIN (*in a similar manner*): Bolosnin, Ensign in the Russian Liberation Army. (*They shake hands.*)

VOROTYNTSEV *then introduces all the other prisoners one by one, who shake hands with* BOLOSNIN.

VOROTYNTSEV: Kholudenev, Captain in the Red Army.
Klimov, Soldier in the American Army.
Temirov, Captain in the Royal Yugoslav Army.
Halberau, Oberleutnant in the Wehrmacht.
Wrzesnik, Lieutenant in the Polish Army.

Fiacente, Corporal in the Italian Army.
Pryanchikov, a fighter in the Belgian Resistance.
Professor Mostovshchikov.
Kuzma Kulybyshev, President of the Collective Farm
named after Ivan Susanin[4] . . .

Scene 3

*A small room, the sun shines through the window. There is a
large portrait of Stalin* MAJOR OGNIDA *and his typist*
NINEL *sit side by side at a table.*

OGNIDA (*dictating*): "A Decree. I, Major Ognida, having
examined and studied the anti-Soviet activities of
Lieutenant-Colonel Alexander Ivanov of the Guards,
which took the form: a) that in the period from 1941 to
1942 he slandered the planned retreat of the Red Army
and attacked the unpreparedness of the Soviet
Government for the war; b) that during 1944 he praised
American war technology, as well as the part played by
the Allies in the destruction of Hitler's Germany; c) that,
having established personal contact under the guise of
friendship with pilots of the American Air Force, George
Fletcher . . . George Fletcher and William Rigby . . .
William Rigby . . ., I have decided to cut short the
intricacies of this investigation by arresting him. Signed,
Major Ognida." Full stop. Next.

NINEL: Do give me a bit of a rest, my arms are dropping
off.

OGNIDA: Now, listen, Ninel, you are supposed to be the
best typist in the department.

NINEL: Best typist, maybe, but I'm not a camel. Look, just
look how much we have done since the morning.

OGNIDA: Splendid. When we get to half a hundred – we'll
stop for a cigarette.

NINEL: But my fingers are numb. (*She stretches them out.*)
Feel them – they're numb!

136

Scene 3

OGNIDA (*frowning, speaking rapidly*): Ninel! The Party, the Government and Comrade Stalin, personally, demand that we should *work*. Is that clear? Go on typing . . . "I confirm . . . (NINEL *types*) Deputy Commissar of State Security, Lieutenant-General dot, dot, dot. Deputy Prosecutor of the R.S.F.S.R., Major-General dot, dot, dot. A Decree. I, Major Ognida, having examined and studied the criminal, anti-Soviet activities of Hero of the Soviet Union Lieutenant Ilya Petrov, which found expression in the slanderous perversion of Stalin's humane National policies in the regions of the Volga, of the Crimea and of the Caucasus – I have decided to cut short the intricacies of this investigation by arresting him. Major Ognida." Full stop. Next.

NINEL: I'm surprised at the amount you've found time to write.

OGNIDA: During the nights, Ninel, during the nights.

NINEL: Tell that to the Marines! What patriotism! No sooner do you get to Poland than you're surrounded by Polish girls. As soon as you get to Germany – it's all the German ones.

OGNIDA: That's an old-established law of war, Ninel – all the girls of a vanquished nation belong to the conquerors.

NINEL: But Hilde is still a schoolgirl, she's only sixteen.

OGNIDA: Seventeen. And what's more, by private agreement, her mother gets my rations.

NINEL: One could accuse you too of "having established a personal contact" . . . I remember the North-Western Front . . . ; The local population had disappeared and you swarmed all over us. I used to say to you then: Edward, I don't feel like typing today. Do it yourself. And you used to sit down and bash out: "I, Lieutenant Ognida . . ."

OGNIDA: "Have resolved, that the Deputy Commissar of the National State . . ."

NINEL (*typing*): They used to ask me – Ninel? Ninel?

137

Where did you get such a wonderful name? Are you
French? But you know Ninel is only Lenin – backwards . . .

OGNIDA: "A Decree. I, Major Ognida . . ."

NINEL: Let's make a change and do one about a
woman . . .

OGNIDA: Don't fool around. The women's turn will come.

NINEL: Do you remember the story about this woman in
Oryol who got pregnant by a German Sergeant-Major,
and when our Army arrived, she hanged the baby and
stuck a note on him which said "Death to the German
Occupiers". (*She continues to type after* OGNIDA's
impatient gesture.) . . . Having examined and having
looked into . . . I love it when women are arrested . . .
the criminal, anti-Soviet activities . . . Why do they
always arrest men? Always men . . . Your approach is
not statesmanlike.

OGNIDA: . . . the serving officer . . . Calm down. Nobody
will arrest you after your war service . . .

MAJOR KAPUSTIN *enters. He is plump and bouncy. He
carries a batch of papers. A* SERGEANT *stops at the door.*

KAPUSTIN: Edward, listen.

OGNIDA: Well?

KAPUSTIN: I have to move you out of here for a couple of
hours.

OGNIDA: And why is that?

KAPUSTIN: I've got to read out the Instructions of the
Special Conference of the J.K.V.D.

OGNIDA: Why don't you go to Mironov's room?

KAPUSTIN: There's an interrogation going on in there.

OGNIDA: What about Vasiliy's?

KAPUSTIN: Another interrogation. I've been to all the
offices – they're all having interrogations.

OGNIDA: I'm short of time too. By seventeen hundred
hours I've got to get everything ready for signature.

KAPUSTIN: Well, I don't know. Rublyov told me to come
here. It's no joke. But we don't get enough time to

announce all the sentences, or to deport everybody on
time, and the General is due back today – you know
what that means?

OGNIDA: It's a job and a half. You'll have to put forty
people in a cell instead of twenty. I must hurry with my
batch. They're walking about quite free.

KAPUSTIN: Go to the typing pool.

OGNIDA: But they've got ten typewriters going there, like
so many machine guns. It's unthinkable to work there.

KAPUSTIN: Well, go to the tower then. The tower is free.

OGNIDA: It stinks of rats. You go there yourself.

KAPUSTIN: We can't take the prisoners all the way up
those stairs. What's more, the stairs haven't got safety
grids. You go. Off with you.

OGNIDA: Oh, hell! No sooner do we get settled down . . .

NINEL: I'm not going to carry the typewriter up those
stairs.

OGNIDA: Are you expecting me to carry it for you?

KAPUSTIN: You can use my soldier. Stop squabbling. (*He
makes a sign to the* SERGEANT. *A Soldier enters.*) I shall
be quick. (*Leafs through his thick file.*) You can come
back in an hour and a half. (*The* SOLDIER *picks up the
typewriter.*)

NINEL: Everybody's nervous, everybody's rushing around,
all the papers will get mixed up. I hate these moves. (*She
picks up the papers and hurries after the* SOLDIER.)
Soldier, take care. There's one letter falling out!
She leaves, together with OGNIDA.

KAPUSTIN (*to the* SERGEANT): Well, start shoving them
in, according to the list. While one of them's here, you
get the next one out of the cell. It'll go smoothly that
way.
The SERGEANT *goes out.* KAPUSTIN *arranges the table in
his own way, spreads his papers out and throws open the
window.*

KAPUSTIN: Just look at this weather – sheer bliss.
Wouldn't it be lovely to go fishing on the river, stay the

night? Might get shot by the Germans, though . . . Oh, what the hell. I won't be able to escape even on Sunday, there's so much work. They say that there's never been such a load of work, not even in 1937. (*He walks towards the table and yawns.* SIDOROV *enters. He looks like a factory worker. He looks sullen.* KAPUSTIN, *speaking through his yawn*): Name and surname?

SIDOROV: Mitrofan Sidorov.

KAPUSTIN: Date of birth?

SIDOROV: I never learned to write, Squire.

KAPUSTIN: What d'you mean – Squire? There have been no squires since the Revolution. (*He rummages among the papers.*) Didn't you know? Born in 1895, is that right?

SIDOROV: That's how I'm registered.

KAPUSTIN (*indicating*): Sit down. (*Speaking in a rapid monotone*): "By the decree of the Special Conference of the N.K.V.D. of the fifteenth of the sixth, 1945 Mitrofan Sidorov, born in 1895, is to be imprisoned in the corrective labour camp for ten years for having betrayed his country." Sign here.

SIDOROV (*rising from the edge of his chair*): Comrade Major! The Germans took me away by force. How can I be guilty? . . .

KAPUSTIN: I've read it out to you – for betraying your country. Sign. Right here.

SIDOROV: Ten years. That's quite something . . . It's no good shoving it at me. I can't write, I've told you.

KAPUSTIN: Make a cross, then.

SIDOROV: I'm not going to do it. You make the cross.

KAPUSTIN (*writing*): On behalf of the illiterate . . .

SIDOROV: A five-cornered star . . .

KAPUSTIN: None of your lip. You're quite some illiterate, I see! Hullo! The next!

The SERGEANT *lets* YELESHEV *in.*

KAPUSTIN: Name-surname-date-of-birth?

SIDOROV *leaves reluctantly, looking back. The* SERGEANT *hurries him out.*

YELESHEV: I'm a Moscow architect, fairly well known, a pupil of Shchusev . . .

KAPUSTIN: Who did you say? Shchukov?

YELESHEV: Do you mean my name? No. Yeleshev, Anatoliy. I was responsible for the building . . . (*He sits down.*)

KAPUSTIN: Date of birth?

YELESHEV: Mine?

KAPUSTIN: Naturally. I know my own.

YELESHEV: I'm forty. Born in 1904. If you've ever been to . . . you might have seen my building . . .

KAPUSTIN: Sit down. (*Reading in a rapid monotone.*) "By the decree of the Special Conference of the N.K.V.D. of the fifteenth of the sixth 1945 the former soldier, Second Lieutenant of the Red Army Anatoliy Yeleshev, born in 1904, is to be imprisoned in the corrective labour camp for ten years for having betrayed his country." Sign.

YELESHEV: Excuse me, from a strictly juridical point of view . . .

KAPUSTIN: You can write about that from the camp. Sign. Right here.

YELESHEV: You must hear me out, please. I yielded at the interrogation, because I had hoped that in the course of the trial, during cross-examination in court . . .

KAPUSTIN: It's for just such cross-examinations that we have no time. Sign.

YELESHEV: I refuse to sign. It's monstrous! Who is the judge here? Where's the court? Are you the court?

KAPUSTIN: I think I read it out to you clearly enough: a Special Conference.

YELESHEV: But where is it?

KAPUSTIN: In Moscow.

YELESHEV: But how can it pass judgment on me when it has never set eyes on me?

KAPUSTIN: Prisoner Yeleshev! I do not propose to explain this to you. Sign.

YELESHEV (*with heat*): There is not a grain of truth in any

141

of the accusations in my case. It's like some fantastic
novel. The Investigator put down anything that came
into his head, and forced my signature by the threat of
solitary confinement, or danger to my family.

KAPUSTIN: So! You're even prepared to slander Soviet
Investigations methods. Slander the Organs of State
Security. Your sentence obviously isn't long enough.

YELESHEV: No. Don't say that. But the verdict . . .

KAPUSTIN: This is not a verdict but a decree. What you're
signing is the fact that you've read it.

YELESHEV (*with animation*): I never read it!

KAPUSTIN: Then say so. Here, read it, the devil take you!
(*He throws the decree towards him, and lights a cigarette.*)
Only, hurry up! Come on!

YELESHEV (*having read it*): Ten years! My God! I was
thirty-six years of age when I was taken prisoner of war.
I shall leave the camp as an old man of fifty. For what?
For the fact that in 1941 officers floundered around like
blind puppies without maps, compasses or pistols.

KAPUSTIN (*in a rapid monotone*): It was your duty to die on
the field of battle. Sign.

YELESHEV: No! This is monstrous!

KAPUSTIN: Take care you don't regret it later on. (*Takes up
his pen.*) So-o . . . He refused to sign and expressed . . .

YELESHEV: No! I expressed nothing. I did not refuse!

KAPUSTIN: Then sign, blast you! You've wasted ten
minutes of my time.

YELESHEV: To the effect that I've actually read it?

KAPUSTIN: Well, yes, yes.

YELESHEV: But that doesn't mean that I accept the
correctness of the verdict or that I admit to being guilty.

KAPUSTIN: No, no, of course not.

YELESHEV: What about the amnesty?

KAPUSTIN: Yes, of course, there'll be an amnesty.

YELESHEV (*timidly*): There's been one? . . .

KAPUSTIN: There's been one, there'll be another.
Everybody will go free.

YELESHEV: Well, you put my mind at rest. (*He signs. Like a king, who has abdicated his throne, he drops the pen in a state of exhaustion.*) O my God. What is the price of human individuality?

KAPUSTIN: Hullo, there! Next!

A little peasant, who looks like an illustration from a folk tale, stands on the threshold, holding his fur hat in his hand. It is PAKHOMOV.

KAPUSTIN: Name? Surname?

YELESHEV (*without leaving his seat at the table*): We weren't allowed any writing paper in our cells, so that we couldn't put down our complaints or statements. If they do issue paper, it's tiny bits of blotting paper, so small you can't sign your name. I request that you give me an opportunity here, before I leave your study, to write an appeal on my case.

KAPUSTIN (*impatiently summoning* PAKHOMOV): Against regulations. (*To* PAKHOMOV): Name? Surname?

YELESHEV: How do you mean, regulations? What are the regulations?

SERGEANT (*pulling him off his chair and pushing him out*): Regulations are what we say they are. Out!

PAKHOMOV (*bowing*): Pakhomov, Theodore.

KAPUSTIN (*irritated by now*): Date of birth?

PAKHOMOV: 1901.

KAPUSTIN: Sign. (PAKHOMOV *signs.*) You may go. (PAKHOMOV *goes.*) Hullo! Next . . . Hey you! Did I read it to you!

PAKHOMOV: Read what?

KAPUSTIN: What a fool! What did you sign then? Come here and sit down. "The Decree of the Special Conference of the N.K.V.D. of the fifteenth of the sixth, 1945 states that Pakhomov, Theodore is to be imprisoned in the corrective labour camp for ten years for betraying his country; for undertaking an armed uprising; for working with the enemy and for contacts with world bourgeoisie; for undermining productivity in industry,

agriculture and transport; for terrorist intentions, shortfall of provisions, as well as for connections which lead to suspicions of espionage." Now, sign.
(PAKHOMOV *takes up the pen.*) No, not again. (*Removes the pen.*) Is it clear?

PAKHOMOV (*looking enviously at a cigarette stub in the Major's mouth*): Permission to finish your cigarette, Comrade boss. (KAPUSTIN *passes on the stub.* PAKHOMOV *bows deeply.*) God give you health, Comrade boss. (*Exit backwards, bowing, and pulling on the cigarette.*)

KAPUSTIN: Here, grandpa. (*He rapidly takes out a couple of cigarettes and offers them to* PAKHOMOV *who bows.*) Hullo! Next!

Scene 4

We can see, one by one, four investigation rooms which are absolutely identical as to size, position of the door and barred window, the desk of the Investigator, the position of the prisoner and the portrait of Stalin. It is only the Investigator and the prisoner who change, while the lights go out completely – to the tune of "Stalin's Windmill".

The tune of "Stalin's Windmill". The lights come up.

PART I

MYMRA *and* KLIMOV

MYMRA: Question two. What was your rank and calling at the moment of being taken prisoner of war?

KLIMOV: Sergeant. In charge of the infantry section.

MYMRA (*writing down*): . . . of the infantry section.
Question three. (*Absolutely expressionless.*) What was your aim when you gave yourself up? Why didn't you shoot yourself?

KLIMOV: Terrific! Would you have done?

MYMRA (*still expressionless*): Prisoner Klimov. You are here
to answer questions, not to ask them. You could be
locked up in a cell for refusing to answer questions.
Personally, we are ready to die for our leader. Question
three: what was your aim when you gave yourself up?
Why didn't you shoot yourself?

KLIMOV: I was waiting to see if the Divisional Commander
would shoot himself first. However, he managed to
escape to Moscow by 'plane out of the encirclement and
then got promoted.

MYMRA (*writing down*): Answer. I gave myself up, my aim
being to betray my Socialist country . . .

KLIMOV: We-el, well; you can put it like that . . .

*The lights go out. The tune of the "Windmill". The lights go
up.*

PART II

SVERBYOZHNIKOV *and* PECHKUROV

SVERBYOZHNIKOV: Question two. What was your rank
and calling at the moment of being taken prisoner of
war?

PECHKUROV: What calling? I'm called Ivan. I humped an
anti-tank gun about. I was number one.

SVERBYOZHNIKOV (*jumping up*): Don't you dare tell lies,
you scum! Soviet Intelligence knows everything! I can
see three yards into the ground beneath you! Commander
of the Unit, eh? Did you remove your unit badge?

PECHKUROV: Ah, n-no. Didn't have a sickle, did I?

SVERBYOZHNIKOV: Not much of a soldier. Once a wild
animal, always a wild animal, despite the training. A rich
peasant's pampered son, maybe?

PECHKUROV: Agricultural labourers, both father and
grandfather.

SVERBYOZHNIKOV: Soviet Intelligence knows everything!

(*He sits down and writes.*) Question three. What was your aim when you gave yourself up? Why didn't you shoot yourself?

PECHKUROV: Ever seen an anti-tank gun? How do you think you can shoot yourself with that?

SVERBYOZHNIKOV (*getting angry*): You're getting insolent, you oaf. You had no arms? The Soviet Government was short of arms?

PECHKUROV: Don't know about the Government, but I carted the anti-tank gun without ammunition for a week.

SVERBYOZHNIKOV (*jumping up*): You snake! You vermin! We'll shoot you for this slander. We'll find a bullet for you; we'll order *nine grammes* to make a hole in your forehead! (*Returning to his desk he reads from a different piece of paper.*) "I gave myself up my aim being to betray my Socialist country." That's the sort of answer we want. *The lights go down. The tune of "Stalin's Windmill". The lights go up.*

PART III

NEKLYUCHIMOV *and* KULYBYSHEV

NEKLYUCHIMOV: Question two. What was your rank and calling at the moment of being taken prisoner of war?

KULYBYSHEV: What, in a penal company? I was there making up the numbers. I was working in the stables as the regimental goat.

NEKLYUCHIMOV (*laughing*): You funny old man . . . Still, I've got to write something.

KULYBYSHEV: Well, if they demand to know my calling, write President of the collective farm named after Ivan Susanin.

NEKLYUCHIMOV: Susanin? . . . Wait a sec. Where did you say you come from?

KULYBYSHEV: How am I to answer that? Not too far from Kostroma.

146

Scene 4

NEKLYUCHIMOV: Oh I see. So Ivan Susanin and you are from the same district?

KULYBYSHEV: Fancy you knowing him. What a small world. Ivan, Michael, Theodore, Gleb – we're all from there. There's just one awkward thing – they're all Kulaks.

NEKLYUCHIMOV: How do you mean?

KULYBYSHEV: Simple. Under the Tsar, they gave them a pension. No wonder they become Kulaks.

NEKLYUCHIMOV: A pension?

KULYBYSHEV: They must have obliged somehow, see. Now. In the 'thirties they got dispossessed, packed off to Siberia. Not a squeak from them for six years, so in our fervour we name our collective farm "Lenin's Path" – but in '36 we get a piece of paper, which says Ivan Susanin was your respected fellow-citizen and you are to call your farm after him. Well, we'd nothing against that, the Government knows best. On the other hand, we're a bit ashamed before our neighbours. It would have been all right if they'd told us to call it after Michael or Theodore or his brothers. But Ivan, of all of them, was the most useless – he drank and rioted and brawled. To hell with him! Still, I suppose he managed to get to the top . . .

While he is talking NEKLYUCHIMOV *has taken a plate of sandwiches out of his drawer.*

NEKLYUCHIMOV: Oh dear, Kuzma, you're a nice old man, you know. It's a shame that you got yourself into a prisoner of war camp. Here, have one. (KULYBYSHEV *takes a sandwich, sniffs it and puts it back on the plate.*) Why don't you eat it? It can't be that you're not hungry.

KULYBYSHEV: Why . . . ?

NEKLYUCHIMOV: Eat, then! Eat as much as you can. I can't give it to you in your cell, but you can eat here. (*Looks at* KULYBYSHEV *intently.*) Wait a minute. Why are you refusing to eat?

KULYBYSHEV: Well, you see . . . I don't want to upset

147

you, truly . . . But . . . perhaps . . . it's poisoned.

NEKLYUCHIMOV: Kuzma, Kuzma! (*He is hurt.*) Do I look like someone who'd poison? (*He looks at himself in the open window pane, as if it were a mirror.*) Eh? We-ll . . . Let me take the one you're worried about. I'll eat it myself.

KULYBYSHEV *indicates the sandwich:* NEKLYUCHIMOV *eats it and walks towards his desk.* KULYBYSHEV *eats also.*

NEKLYUCHIMOV: Last time . . . you told me about how the penal company crossed the Dniepr on logs . . . and how some were shot and others fell off and were drowned; and how only a handful of you managed to clamber up the steep banks, but were taken prisoner . . . So, now, question three: what was your aim in giving yourselves up? Why didn't you shoot yourselves? (*KULYBYSHEV is eating his sandwiches hungrily.* NEKLYUCHIMOV *writes.*) Answer. I gave myself up my aim being to betray my Socialist country.

The lights go down. The tune of the "Windmill". The lights go up.

PART IV

KAMCHUZHNAYA *and* POSVYANTSEVA

KAMCHUZHNAYA: Here. This is for Anastasiya Posvyantseva. This letter was found in the pocket of the dead man's jacket.

POSVYANTSEVA: Give it to me! Give it to me!

KAMCHUZHNAYA: That depends on your behaviour. (*Skims through the letter.*) "Anastasiya, my love . . . Whatever I do, wherever I am, my thoughts . . ." There are pages and pages of sweet nothings here.

POSVYANTSEVA: Listen to me, Captain Kamchuzh-naya! . . .

KAMCHUZHNAYA: "The lands around Oryol disappear

148

from beneath our very feet . . ." That's sufficiently
straightforward. "We are retreating, in order to take up
defences at Oryol itself. Oh, the blue-green stalks of
wheat all blackened by the blast of bomb explosions
. . ." Quite a poet, isn't he? . . . "No, we will not
surrender the town . . ." He's quite an educated little
officer, that husband of yours, I see . . . "But since
you're ten miles from the front your life will be
impossible. I beg you to go to our relatives in Saxony
. . ." Well, he begged unnecessarily. You'd thought of it
yourself . . . By the way, there's a postscript here in
someone else's handwriting. Whose is it, eh?

POSVYANTSEVA: I can't see.

KAMCHUZHNAYA (*approaches, showing it*): Here.

POSVYANTSEVA: I can't see when someone else is holding
it. Let me take it.

KAMCHUZHNAYA (*with a sneer*): Don't think you can fool
me, you idiot. This is Captain Theodore Kolosovitov's
handwriting! Did he come to your house?

POSVYANTSEVA: No.

KAMCHUZHNAYA: What about Ensign Igor Bolosnin?

POSVYANTSEVA: I don't remember.

KAMCHUZHNAYA (*holding the letter in front of
POSVYANTSEVA's face*): You'll soon be able to read the
whole letter. It is the *last* letter from your husband!
There are eight pages of it. Eight tender pages. What do
you know about Igor Bolosnin?

POSVYANTSEVA: Bolosnin? I don't remember.

The light goes out.

Scene 5: A Flashback

*In the light of the setting sun we can see a small garden, which
contains a single-storey house with a summer terrace. There is a
table fixed to the ground and some benches.*

A church bell tolls regularly, a thin, makeshift sound.
Anastasiya is laying the table, putting on a cloth and placing
tea cups. Bolosnin, who is wearing a German uniform, has a
badge on the sleeve which says 'R.L.A.' (Russian Liberation
Army).

BOLOSNIN: They are ringing the bell. They are ringing for
    Vespers . . . O Russia, can this ever come back again?
    Will you ever be yourself? I have lived on your soil for
    twenty-six years, I spoke Russian, listened to Russian,
    but never knew what you were, my country! . . .

ANASTASIYA: And you, yourself, where are you from Igor?

BOLOSNIN (*unloading food from a basket*): I come from, I'm
    a citizen of a town which I'm so fond of I don't know
    what a suitable name for it would be. Saint . . . ? That
    got lost long ago. Especially since this town was not
    named after any apostle. Petersburg – that's German.
    Petrograd? – I don't see that name making Russia rear
    up under the reins of Peter the Great.[5] This town does
    not belong to Pushkin, or to Dostoyevsky. There is no
    one name that would cover it in full. To myself I call it
    . . . shall I tell you?

ANASTASIYA: What?

BOLOSNIN: I call it Never-grad. I'm a citizen of
    Never-grad.

ANASTASIYA: Never-grad. That sounds like the Novgorod
    that never was. It has a very Russian sound. You know
    those fragrant Russian words which have a stress on the
    first syllable?

BOLOSNIN: Added to which, it is completely correct. There
    is no other large city on the Neva. (*A pause.*) My father
    is there. He's a high-ranking officer – a General. They
    used to spoil me, they thought of giving me a car before
    the war . . . O Lord, how hard it is to realise at the age
    of twenty-five how blind one's been, how blind and
    insignificant! In the louse-ridden prisoner of war camps,
    to be rejected by one's country, to be horrified by one's
    shameful Komsomol youth! . . .

150

Scene 5: A Flashback

ANASTASIYA: You know, Igor, I have a brother not far from Leningrad – on the other side . . . He's in the artillery too. Very young. His last letter came from Pulkovo, but was unfinished. While my husband is now here . . . What is the truth? How will it all end? . . . (*A pause. The tolling of the bell speeds up and then stops.*) Vsevolod used to say – you two are fine, only your outlook on life is too gloomy.

BOLOSNIN: Was anyone unkind to him? They had told him all sorts of rosy things about Russia while he was abroad. (*He opens the wine bottles and the conserves.*) It's silly to go on repeating that the White Army consisted of landowners. My father, for instance, came of an aristocratic family, but goodness knows why he joined the Bolsheviks, while your husband's father was a simple telegraphist, not a member of the nobility, had no money and yet spent the whole Civil War in the White Army; took his wife and children down south, retreated to Gallipoli and did not stay in Red Soviet Russia . . . Incidentally, they told me, while I was visiting them in Saxony, that Vsevolod's elder sister went to school . . . where . . .

ANASTASIYA: Yes, where my mother was the headmistress. They come from Oryol.

BOLOSNIN: Then, both you and your mother are teachers. And both teaching Russian language and literature . . . (ANASTASIYA *nods.*) I met so many nice people during those two years when I stopped being a Soviet citizen, they were so generous and we understood one another so well . . .

KOLOSOVITOV (*in the same uniform as* BOLOSNIN; *he is huge. He wears glasses and carries a book. As he comes down from the terrace he is humming*):

O, Anastasiya, you flourished here,
You sang your songs,
You wove carpets for me, your groom,
But where are you now? . . .

151

ANASTASIYA: Theodore, take off your glasses when you're
with me. They ruin your image.

KOLOSOVITOV: What's one to do, Anastasiya? There are no
more giants in the twentieth century. I have put Alexei
Tolstoy back on the shelf, but have borrowed Herzen. Is
that all right? (*He takes off his glasses.*)

BOLOSNIN: Why Herzen? He's not your kind of thing.

KOLOSOVITOV: Why not? He was an extremely intelligent
fellow. Do you know what he called Marx, *et al*? *A
sulphuric band*! He does not belong to the Bolsheviks.
Just bear that in mind. We might yet have to start
publishing *The Bell*,[6] you know.

ANASTASIYA: You have hundreds of plans, Theodore. And
look at all the things you've brought. (*She walks back to
the house with a purposeful air.*)

KOLOSOVITOV: There's one plan, the most important one,
I never completed. I didn't stamp out Stalin.

BOLOSNIN (*staggered*): Were you intending to?!

KOLOSOVITOV: Why do we have to suffer him? Don't you
see, Igor, my life's been like a rolling stone. I've been all
over Mother Russia: to the Aldan and the Yenissey, to
Chukotka and to the Kolyma, and Norilsk, and even to
places where bears never get to – I got as far as that. I've
been going round as a research geologist ever since 1926.
But let me tell you this extraordinary thing – I come to a
place for the first time and there's nothing there; I come
a second time and there's a camp there. Camps, camps,
camps, nothing but camps. Entire continents behind
barbed wire – GULAG ARCHIPELAGO. Nothing left
of Russia! All roads were barred, I felt enmeshed in that
blasted barbed wire. I wanted to walk straight through
it, tearing it up, tearing it up. And the people I had to
work with! It was either a camp prisoner under guard, or
a camp prisoner without a guard, either a former
prisoner or a future one. It was desperate; what was one
to do? To organise a political party? Some underground
movement? But there were no real people left, just a

Scene 5: A Flashback

lowing herd; all the G.P.U. herdsman had to do was to
crack his whip for them all to fall on their front legs.
And a thought occurred to me that I might knock off the
pock-marked cretin responsible for it all myself. It was
just then that I published a book on geology, got
transferred to Moscow, became known; was taken up by
the Academy, became a member of the All-Union Society
for Cultural Relations with Foreign Countries. They held
receptions close by the Kremlin. "The Father of all the
Peoples, the Leading Light of all the Sciences" would be
around. Glory to the old Blackcock with his feathered
feet! Of course, within the Kremlin it would have been
more resounding – there's resonance there, but I
examined all the week-end dachas.

BOLOSNIN: But it's impossible to take any arms into the
Kremlin. One's searched a hundred times. It's
tricky.

KOLOSOVITOV: Tricky things are for tricksters. What the
hell did I need arms for? *These* are my arms. (*He stretches
out his two hands.*) All I needed was to find myself within
ten paces of him and, in some cold place, one leap . . .
But there's another problem. They say he has at least six
doubles . . .

BOLOSNIN: Just think! It's possible you weren't alone;
maybe there were a half dozen like-minded people
milling around him, not knowing one another – and not
one got within reach!

KOLOSOVITOV: I would have reached him. As a schoolboy
of fourteen I experienced gun-fire and got gassed in
Yaroslavl – they used to shoot chemical shells at us then.
The Cheka shot me, but I survived. I would have
waited, if necessary, till I was an old, bald Academician
to get within reach – but the war came . . . Stalin went
East from Moscow and I, after some thought, decided to
go West for the time being. Just then they were
recruiting for the People's Militia among the
Academicians . . .

BOLOSNIN: From the Academy of Sciences? From there into the People's Militia?

KOLOSOVITOV: Indeed, yes. Full speed. Everybody wanted to show off, nobody wanted to be left behind. Everyone signed on. Later on the party bosses were transferred to the rear to form the nucleus of scientific cadres, but those of us who weren't quite so good – off to the wars with us. We were beaten hollow at Vyazma . . . Kulik, for instance, you know – the famous Tungus meteorite of 1908. Well, Kulik – he was in my company. He died in a prioner of war camp; Kachalov's son also. I can't enumerate them all . . . The prisoner of war camp! D'you know, Igor, I expected all sorts of vile, low-down tricks from the Bolshevik government, but I didn't expect that it would betray its own prisoners of war!

BOLOSNIN (*very agitated*): Don't talk to me about that, Theodore! In two hundred years time I will be croaking from my grave about those Russian prisoners! In there I survived typhus, hunger; my love for the Revolution died there, my love for my father and my faith in man nearly disappeared there! They beat each other over the head with sticks, with mess tins to get some of that miserable soup, that filthy prison soup; ten thousand of them queuing up, starting at midnight. They used to gnaw tree-bark to the last shred. And then we are told that we are traitors to our own country. The swine, they should be put in there! The English, the French, the Serbs, the Norwegians – all prisoners of war like us – were our neighbours behind the barbed wire. They received their pay-packets for the years in prison, they received rewards for their years of service, promotion, letters from home, parcels from the Red Cross. They didn't even have to queue for the German soup cauldron and threw chocolates and cigarettes to us over the fence.

VSEVOLOD, *wearing the same uniform, comes from round the corner of the house, carrying a samovar with a teapot on top.*

Scene 5: A Flashback

BOLOSNIN: Only "Ivan" is unwanted in the world, only "Ivan" belongs to no one. How can Stalin be forgiven for that?

KOLOSOVITOV: But, Igor, all of them, every one of them was like that. All those Lenins and Tomskys, Trotskys and Shchatskys. Russia, Mexico – what did they care? They never wore a caftan.

VSEVOLOD: And did you imagine, gentlemen, that our émigré leaders were any brighter? Do you think they would bother to consult the Russian people? Not a chance! Each one of them could only go on repeating that he had been right. They did not care that some fifteen, twenty years had passed during which time the nation suffered, grew up, had its own thoughts. How we argued with them! And we left them! A new movement arose among us, the younger ones. It was against *pre-deter-min-ation*. We do not force our decisions on the people. We intend to free the people, but since the burden was not carried by us, it is not up to us to decide how: to the point that if the Russian peasant likes his collective farm, let him have it. If the Ukraine wants to become separate – let it. As to Georgia especially, the sooner it floats off the better. At least, that way, we wouldn't be governed and marketed by Georgians. Our motto was: better less, but better! Do we need territories, friends! God gave us a lot of land. What we need is loving rulers, stable laws . . . (*He is out of breath.*)

We can see ANASTASIYA *on the terrace in a different dress.*

ANASTASIYA: Comrades . . . uhum . . . Gentlemen! It's so good of you to come. The best kind of party is an unexpected one. Do sit down, or the samovar will get cold.

They settle down.

KOLOSOVITOV: O samovar, O pot-bellied urn! How you have been reviled by the enemies of mediocrity – by all

155

the Chekhovs, the Gorkys, the Kuprins. There they go
on the stage for three hours on end and putting on airs
and wailing: we're summer folk, we're dacha dwellers!
But what's wrong with that? Gentlemen, I drink to the
middle classes.

BOLOSNIN: Me too. Food, drink, love, home, the
upbringing of children have all been declared shameful
activities. That's not progress, it's Bedlam. They should
try living in hostels building Communism.

KOLOSOVITOV: Into camps with them! Into that coach, on
to the top bunk! (*Holding a bottle in one hand.*) I hope,
Anastasiya, you'll allow me just one toast. Only one,
because now we find ourselves in a pure feminine world;
thereafter we shall be drinking tea with milk. Anastasiya,
I want to express my admiration for the noble work you
are doing. For two years now, in a Russian school, which
is situated at a hair's breadth distance from Soviet Russia
and a Russia whose future is unknown, you have been
unfolding before children the might of our language, the
might of our literature, the joyless history of our people.
And you've been doing that, not through official text
books, but guided by your own conscience and sense of
truth. At the moment we are killing Russians, for no
good purpose, while you're bringing them up for the
future. I want to thank you and others like you, dear
Anastasiya. Your good health! (*They drink.*)

ANASTASIYA: Thank you . . . Thank you, Theodore.
You're a great support to me. The times are so strange,
they hang heavily, just now. Over there, near Bryansk,
schools are being burned down by partisans, while here
in Oryol we get anonymous letters, telling us not to dare
to teach anything while we are under German
occupation, or we'll pay for it. What sort of drunken
louts write such letters? Are they afraid that children will
grow up all wrong, not to mention that they'd lost not
just months, but years of schooling. It's not their fault.
If a child leaves his school desk, he will never return to

Scene 5: A Flashback

it . . . I wish you knew how difficult I find it all! (*She bows her head.*)

KOLOSOVITOV (*humming*):

> You languished and pined in your room,
> While I, in my powdered wig,
> Went to pay my respects to the queen
> And never saw you again . . .

ANASTASIYA: What crude and unfeeling barbarians! How can I stop teaching? After a day's work, I come home refreshed, excited, so happy, I can hardly get to sleep. Before 1941 we had this continuous indoctrination. We had to mouth some class-ridden rubbish about the petty-bourgeois, who'd gone mad. We had to harp on some bad moment in history about this or that; to throw Don Quixote into the rubbish bin of history; had to say that the poet, limited by his gentry background couldn't quite grasp . . . Leo Tolstoy, according to them, couldn't quite grasp, while some Kirpotin grasps everything! . . . But, at least, there was a sense of certainty, however stifling, of some permanence, however bad. But now everything is topsy-turvy. The official pecking order of prescribed quotations has gone, everything is in flux, you don't know what to serve with what – no one knows, teach any way you like; the Dostoyevsky once forbidden is now available – but I can now teach from the heart. I have grown wings. The trouble is, I have no cushion of air to lift me up. There's no firm ground either, come to that. What's going to happen? And how?

VSEVOLOD (*squinting at the sunset*): Look at these fiery clouds. And as soon as the sun sets, it will be like it is on the front line – a warm, bright west and a gloomy, threatening east. (*To* ANASTASIYA.) Our dug-out faces east. How severe the east becomes after the sun has set – I never noticed it before, because we tend to admire the sunset . . . There's some specially bitter charm in this spring of 1943. The Oryol-Kursk line lies on the map like a huge question mark. It is still, like a sleeping

snake and no one knows where its tail will strike. Here,
three versts from the front line, we have kitchen gardens,
the wheat's growing, villages full of people; and over
there for twenty miles everybody's been chased out, no
one lives there, nothing grows apart from steppe grasses,
wild flowers and thistles, as in the days of Batiy.[7] But
both they and we are on the same mid-Russian lands –
hills, sparkling gullies, the waving green foliage of
woods, and the nightingales, nightingales at night! . . .
The region of Oryol. The dream of my childhood. I
wouldn't mind dying in a place like this, truly.

ANASTASIYA: Don't even think it. The very thought might
make it happen.

VSEVOLOD: After it has grown dark, for a short time there
are no rockets, no rattle of machine guns, those *coffee-
grinders* cease their noise, the lonely nocturnal Henschels
do not drone – the wild grasses are fragrant over the
battle front . . . O Anastasiya, come with us there for a
day. It's worth visiting! . . .

ANASTASIYA: I shall, I shall certainly come with you. May
I, Theodore?

KOLOSOVITOV: Better not, Anastasiya. Here we appear to
you like some kind of knights in shining armour, we
come here all fresh, we speak of beautiful things, while
over there we drink and drink and drink, our eyes
pewter-coloured, we play cards . . . It's better not!

ANASTASIYA: But why so? When you're in this house
you're not like that?

VSEVOLOD: I don't know why they behave like that. I
never drink.

BOLOSNIN: But what's one to do? – just consider. I
stopped at a cottage in Stanovoy Kolodez and got to
talking with the peasant woman. She said: "God only
knows what sort of person you are – you seem to be
neither Russian nor German." That's the horror of it –
during the course of this war, in the eyes of ordinary
people, it is the Bolsheviks who have usurped the right

Scene 5: A Flashback

to be called Russian. And indeed, to look at us from
outside in – we are a suspect lot of companies, inserted
into the Wehrmacht. Where here would you find
independent, solidly Russian regiments, divisions? Our
own sections of the battle front?

VSEVOLOD: But we could have marched on, given the
chance. Boy, how we could have marched! Like an
avalanche, ever increasing, growing . . . Some three
hundred versts to Moscow, through towns and villages –
there would have been flowers, caps tossed into the air,
embroidered towels!

KOLOSOVITOV: Those cheap towels, Vsevolod, are now
worn to a frazzle; as to caps, people treasure them.

BOLOSNIN: What sort of uniforms are we wearing? What
are we fighting for? This military jacket is burning on
my back! I'm as ashamed of the German eagle as I would
have been of the Red star! . . . What is it that we are
doing? Side by side with the German soldiers, we're
killing Russians so as to liberate the Russians! That's
how far we've been cornered. On my latest assignment
I've been introduced to General Vlasov.[8] He wanted to
know about morale at the front. I told him straight out:
we cannot see any other Russian governments emerging,
in our heart of hearts we consider the Anglo-Saxons our
true allies, but in the meantime, to the wonder of the
S.S., we're aiding and abetting Hitler.

KOLOSOVITOV: Do you know, Igor, the devil himself tried
to brew beer with the English but had to refuse their
malt.

ANASTASIYA: So what did Vlasov say?

BOLOSNIN: He made a face. I have a feeling that he's
rather confused. Bitten off more than he can chew.

KOLOSOVITOV: Well, of course, no leader in Vlasov's
position can do a damn thing.

VSEVOLOD: Then what did he start it all for? And why does
he go on dragging it out, this muddle? Why does he
encourage, deceive so many ardent young lives?

159

KOLOSOVITOV: But what are these ardent young ones to do, anyway? Die off in prisoner of war camps? He's doing right. You either get hanged or cut the noose.

BOLOSNIN: There's just one hope: to join up with the Allies even if it is only at Hitler's death.

VSEVOLOD: Then why don't we issue an ultimatum to Hitler! We should demand . . .

KOLOSOVITOV: . . . Squeeze a drop of water out of a stone! That wasn't the way to fight the Bolsheviks. It's easy to see what we should have done: we should have landed forces outside the labour camps! All one needed to do then was to knock out the miserable camp guards and hungry hands would be stretching out for armaments. We would have had an army twelve-million-strong, and in the rear, what's more. But Hitler, that arrogant idiot who imagined he could conquer Russia without Russian help and against the Russians – he more or less continued with the collective farms, he burnt down villages, he was afraid to create independent regiments from us. No wonder the Kremlin moustachio is rubbing his hands – there's a know-nothing in the world even thicker than him! Hitler won't understand even on his deathbed that the Russian Liberation Army[9] was the fulcrum to overthrow . . .

ANASTASIYA (*fixedly*): *Was?* Theodore – why *was?*
It is getting quite dark.

BOLOSNIN: If the new Russia is to be created by Hitler – to hell with such a Russia!
It is quite dark. The tune of "Stalin's Windmill". The lights go up. We are back in the investigation room.

KAMCHUZHNAYA: And do you imagine that your romantic little garden has not been surveyed and bugged by honest Soviet patriots? What about Bolosnin? Lieutenant Igor Bolosnin?

POSVYANTSEVA: I don't remember.

KAMCHUZHNAYA: You don't remember, you slut! What if I bring him in?

Scene 4 (resumed)

POSVYANTSEVA: Go on, then.

KAMCHUZHNAYA: And Kolosovitov as well?

POSVYANTSEVA: You won't be able to get them. Your N.K.V.D.'s arms are too short.

KAMCHUZHNAYA: Go on, kneel, you filth, kneel! (*She pushes her into a corner on to her knees.*)
The lights go out. The "Windmill" melody. The lights come up.

Scene 4 (resumed)

PART V

MYMRA *and* KLIMOV

MYMRA: Question six. Who gave you the task of developing spying activities in the Soviet Union?

KLIMOV: That's something new. I never studied in a spy college.

MYMRA (*in level tones*): Don't try to confuse the investigation. You did serve in the American Army from 1944?

KLIMOV: Yes, I did serve with the Allies.

MYMRA: The fact that it was with the Allies is of no importance. Did they not rope you in?

KLIMOV: How do you mean? The very fact that I served?

MYMRA: O.K. As an American soldier you could have got a passport to the U.S.A., or Canada, or . . .

KLIMOV: Anywhere at all.

MYMRA: Now *you* are confused. How, then, do you explain your voluntary return to your country?

KLIMOV: How . . . do I explain . . . my voluntary . . .?

MYMRA (*nods and writes with glee*): Answer. In some confusion . . . I testified untruthfully. I was given a task by American Intelligence.
The lights go out. The "Windmill" melody. The lights come up.

161

PART VI

SVERBYOZHNIKOV *and* PECHKUROV

SVERBYOZHNIKOV (*writing*): Answer. I was given a task by American Intelligence.

PECHKUROV: Citizen Investigator! I've never set my eyes on any Americans. I was liberated by our own people.

SVERBYOZHNIKOV: Who's *ours*? Who's *yours*? *Yours* are running around on all fours in the Krasnoyarsk region of Siberia. (*A pause.*) Well, O.K. Let's say by American Intelligence through an officer of the German Army . . . what was his name?

PECHKUROV: Whose?

SVERBYOZHNIKOV (*writes*): Richard Bauer. (*Rubbing his hands.*) There, now. The charge sheet's complete! (*He sorts out his papers, humming.*) "But he who marches through life with a song . . ." Hey, do you get enough grub over there?

PECHKUROV: Enough, my foot! A piece of bread this small and a couple of half-full tins of prison soup . . .

SVERBYOZHNIKOV (*brings the charge sheet and a pen dipped in ink to* PECHKUROV's *table*): I'll tell them to give you extra food; you'll be getting some gruel and a hundred grammes of bread. Here, sign.

PECHKUROV: I refuse. It's all a tissue of lies.

SVERBYOZHNIKOV: You carrion! Who taught you to give answers like that?

PECHKUROV: I taught myself.

SVERBYOZHNIKOV: Not taught enough. You've not yet sat on a steel hedgehog. (*Advancing slowly.*) You've so far been eating boiled corn and had quiet nights. You wait till we scramble your balls like so many eggs. Would you like that?

PECHKUROV (*downcast*): Well, governor, if I'm to die, then I'm to die. I'm fed up and tired of this whole business. I've no wish to live.

SVERBYOZHNIKOV (*stops, flabbergasted*): What? No wish to live, you son of a bitch?

PECHKUROV (*peaceably*): That's right, no wish to live. You occupy a nice cosy niche, see, you have it off with girls, so you want to live – and you think everybody's the same. But no. I've been through it these last five years. If I'm to get another ten – there's no point in living.

SVERBYOZHNIKOV (*at a loss*): Hum. That's psychologically decadent. How can you not want to live? (*Becoming animated.*) You speak with a voice that's not your own. Soviet Intelligence knows everything. You've been taken out of your isolation cell too soon. I didn't want to do it, but I'll have to remove your old Mum and Dad from Smolensk and pack them off to Siberia . . .

PECHKUROV (*calmly*): We'll thank you for that. Perchance, there are no collective farms there.

SVERBYOZHNIKOV (*utterly at a loss*): Hell's teeth! What am I to do with you, you reptile?

The lights go out. The "Windmill" melody, which stops, as if the record got stuck. The lights go up.

PART VII

NEKLYUCHIMOV *and* KULYBYSHEV

NEKLYUCHIMOV: Question six. Who instructed you to organise a spy network within the Soviet Union? Eh? Old man. Eh? (*He laughs.*) Who gave you this assignment? (*He laughs louder and* KULYBYSHEV *joins him. The laughter increases.*) Eh? You mole? (*They laugh.*) Answer. I was recruited by American Intelligence. Why aren't you eating? Do finish.

KULYBYSHEV: I've eaten my fill,
              Sufficient to kill.
              I must take rest
              And recover my zest.

NEKLYUCHIMOV: Always joking, eh? You're a cheerful
  soul.

KULYBYSHEV: Were it not for the frosts,
              The hop plants would grow –
              Maybe fast, maybe slow –
              But as tall as these posts.

NEKLYUCHIMOV (*moving to sit down closer to* KULYBYSHEV,
  in a confidential tone): All right, Kuzma, let's leave all
  that aside. Tell me, rather, what it was like working for
  a *Bauer* as a farm labourer.

KULYBYSHEV: Eh, m'dear. Let's say, that wherever there's
  plenty, your life's O.K. This word – *Bauer* – it means a
  peasant, but just go into the cellars, or climb up into the
  attics! From one summer to another – there are apples
  this size! And the grapes, and the wine . . . They gave
  me a litre a day – to drink as you please . . . Just
  consider, what kind of village is it if the houses are two
  storeys high, built of brick? You wake up in the morning
  under your feather bed and you lament – Kuzma, you're
  a slave. Talk of cattle, or poultry in the farmyard . . . As
  old men of the village used to say, you may be living
  under a yoke, but you're still well off. Well, then they
  sent us beyond the Rhine into the trenches – and I found
  myself with the Americans. A Russky, they said, a
  Russky! So I looks around and I likes it there, too. The
  Germans are bright, but the Americans are even
  brighter. They value people more than possessions. But
  the Russian seems to be under an evil spell. He may visit
  every blacksmith's in the region and yet returns without
  a horseshoe. He's got a longing to go back to his own
  place. Shall we ever see it? They entice you: "Come
  back, little lamb, come back!" And when you are back:
  "Here's the big bad wolf."

NEKLYUCHIMOV: There you go, old man, there you go.
  You're saying these things to me! – to the Investigator of
  State Security. Should we let you go back to your
  Kostroma region, what sort of things would you be

saying there? Who would want to work in the collective
farms after hearing your kind of stories? You must admit
that's true.

KULYBYSHEV: I s'pose, it's true . . .

NEKLYUCHIMOV: Well, there you are, as you see. I can't
let you off, old thing. You're being imprisoned not
because of you, whether you're guilty or not; it's because
you've seen things, do you understand, it's because
you've seen things! But whatever's written in this charge
sheet – makes no odds. (*A pause.*) So, that's your choice:
if you sign now, you'll be sent into a camp, you'll work
there, you'll get your kilo of rations – and look, you've
done your ten years and come back to the old woman.
But if you don't – I get a reprimand, but then I've had
lots of them and I'm used to it, but you'd be passed on
to another Investigator, and you'd be kept miserable in a
cell, and getting only three hundred grammes and no hot
food – and you'd come crawling on all fours: let me have
the charge sheet, let me sign! . . . So, why don't you
take pity on yourself? (*He brings over the sheet and the
fountain pen.*) Come on, old man, scribble your name, go
on, scribble. "I was recruited by American Intelligence."
KULYBYSHEV *rubs his head. He signs, his lips moving.
The lights go out. The "Windmill" melody. The lights go up.*

PART VIII

KAMCHUZHNAYA *and* POSVYANTSEVA
   POSVYANTSEVA *is in the corner on her knees.*
   KAMCHUZHNAYA *is sitting on a couch.*
KAMCHUZHNAYA: Do you know, Your Highness, I can't
understand your grief. While you're a strong and lusty
female – your life's in your own hands, wherever you
are. In any camp you can get men, any your heart
desires. Should you find yourself in a men's camp centre,
you'll get the red carpet treatment, you silly fool! I envy

you in some ways, would you believe? Get up! I'm
talking sense.

POSVYANTSEVA (*rising*): All I ask is that the child should
be given to her grandmother. What a disaster it was that
I was arrested on my way home. They could have done it
when I got there.

KAMCHUZHNAYA: We might do that. Although, perhaps,
your daughter would be brought up better by the State.
She will grow up a true patriot, will not get married to
the first émigré bandit and will not go off to Saxony.

POSVYANTSEVA: I'm not the only one brought up here. My
brother was too and he's an officer in the Red Army.

KAMCHUZHNAYA: Well, who knows. He may be a traitor
too. We'll have to look into that. (*Changing her attitude
sharply.*) He's been killed! Your brother's been killed in
East Prussia, he's been killed by the friends of your
husband, he's been killed by Vlasov's Army!

POSVYANTSEVA: He's alive!

KAMCHUZHNAYA (*jumps up, sorting papers on the
table*): Here, read this. Go on, read it! He found himself
surrounded, was killed in the village of Orendorf, having
heroically spent all his bullets in an unequal struggle.

POSVYANTSEVA, *having read it, weeps.*

KAMCHUZHNAYA (*standing next to her, tenderly*): Anastasiya,
my dear, who did you get tangled up with? What sort of
mire did you descend into? All these Kolosovitovs, and
all these Bolosnins! An empty, amoral lot, who have
nothing to recommend them but hatred. You do
understand it now?

POSVYANTSEVA (*lifting her head, no longer weeping*): Yes, I
do understand it now. I have understood, within these
walls, that if my brother had survived, if he had escaped
from the encirclement, you wouldn't have believed him,
you would have asked him why it was that he wanted to
return to his country voluntarily, you'd have torn off his
epaulettes and given him ten years!

KAMCHUZHNAYA (*in a monotone*): How come you're so

clever? How come you're so clever? (*She advances and pinches her.*)

POSVYANTSEVA (*tearing herself away*): Don't touch me!

KAMCHUZHNAYA: You wide-eyed lump! Are you proposing to testify against Kolosovitov?

POSVYANTSEVA: No!

KAMCHUZHNAYA: Are you going to remember Bolosnin?

POSVYANTSEVA: No!

KAMCHUZHNAYA: I'll kill your kid. I'll strangle it myself!

POSVYANTSEVA: I wouldn't put it past you!

KAMCHUZHNAYA: I'll do it! I'll do it! (*Beating her over the head.*)

POSVYANTSEVA (*reeling*): Ah-ah-ah!

KAMCHUZHNAYA: Shut up, you slut! Shut up, you pig! (*She pulls her hair.*)

POSVYANTSEVA (*screams*): Help, help!

KAMCHUZHNAYA (*beating her over the mouth*): Shut up, you rubbish! Shut up!

POSVYANTSEVA (*tearing herself away, rushes to the window, jumps on to the window-sill, breaks the window and holding on to the bars, shouts out*): Save me, save me! They're killing me! Killing me!
Two stalwart SUPERVISORS *run in and pull* POSVYANTSEVA *down from the window-sill.* RUBLYOV, *a gloomy-looking Colonel with rings under his eyes and grey streaks in his black hair, appears in the doorway.*

RUBLYOV: What's going on?

KAMCHUZHNAYA (*trembling in her agitation*): This White Army slut we haven't killed off . . .

POSVYANTSEVA (*her hands and face are covered in blood*): All right! Lock me up! Strangle me! I hate you! You get hold of an unfortunate Russian prisoner of war . . . You get hold of innocent Russian girls (*The* SUPERVISORS *try to stop her talking.*) You prevent Russian school children! . . . Your hour will come, you executioners!!

RUBLYOV *makes a sign for her to be taken away.*

Scene 6

*The vast courtyard of a landowner's manor house, which is
occupied by Counter-Intelligence SMERSH. To the right we
can see the pediment of a large building, the top of which is
invisible. There are steps leading up to a wide entrance door.
The windows of the first floor are fitted with widely-spaced bars.
At the back of the stage we can see an even larger brick
building, without any embellishments, the top of which is also
invisible, but we can see a semi-basement – it is the same
building which was seen from the back in Scene 1. It has been
turned into a prison: on its generally dark brown background we
can see the windows, which have been freshly bricked up with
bright pink bricks all the way up to a small spy hole. To the left
of the stage, right across it, there are wrought-iron gates, next to
which there is a lodge; it has been turned into a watch-tower.
There are a couple of flower beds and a defunct fountain. A
network of asphalt paths connect various doors of the building on
the right with those at the back. By one of the paths, at the
crossing of them and almost in the centre, there stands a crude,
wooden sentry-box, in which a soldier with colourful little flags
directs the traffic; his gestures are elegant, picturesque. All the
exits and entrances are at his command. The sentry-box has a
loud-speaker. It is a blinding July midday.*

*The whole scene lasts no more than eight to ten minutes. It is
a* Pantomime, *which consists of constant and tense movements
about the yard, the result of the activities of a large and well-
ordered establishment.*

*Along the paths at the back of the stage, guards conduct
prisoners from the prison into the building on the right and back
again, in particular they lead* PECHKUROV, KULYBYSHEV
and KLIMOV *back from their interrogation. In order to
announce their presence and in order to avoid the possibility of
the prisoners meeting each other, the guards click their tongues,
clank their keys against the buckles of their belts; they move their*

168

prisoners quickly along, putting their charges occasionally into the sentry-box because they must not see each other.

During the time of arrival and departure of prisoners, the traffic-regulating soldier stops the movement of those under investigation. In the course of this scene a couple of small batches of prisoners are brought in and two large ones are being sent off – one, on foot, marches off through the gates, five prisoners to a line, the other by an open lorry, which backs towards the gates; the prisoners sit on the floor of the vehicle, while the guards stand with their backs to the cab.

Among the prisoners there are young women, dressed in West European clothes, as well as Russian peasant women wearing head scarves and carrying bags; young men in soldiers' uniforms and peasants in jerkins; there are many in military great-coats made of Russian cloth, some have white markings "S.U." on their backs, but among them there are army uniforms from all over the world. One of the batches of prisoners includes women with children. Some prisoners carry heavy luggage, others have hardly any. The prisoners who are being dispatched emerge from the prison doors, carrying some bread and herring. They talk to each other in a dumb-show, while those who have just arrived are quickly sorted out and taken in. Among those who are about to leave are YELESHEV, SIDOROV *and* PAKHOMOV.

Numerous Supervisors are rushing around the yard, either attending the prisoners or carrying heaps of files. Sentries come and go, while Sergeants receive or dispatch groups of prisoners.

This silent pantomime is accompanied by the sound of a children's song, which is being rehearsed on radio: it is first performed in toto *by a choir, then a solo voice dictates and performs one couplet after another and at the end the whole song is performed again. At the last refrain the curtain comes down.*

Happy, victorious
Our country is glorious,
The Kremlin is sparkling with gold.

Stalin, Leader and Guide,
Says we must struggle and fight,
Calls us all to join the fold.

Refrain:
  Our country is happy and free,
  Just look around you and see,
  Don't let it be wasted or sold.

But behind the glorious rainbows
There are enemies lurking about.
We must sweep every one of them out.

Refrain.

The pantomime is interrupted during this song by distant calls regarding prisoners, as for instance:

SERGEANT: Solovyova!

ANSWER: Oktyabrina, born in 1924 in the town of Hommel, 58-one-A. Ten years.

SERGEANT: Makarova!

ANSWER: Vladilena, born in 1921. Leningrad. 58-one-A. Ten years.

A second time.

SERGEANT: Chugrev!

ANSWER: Ivan. 1918. Village of Lugari, Tambov district. 58-one-B. Ten years.

SERGEANT: Nekurepov!

ANSWER: Gavrila. 1912, village of Merigorye, 58-one-B. Ten years.

He who answers moves over, carrying his belongings from the group which has not been summoned to the group which has. Or the pantomime is interrupted by instructions issued by the Duty Officer ("a prayer").

"Attention, prisoners! While you are *en route*, you're not to bend down, not to pick up anything from the ground, not to turn round, not to change places from line to line, not to lag behind or get out of line. You are to obey all the orders of your guards. One step to the right, or one

170

Scene 6

step to the left will be considered an attempted escape
and you'll be shot *without* warning!"
Or interrupted by his own command:
March, you in front!
Or by the arrival of the GENERAL *in his limousine. At this
point all movement ceases.* SENTRIES *jump to attention.*
SUPERVISORS, *who find themselves in his path, salute
awkwardly, the ones further back try to disappear.*
Short, fat, pock-marked COLONEL OKHREYANOV *comes
dashing out from the building on the right and arrives just as
the tall young* GENERAL *emerges from his car.*

OKHREYANOV (*making his report*): Comrade Major-General.
During your absence everything's been in order at the
Department of Counter-Intelligence SMERSH, which is
under your command!
*The window panes of one of the windows on the second floor
of the building on the right are broken with a loud noise.*
POSVYANTSEVA *appears in the window.*

POSVYANTSEVA: Help, help! They're killing me, they're
killing me!
BOLOSNIN, *who is being conducted along one of the paths,
jerks his head upwards and stops still. His guard tries to
push him on.* BOLOSNIN *resists, his eyes fixed on the
window. Another guard comes running and the two of them
grab his arms and hustle him along.* POSVYANTSEVA *is
removed from the window.*

GENERAL: How do you work here? (*Wincing.*) Is it always
like that?

OKHREYANOV: Comrade General . . .

GENERAL: No excuses. Investigate and report. There I was
in a good mood, coming here, and all you can do is ruin
everything. Why haven't these flowerbeds been watered?

OKHREYANOV: Comrade Major-General! We water them
every morning and every evening . . .

GENERAL: You call that watered?! The earth's quite dry.
Look. (*He picks up a handful of earth and shows it to him.*)
Dry! (*He wipes his hands on a handkerchief and with a*

171

wave of his handkerchief dismisses his car.) Do I really have to look into everything myself? You're to get the heads of departments for a conference with me at 8 o'clock.

OKHREYANOV: Certainly, sir. A conference!
They walk to the building on the right.
After the curtain comes down, the record is obviously stuck and it plays "Our country is happy and free" at such an unbearable volume that the audience must escape.

Scene 7

A cell. It is day time. A tiny bit of bright sky is visible under the shutter of a spy hole. But the light, on the whole, is grey. There are the same prisoners, with the exception of YELESHEV, DAVYDOV, WRZESNIK and the PRISONER WITH A BLACK EYE. Their "dinner" is almost over; they have finished drinking the liquid from stew tins and are eating the grain – they have no spoons so that some pour it straight from the tins into their mouths, while others pick it up with their fingers. HALBERAU is noticeably methodical in his consumption of the grain, which he eats imperturbably to the very end of the scene. The tins, which stand in the places of MEDNIKOV and BOLOSNIN are untouched, since they are absent.

The curtain has not quite come up yet, but we hear a fierce argument going on, which distracts the prisoners from their precious food. The argument is not just heated, it is painful. Apart from the remarks which we can distinguish, there is a constant hum of "rhubarb" going on, and which is delivered with great speed.

RUBIN is attempting to eat his food automatically, but he has to defend himself from everybody, like a cornered wolf. He is not enjoying his food.

Owing to this argument, BOLOSNIN's entry is unnoticed. He

*tries to convey his experiences, but having heard some of the
argument, he becomes incensed.*

  *To start with, prisoners are sitting down, but one by one they
jump up, and it is only the German and the Italian who remain
sitting and observing the Russian argument with consternation.*

PECHKUROV: Listen, Rubin, have you ever been to a
  collective farm?

RUBIN: Yes, I have.

TEMIROV: As a correspondent, no doubt.

KLIMOV (*advancing on* RUBIN): So what did you think, tell
  me, what did you think when the peasants were being
  destroyed?

RUBIN (*to someone else*): But then we have the underground
  – the best in the world.

TEMIROV: Nothing but show. Everything's for show. "The
  bridges may be made of iron, but their supports are of
  wood."

DIVNICH: Yes, I must say, the Soviet people are beggars!
  When they come to Europe, they're ready to pinch
  things from the shop counter.

PECHKUROV: What does a collective farmer earn a day?
  How much per day?

RUBIN: Well, that's because their work is badly organised.

PECHKUROV (*shouting*): Fuck off, you and your
  organisation! Just give me some land and I'll manage
  without your organisation.

DIVNICH (*advancing even closer*): Your country is in a state
  of collapse! It's up the spout! Crazy prices, empty
  shops! . . .

RUBIN: Well, things were just getting better, when the war
  got in the way.

KULYBYSHEV: Tell that to the Marines! Ah! War!

KLIMOV: How do you mean, getting better. In 1939 there
  were thousands of queues for bread all over the country
  – was that due to war?

GAI: Why did you starve the Ukraine to death? Was that
  because of the war?

173

RUBIN: You starved yourselves to death. You left the grain
to rot in rubbish dumps.

GAI: We refused to sow it. That's true.

RUBIN: You should have sown it!

GAI: Who for?! Why did you set up a blockade against us?
(*He shouts to everyone in the cell.*) Quiet, there! Friends!
Does anyone know about the blockade of the Ukraine in
1931? When a komsomol would come into your house
and prevent you getting water from your own well!
Cattle died off from thirst. My baby sister died!

DIVNICH: In the twentieth century we have come round to
slave labour!

RUBIN: I can't answer you all at once. Let me speak! (*He
rushes into the centre of the cell, speaks to them all round, for
he is surrounded by enemies.*) Remember what sort of
country we had inherited . . .

VOROTYNTSEV: Well, what?

BOLOSNIN (*by the door, furiously*): We should have squashed
the bed-bugs first and started the Revolution second!

RUBIN (*twisting and turning in the middle of the cell*): You're
all mad! How do you mean "second"? Human history
has lasted ten thousand years and never yet has it seen
any justice! Slaves, driven to despair, would rise with
Spartacus and Wat Tyler, in copper rebellions or in salt-
mine revolts, they would storm the Bastille, there would
be Taborite[10] revolts or revolts of the Communes of
Muenster and Paris. More often than not they would
perish, even before they had had time to rise up from
their knees, hardly ever did they manage to get to power
and even more rarely did they manage to cling on to it –
but never, never did they succeed in embodying the
great dream of justice on earth! That is because they had
too much trust in yesterday's oppressors, too much
charity towards their foes! It was because they took the
path of terror and dictatorship with too much doubt and
timidity. And so now, when at last, for the first time in
many thousands of years, there arose and matured an

174

unconquerable *Science of Revolution*, when an immutable
tactic of *Dictatorship* has been evolved, when all the
former mistakes of all the previous revolutions have been
taken into account, when this tactic has finally
succeeded! – when a new world is ready to grow for tens
of hundreds of years . . .

DIVNICH: . . . on the bones of a million of . . .

RUBIN: . . . but has had only some miserable twenty-five
years . . .

BOLOSNIN: . . . that's half of a human span . . .

RUBIN (*putting one foot on top of the slop bucket*): . . . you
unhappy, miserable little people, whose petty lives have
been squeezed by the Revolution, all you can do is
distort its very essence, you slander its grand, bright
march forward, you pour slops over the purple vestments
of humanity's highest dreams! There! (*He swiftly sits
down on the slop bucket the way one does and, turning his
hands into the lenses of binoculars, surveys the world around
him.*) Here you are! That's your observatory – this slop
bucket! It is from this vantage point that you observe
and learn about the world!

PRYANCHIKOV (*waving someone's torn garment, as if it were a
flag*): Purple vestments, Rubin? Don't make me laugh!

BOLOSNIN (*throws himself at* RUBIN, *but is held
back*): While I was at liberty I did my best to destroy
you, you horrors, but not in order to put up with you in
a cell!

RUBIN (*jumping up from his slop bucket*): Do you know what
you are – you're Vlasov's lap dog! (*He rushes at
BOLOSNIN, *but is also held back.*)

TEMIROV: These troubadours should be shot: ten years is
not enough!

GAI: Who are the troubadours?

TEMIROV: Any idiot who blows a trumpet is a troubadour!
The hatch is opened. Everybody falls silent, as if cut off.

7TH SUPERVISOR: Anyone with the letter "K"?

KHOLUDENEV: Kholudenev.

7TH SUPERVISOR: And "D"?

DIVNICH: Divnich.

7TH SUPERVISOR: Take your things.

The hatch is closed. Nobody rushes at anybody. Nobody is held back. There is immobility.

KHOLUDENEV: M-m-m-yes. The conference continues.

Both he and DIVNICH *begin collecting their belongings. Everybody observes them in silence.*

DIVNICH: Even though they give you ten years, there's no time to argue.

BOLOSNIN (*pouring some tobacco from his own pocket into* DIVNICH'S): You'll get nervous there, have a smoke.

KHOLUDENEV: Oh dear. We've not had time for a proper chat. Igor! You have such a clear head, whatever brought you back to the Soviet Union? What for? And left your wife behind.

BOLOSNIN: I ask only one thing – don't mention Galina. This question only Mr. Churchill can answer! How I trusted the English! People were warning me, but still I trusted them. It was incredible, it was monstrous, but while they were digging the grave of their own Empire, they disarmed us by deception and gave us up to the Bolsheviks. Hundreds of officers and tens of thousands of soldiers!

VOROTYNTSEV: Mr. Divnich, you were going to tell us what the difference is between the Gestapo and the G.P.U. and you never did.

DIVNICH: Well, it's quite clear that it sounds similar and from the ideological point of view there's no difference at all. In terms of practical application the Gestapo's approach is mediaeval and direct, when they try to find out the truth; they will savagely beat you, torture you, hang you upside down. But if they find that according to their laws you're innocent, they'll let you go, as they let me go. But the N.K.G.B. do not even attempt to find out the truth unless they're trying to unearth some sort of subversive organisation; that's because they're

176

profoundly uninterested in finding out whether you're
innocent or not. Whatever happens, you get ten
years.

VOROTYNTSEV: Unless they shoot you. Many thanks. It's
quite clear.

DIVNICH *and* KHOLUDENEV *carry their bags towards the
door.*

BOLOSNIN (*accompanying* KHOLUDENEV): Just think! An
extraordinary encounter: they were taking me through
the yard, suddenly I heard the window pane breaking
and in the window I saw a woman who was clinging to
the window bars: "Help! They are killing me!" And I
recognised her as the wife of my war-time friend who got
killed. She's a good, charming woman, being tortured
right here and you can't do anything to help, and
(*gesturing towards* RUBIN) there they go trying to prove
that it's all within the law.

DIVNICH: Well, friends, since you haven't got a song of
your own yet, let's sing one of ours. (*He puts his arms
round the shoulders of two of them.*)
Several voices sing:
    Say your prayers, friend, when you're away
    Pray for your country, pray and say:
    Let God protect all those you love
    Let Him protect them from above.
*There is a bang on the door and an order to stop the singing.
But instead everybody, including* RUBIN, *joins in the song,
arms around each other's shoulders and facing the audience.*
    Pray to our Lord to give us strength
    To overcome our foes' intents,
    Then peace and love we'll see again
    Above our fields resume their reign.
*The door is opened wide with a crash. They all embrace each
other in silence.* DIVNICH *and* KHOLUDENEV *leave, the
door is shut again, the German continues the methodical
eating of his grain. Those who remain embrace each other
more closely.*

We are deprived of our land,
We know we need a helping hand,
But we believe the time will come
When we shall win, we'll overcome.

Scene 8

*To the left there is a summer pavilion; its façade, with three
windows and a porch, faces the audience. The porter is either
opening or shutting the door. There is a large notice:
RESTAURANT NO. 2, SPECIALITIES. To the right there
is an avenue of trees leading away. In front there are two garden
benches, one of which is hidden from both the restaurant and the
avenue by a semicircle of thick shrubs. There is a lawn in front
of the restaurant and in the flowerbed a colourful inscription
reads "Glory to Stalin". The windows are wide open and by
each window there is a small table, while further back there is
lively restaurant activity and we can hear cheerful music.
Counter-Intelligence Officers walk up and down the avenue
entering or leaving the restaurant. There are a few prostitutes. It
is a sunny afternoon. As the curtain rises, there is general
movement, music, conversation.*

Behind one of the windows:

Listen, Miss, I ordered one glass of Château Yquem and
one glass of Rhine wine.

I'm sorry.

Well, you should listen carefully.

In the avenue:

Heard about Mymra?

What about him?

He's been appointed Head of the Department.

Okhreyanov seems to like him.

Well, he works with clockwork precision. You should
take lessons from Mymra.

NEKLYUCHIMOV *and* FILIPPOV *approach.*

Scene 8

FILIPPOV: I was trained as an infantryman, became Commander of a machine-gun platoon. I spent almost the entire war at the front or in hospitals, so I find it rather uncongenial now to be on prison escort duty; it goes against the grain.

NEKLYUCHIMOV: Yes, Captain, each sort of duty bends you to its requirements. I don't usually drink, but I would like to have a drink with you. Let's go.
Behind another window:
We're just routine investigators – donkeys, you might say. We pull the cart and it's the cart that gets the medals, wouldn't you agree?
Along the avenue:
That's what Okhreyanov decreed! (*They go past.*)
Comrade Major, is there a political seminar today? It is Monday, isn't it? No need to ask. At seven. (*They go past.*)

KAPUSTIN (*to* OFFICER NO. 3): Let me tell you about dace. First of all, it's tasteless, second, it's too dry, third, it's skittish, while carp . . .

OFFICER NO. 4 (*coming towards them*): Kapustin, lend me twenty roubles.

KAPUSTIN (*tapping his pockets*): You owe me twenty already.

OFFICER NO. 4: Ten.

KAPUSTIN: Not twenty?

OFFICER NO. 4: No, no. I borrowed and returned it at once. There was even an I.O.U.

KAPUSTIN (*opening his wallet*): Well, you ought to know; just before pay day. When will you pay it back?

OFFICER NO. 4: I'll pay it back, don't worry. (*Snatching the note, he walks quickly away.*)

KAPUSTIN: They snatch half your salary this way . . . Yes, as to carp . . .

OFFICER NO. 3: Can you lend *me* thirty roubles?

KAPUSTIN: When will you pay it back? (*Gives it to him.*)

OFFICER NO. 3: I'll pay . . . it back . . .

They enter the restaurant. One of the tables at a window is now free. NEKLYUCHIMOV *and* FILIPPOV *have taken it. Along the avenue:*

TYPIST NO. 1: I know. I've also seen her brother – striped trousers, wide flares, provincial.

OFFICER NO. 5: What's she like?

TYPIST NO. 1: Well, what do you expect? A plunging neckline, pink embroidery, got a bow stuck right here, and she struts like a fool.

OFFICER NO. 5: No, I'm talking about her work. She's been sacked, after all; they've opened a file on her . . .

TYPIST NO. 1: Oh, I forgot to ask. I never asked. (*They go past.*)

Behind the window:

OFFICER NO. 1: There you go – you live, you breathe, you know nothing, while they compose secret files about you. Each and every year! They can smear you with tar, but if you try to clear yourself . . . they never let you see it.

Along the avenue:

NINEL (*clinging to* MYMRA'S *arm*): Mymra, you ought to be ashamed of yourself! You've just been promoted and you refuse to treat me.

MYMRA (*as dispassionately as in his investigations*): All right, I'll buy you some pastries.

NINEL: Mymra, that's vulgar. Pastries!

SVERBYOZHNIKOV (*coming towards them*): Comrade Mymra. Congratulations!

OFFICER NO. 6: Comrade Mymra. On your new appointment.

MYMRA: I serve the Soviet Union. Thank you, Comrades. (*They enter the restaurant.*)

TYPIST NO. 2: Goodness, it's hot. Isn't it hot! And look at this trollop, clinging to Mymra already!

TYPIST NO. 3 (*deep voice*): Will they have iced beer, I wonder?

(*They enter the restaurant.*)

KAMCHUZHNAYA (*to* OFFICER NO. 7): I collect colour

photographs. I have a passion for colour photographs.

OFFICER NO. 8 (*to* NO. 9): Do you think Okhreyanov has succeeded because of this? (*He points to his head.*) It's because of this. (*He points to the small of his back.*) He began twenty-five years ago as a simple supervisor.

OFFICER NO. 9: Be quiet. Here he is.

OKHREYANOV *is still out of sight up the avenue, but everybody is already giving way, and, as he approaches, greets him. The last to pass along the avenue are the two* OPERATIVES. KAMCHUZHNAYA *comes across them by the porch.*

OPERATIVE NO. 1: Hallo, Lydia.

KAMCHUZHNAYA: Hallo, there! Are you free today?

OPERATIVE NO. 1: No, we're on duty.

KAMCHUZHNAYA: What, here?! (*She drags him excitedly on to the bench, which is in the middle of the stage. The* 2ND OPERATIVE *sits down next to them.*) Come on, boys. Who is it? Do tell!

OPERATIVE NO. 1: Why do you have to know? Anyway, you'll see in a minute.

KAMCHUZHNAYA: Come on, Mike. Do tell. I'm one of you. I've never had the chance to do it myself . . .

There is a procession, headed by OKHREYANOV *and* KRIVOSHCHAP, *which approaches the porch.*

OKHREYANOV *moves very slowly; he carries his body as if it were a monument. Some* MAJOR, *who was coming towards him, is being detained and is apologising about something. The movement along the avenue stops. Those who were behind, having come across this group, wander off; the ones in front return to the restaurant.*

FILIPPOV: Why do they call you an astronomer? Are you really an astronomer?

NEKLYUCHIMOV: People can never endure to see someone who's unlike them. I did want to become an astronomer, joined the University of Moscow, but in my second year I was taken away, owing to the Komsomol mobilisation and put into the N.K.V.D. training school. And it was impossible to get away, quite impossible.

OKHREYANOV (*in front of the porch*): Do I really have to examine everything myself? I came here in a good mood, and all you can do is ruin everything. Write me an explanatory memo. (*The* MAJOR *salutes and leaves rapidly. To the* ADJUTANT.) Do they prune those trees, or not? Where's the Manager?

ADJUTANT: He's away on a job, Colonel.

OKHREYANOV: Issue a reprimand.

ADJUTANT: Yes, sir. (*Making a note.*)

OKHREYANOV (*mollified*): Well, Krivoshchap, since we've got so far, shall we drop in? They say they've got vintage bottles here from the Count's cellar . . .

KRIVOSHCHAP: Let's dive in, sir.

They enter the restaurant. The movement along the avenue resumes. At a window:

OFFICER NO. 1: Who said "donkeys"? Who said that?

OFFICER NO. 2 (*very drunk*): You . . . s-s-said it! You al-l-lso cr-criticised the f-f-f-iles.

OFFICER NO. 1: Are you off your head? I couldn't have said it. Anya, another bottle, quick!

Along the avenue:

Beef Stroganoff, that's quite something!

I have just sent a typewriter home. Do you think I'll get five thousand for it?

Has it got Russian letters?

No, German.

The adaptation will cost you a cool thousand.

KAMCHUZHNAYA (*indicating the concealed bench*): Over there, all right? (*She walks slowly towards the window.*)

OPERATIVE NO. 2 (*sitting on the bench in the centre*): You shouldn't have told her.

OPERATIVE NO. 1: No matter, the bitch is drunk.

KAMCHUZHNAYA (*from below the window*): Hallo, Astronomer. You're drinking, I see. What's happened?

Scene 8

NEKLYUCHIMOV: Captain Kamchuzhnaya, my surname is Neklyuchimov and my first name is Alexander.

KAMCHUZHNAYA (*humming*): Do you remember, Alex, our brief encounters? . . .

NEKLYUCHIMOV: I don't seem to . . .

KAMCHUZHNAYA (*with a break in her voice*): Listen, how can you? . . . How can you? . . . (*She moves away.*) *Along the avenue:*

OFFICER NO. 10: I admire the way you work, Comrade Colonel. You have managed to become an indispensable specialist.

MORGOSLEPOV: My father used to say to me: I'll teach you until it isn't *you* that's looking for work, but *work* that's seeking you out.

OFFICER NO. 11: And how many years did that take? (*They come out towards the porch.*)

MORGOSLEPOV: Seven years at school, six years of factory training, then face-to-face tuition, then correspondence courses. Have you had lunch? I'll go in, my lunch breaks are short. (*He enters the restaurant.*)

OFFICER NO. 10: The bloody hack! But then, even though he managed to displace three Prosecutors, he now works as hard as four.

OFFICER NO. 11: He'll burst from greed, one of these days. He'll even ask five kopecks' change from the waitress. (*He moves away.*)

OFFICER NO. 12 (*nodding after him, to* OFFICER NO. 10): He should talk. He gets twenty packets of cigarettes a month, to soften up prisoners during interrogation, yet he'd sooner choke than part with a cigarette, even though he doesn't smoke. He can't sell them to anyone, so he sends them home in a parcel – his brother smokes. An officer like that should be shot!

FILIPPOV: I saw on a parade ground, with my own eyes, a Sergeant shoot down a couple of Messerschmitts. And now, on my escort duties, who do I see but the very man . . .

183

KAMCHUZHNAYA: Alexander, finish your drink and come here for a minute. I need you.

NEKLYUCHIMOV: This is break time, Lydia. I don't want to talk bnusiness.

KAMCHUZHNAYA: Alex, I need you a lot. I wouldn't have asked . . .

NEKLYUCHIMOV: Wait for me, Captain, I shan't be long. (*He rises.*)

OFFICER NO. 13 (*walking in front of the flowerbed with* OFFICER NO. 14): There's one thing I don't understand, George: why did the Americans let us have the Vlasov lot? And the English the Cossacks? What for? What was their aim?

OFFICER NO. 14: D'you want to know what *I* think? Personally? . . . We shall pay for it, by having to fight the Japanese. That'll be our payment, I'm sure of it!

OPERATIVE NO. 1 (*entering the restaurant with* NO. 2): In the meantime, Lydia, we'll have a . . . (*Makes a gesture of drinking from a glass.*)
The two OPERATIVES *come across* NEKLYUCHIMOV *on the porch.*

OPERATIVE NO. 1: Hallo, Astronomer. How are the stars? All in their appointed places?

NEKLYUCHIMOV (*hostile*): Not all of them.

OPERATIVE NO. 2: Some fallen?

NEKLYUCHIMOV: Uh-huh.

OPERATIVE NO. 1: It happens.
They enter the restaurant. NEKLYUCHIMOV, *following* KAMCHUZHNAYA, *walks towards the hidden bench.* KAMCHUZHNAYA *sits with her face towards the restaurant.* NEKLYUCHIMOV *with his back to it. There is a slow waltz from the restaurant.*

KAMCHUZHNAYA: Alex, did you ever . . . like me . . . a tiny bit?

NEKLYUCHIMOV: Did you call me out for this? . . . (*Attempting to rise.*)

Scene 8

KAMCHUZHNAYA (*restraining him*): It's very important, Alex. Answer me.

NEKLYUCHIMOV: I hate you!

KAMCHUZHNAYA: What for?

NEKLYUCHIMOV: D'you really want to know? A beautiful vase is nothing without . . .

KAMCHUZHNAYA (*triumphant*): So you did . . .

NEKLYUCHIMOV: But I'm married, there's no point in talk like that. Is anything wrong? Are you ill?

KAMCHUZHNAYA: I wouldn't trust your wife if I were you. However, you'll find out about her soon enough. We shan't meet again, Alex.

NEKLYUCHIMOV: Are you going away?

KAMCHUZHNAYA: And yet we might . . . meet again . . . Should you need me . . . When you're in trouble, in very bad trouble, just remember, I loved you once! (*She kisses him and puts her head on his chest.*)
OPERATIVES NO. 1 *and* NO. 2, *having left the restaurant, are walking towards them, but are as yet unobserved by them.*

NEKLYUCHIMOV: What were you about to say?

KAMCHUZHNAYA (*rapidly*): Got anything that should be destroyed? Addresses? Notes?

NEKLYUCHIMOV: What's the matter?

KAMCHUZHNAYA (*rushing him*): Quickly, my love!

NEKLYUCHIMOV (*hesitating for just a moment; passes his note book to her*): But why?

KAMCHUZHNAYA (*hiding it*): In your desk? At home?

NEKLYUCHIMOV: Nothing at all. That's the lot.
KAMCHUZHNAYA *puts her arm round his neck. Almost at once the* OPERATIVES *appear from behind the shrubs.*
KAMCHUZHNAYA, *having noticed them, turns her embrace into a sharp pull with both hands at his epaulettes.*
NEKLYUCHIMOV *jumps up, staring around. The restaurant music has ceased. The* 1ST OPERATIVE, *stretching out his arm, shows* NEKLYUCHIMOV *a piece of paper.*

OPERATIVE NO. 1: You're under arrest!

NEKLYUCHIMOV: Me-e?

He is making an attempt to read the order, but both
OPERATIVES *are already rapidly removing his swordbelt,*
the star from his cap. They empty his pockets, using all four
hands. The 2ND OPERATIVE *collects everything and moves*
on.

OPERATIVE NO. I (*taking out his pistol*): Abo-ut turn!
Hands behind your back! No talking! March!

There is an upsurge of rumba from the orchestra. They march
into the centre through the thick crowd of Cheka officers, who
make way for them, and they turn right into the avenue: the
2ND OPERATIVE *in front, followed by* NEKLYUCHIMOV,
his head bent and his hands behind his back; the IST
OPERATIVE *is behind, his pistol at the ready.*

There is a crowd on the porch and people are looking out of
the windows, FILIPPOV *among them with an expression of*
horror on his face. KAMCHUZHNAYA, *hidden from*
everybody by the shrubs, is motionless, pressing
NEKLYUCHIMOV's *epaulettes to her cheeks. The rumba*
plays on.

Scene 9

A large room, almost a ballroom. There are heavy curtains and
electric light. At the back – a rostrum, on which there is a large
sculpture of Stalin, full-length, with one arm raised. He is in the
uniform of a Generalissimo. On the rostrum there is a table for
the judges and the tribunal of Prosecutors; lower down, there is a
smaller table for the secretary and lower still a place for the
defence counsel and a chair for the defendant. Further downstage
there are two rows of dusty chairs, held together by wooden bars,
with their backs to the audience. There are two doors, left and
right of the rostrum, and another one nearer to us.

As the curtain rises, it is through this door that an USHER
and a GUARD *conduct* KHOLUDENEV, *his hands behind his*
back. They show him his place.

USHER: Arms at the ready!

> The GUARD *levels his weapon, the* USHER *leaves. A pause. The guard gradually relaxes his stance.*
>
> KHOLUDENEV *fishes a scrap of paper from his pocket and after some hesitation, shakes tobacco into it.*

GUARD: What are you twirling?

KHOLUDENEV: A cigarette, as you can see.

GUARD: What's this paper?

KHOLUDENEV: It's a receipt for my medals and for the watch.

GUARD: How will you get them back then?

KHOLUDENEV: Medals? What do I need them for?

GUARD (*after some thought*): What about the watch?

KHOLUDENEV: It'll get rusty in ten years.

GUARD: I would keep it, all the same. Here's a bit of newspaper.

KHOLUDENEV (*taking the torn-off bit and putting the receipt back into his pocket*): It'll get used – either here or on the way to Siberia, what's the odds?

GUARD: Have some shag. (*Offers him some.*)

KHOLUDENEV: Thanks, if you mean it. (*Pours some into his pocket and adds the rest to his cigarette.*) Got a light?

GUARD (*giving him a light*): How many medals?

KHOLUDENEV: I had three.

GUARD: An officer?

KHOLUDENEV: A Captain.

GUARD: What did they arrest you for?

KHOLUDENEV: Well, you see . . .

> *The same door opens. The* GUARD *levels his weapon sharply and moves away from* KHOLUDENEV. KASHEVAROV *enters with a bouncing gait. He wears a silk shirt with short sleeves and white trousers. As he approaches* KHOLUDENEV *he stretches out an accusing hand towards him.*

KASHEVAROV: You . . . You there . . . What's your surname? (*Checking in his notebook.*)

KHOLUDENEV (*smoking and leaning back comfortably*): And what sort of employment do you have here?

KASHEVAROV: I'm your State defence counsel.

KHOLUDENEV: Is that so? I rather thought you might be a Captain of the Volleyball Team.

KASHEVAROV: Your surname, what is it?

KHOLUDENEV: Look, why don't you just buzz off; I never engaged you.

KASHEVAROV: True, but the State can't leave you without a defence lawyer.

KHOLUDENEV: That State of yours, as far as I'm concerned can . . . I'd be glad to exchange your State for a chamber pot and top it up.

KASHEVAROV: How do you mean?

KHOLUDENEV: It'd be a damn sight more useful.

KASHEVAROV (*brightening up*): I say, maybe you're not quite all there. Have you had a medical? I could demand that they give you a medical.

KHOLUDENEV (*laughs cheerfully. In a conciliatory manner*): I'll tell you what, fella-me-lad, I don't get in your way and you don't get in mine. I'd love to give you a tip, but, alas, I haven't any cash.

KASHEVAROV: You *are* off your head! You just don't know the rules. If there's no defence, then there's no prosecution.

KHOLUDENEV: These are excellent rules.

KASHEVAROV: But then how are you to defend yourself? If you're worried about paying me, it's only some paltry hundred roubles. They'll take them off your receipts.

KHOLUDENEV: What did you say? My receipts? (*Rising.*) Get out of here, you idiot!

KASHEVAROV (*jumping up, in a squeaky voice*): Guard! Aren't you watching?

GUARD (*peaceably*): That'll do. Take it easy.

A COURT COMMANDANT *enters quickly through the right-hand door of the rostrum. The door remains open and through it we can hear the voice of* KRIVOSHCHAP *from the neighbouring room:* "The Court will retire for consultation."

COMMANDANT: Everybody rise for the Court!
  KHOLUDENEV *has no time to sit down.* KRIVOSHCHAP,
  two ASSESSORS, *and a secretary come on to the rostrum.*
  Everybody sits down simultaneously.

KRIVOSHCHAP (*rapidly – he is preoccupied*): I pronounce the
  session of the military tribunal open. The prisoner will
  answer the questions. Your name and surname

KHOLUDENEV (*gloomily*): Kholudenev.

KRIVOSHCHAP: First name, date of birth?

KHOLUDENEV: All that's been written down a hundred
  times.

KRIVOSHCHAP: Are there any objections to the members of
  the tribunal?

KHOLUDENEV: That's a matter for the defence. I don't
  want any of this.

KRIVOSHCHAP: The rules are immutable. We cannot judge
  anyone who has no defence. The State allows you to have
  a fully qualified defence lawyer. Will the two sides take
  their seats. (*To a clerk.*) Proceed.
  The defence lawyer, with a sidelong glance at his client, sits
  down.

KHOLUDENEV (*sitting down*): B-b-bureaucrats . . .

1ST ASSESSOR (*mutters rapidly, emphasising occasionally the*
  important, or unimportant passages): "I, Major-General
  and Head of the 2nd Department of Counter-Intelligence
  SMERSH, Central Army Group affirm . . . The
  indictment was concluded in the case No. 01544/S/31 of
  Kholudenev, Andrew S. A. S. Kholudenev was arrested
  and brought to trial by the front-line Counter-
  Intelligence SMERSH. The investigations have
  established that Kholudenev, while being an officer of
  the Red Army, with the last rank of Captain, and a
  Commander of the Sapper Company, actively conducted
  subversive, anti-Soviet activity. This subversive activity
  found its expression, as testified by the Party organiser,
  U. V. Tyrlykov and the Deputy Political Instructor of
  the Battalion, G. M. Visgunov, in his allowing the party

political and mass educational work to lapse in the
subsection entrusted to him (exhibits nos. 25 and 26). In
the spring of 1943 Kholudenev called his deputy in the
political section, Khukhnobratov, who was the chief
political director by the insulting name of 'fool' and
threatened 'to break his legs were he to conduct political
discussions at unsuitable times' (exhibits 45, 47, which
are Major Khukhnobratov's testimonies). It is in this
fashion that Kholudenev has demonstrated his violently
terrorist intentions towards the Party's guiding
principles. Since the summer of 1943, after the
establishment of the deputy commanders in the political
sections of companies had been abolished and when the
whole of the political activity in his company had become
his sole responsibility, Kholudenev, the accused,
neglected these duties, announcing in front of his
soldiers, even, that the best form of political discussion is
'good thick porridge' (exhibit 74). On those rare
occasions when he could not evade conducting political
discussions, the accused would interpret events in a
slanderously untruthful manner and would praise
enthusiastically Anglo-American military aid. When,
prior to entering German soil, the political section of the
division required Kholudenev to give a lecture to the
plenary Red Army meeting of the battalion on the
subject of 'A death for a death, blood for blood',
Kholudenev bluntly refused and expressed his beastly
anti-Soviet instincts by saying that 'Germans are also
human' (exhibit 95). One link in the chain of
Kholudenev's misdeeds is his close relationship with the
chief technician of the same battalion Ivan Novotelov, a
survivor of the bourgeoisie, a fierce enemy of progress
and of socialism, who escaped the punishment of Soviet
Justice by dying on the field of battle. In some of their
conversations conducted in a separate tent, but which
became known to the members of SMERSH,
Kholudenev and Novotelov poured out their hatred

towards the great genius the Leader of the Party and of the Soviet people, throwing contempt and insulting nicknames against his shining person, as well as indecent swearing (exhibits 9, 18, 101–103)."

2ND ASSESSOR (*half rising in a pious movement towards the statue of Stalin*): You didn't dare? . . .

KHOLUDENEV: I dared.

1ST ASSESSOR: "But the accused, together with the deceased Novotelov did not only slander Stalin's brilliant ideas on strategy. In one of their conversations, examining the revolutionary changes in agriculture in 1929–1930 which they interpreted in a criminally incorrect way, they in fact demonstrated that they were defenders of the kulaks and were opposed to complete and voluntary collectivisation. All this gives us grounds for believing that Kholudenev and Novotelov were the instigators of an underground terrorist gang which they failed to form due to the death of one and the arrest of the other. Kholudenev, Andrew, born in 1919, in the town of Tambov, a Russian, who has no previous record and is a citizen of the U.S.S.R., a construction engineer by profession and who served as Commander of a company with the rank of Captain, who was awarded medals of the 1st and 2nd category and of the Red Star, is, on the basis of the aforesaid accused of: conducting base anti-Soviet agitation together with the deceased co-conspirator Novotelov, was preparing himself for active subversion and expressed terrorist intentions, i.e. crimes which are covered by articles 58-10 part two, 58-8 to 19 and 58-11 of the Criminal Code of the Russian Soviet Federal Socialist Republic. Kholudenev has confessed to the charges and is further convicted by the testimony of witnesses. According to article 208 of the Criminal Law Procedure Code, this case is passed on to Prosecutor Morgoslepov for the accused to be sent for trial. The indictment is put together by . . . signature . . . witnessed by . . ." (*He sits down and takes a breath.*)

191

KRIVOSHCHAP: The trial begins. Accused Kholudenev, are you guilty of the crimes you are accused of?

KHOLUDENEV: What's the difference? Whatever happens . . .

KRIVOSHCHAP: In other words, you admit that . . .

KHOLUDENEV: Yep.

KRIVOSHCHAP: And you stick to your opinions?

KHOLUDENEV: No.

KRIVOSHCHAP: Is it really true? Have you truly repented?

KHOLUDENEV: Truly, absolutely and finally.

2ND ASSESSOR: Do you really think that the Court will believe your repentance?

KHOLUDENEV: I don't see why not. Now that I've sorted myself out, I can see that it wasn't only Stalin, but all of you and it didn't start in 1929 but in 1917.

MORGOSLEPOV *comes running in through the door on the left of the rostrum. He stands on the rostrum, looking through some papers.*

KRIVOSHCHAP: Does the Prosecutor have any questions?

MORGOSLEPOV: No, no, everything is quite clear.

KRIVOSHCHAP: The Defence Counsel?

KASHEVAROV: No.

KRIVOSHCHAP: We will then pass on to the arguments of the two sides. Comrade Morgoslepov, the State Prosecutor has the first word.

MORGOSLEPOV (*very rapidly*): Comrade Judges. Who's this we see before us? We see a man who was nurtured and brought up by our own Soviet country, our own Komsomol. And what do we get by way of gratitude? This degenerate mongrel – I cannot find better words to describe him – took up slandering our wise and brilliant Leader, he did not refrain from open terrorism towards Party leadership and was preparing an armed rebellion . . . ehm-ehm . . . ah . . . preparing to prevent the peaceful conversion of the kulak to socialism. Comrade Judges. There's a limit to our patience. You are the avenging arm of Communist society, of the all-powerful

Soviet people. I demand that this accused be given . . .
(*he is already on his way out through the same door*) ten
years of loss of freedom plus five years without civil
rights! (*He has run out.*)

KRIVOSHCHAP: The State Defence Counsel, Comrade
Kashevarov, has the word.

KASHEVAROV: Comrades. Being an honest Soviet citizen, a
true son of my Socialist Motherland, I've taken perforce
the ungrateful duty of defending this bitter enemy, this
criminal, who's been so completely exposed. The proof
of the accusation is incontrovertible and the Prosecutor
could quite rightly have demanded execution for this
aggregate of heavy crimes. Comrade Vyshinsky[11] put it
so well when he said: "Everybody's to be shot, like rabid
dogs." In conclusion of my defence speech, I ask that
you show clemency to my client and limit his
punishment to ten years plus five years without civil
rights. (*Exit rapidly.*)

KRIVOSHCHAP: The accused has the last word.

KHOLUDENEV: You can have it.

The USHER *goes out through the door on the right and we
can hear his voice in the next court room, shouting: "Rise.
The Court is coming."*

KRIVOSHCHAP: The Court will retire for a consultation.
They depart. KHOLUDENEV *lights up the cigarette he did
not finish before the session. A long pause.*

GUARD: I must say, Comrade Captain, your remark about
porridge is quite true. They feed you on newspaper pulp.
(*Pensively.*) And what you said about the Germans . . .
*The lights go out. They go up again. The second court room
is a mirror image of the first. The Prosecutor's rostrum is at
the other end. Stalin's statue has the other arm raised. The
Court session is in full swing.* DIVNICH *is the accused.*
KASHEVAROV *is the Defence Counsel.*

MORGOSLEPOV (*coming to the end of his speech*): . . . Even
during the interrogation he had the audacity to explain it
as follows (*reading*): "Spreading the good news is my

unavoidable duty, and woe to me if I do not spread the good news." How do you like that, Comrades? Clear enough, isn't it? Another interesting feature is that he was arrested by the Gestapo and then released. What does that tell us? It tells us that he had found a common language with the Nazi murderers. He will not find such a language with us, Comrades! The accused came back to the Soviet Union with the intention of continuing his subversive anti-Soviet work, hiding behind the banner of progressive religion and even of the latest discoveries in medicine, such as that "it's not the healthy that are in need of a doctor, but the sick". Comrade Judges, there is a limit to our patience. You are the avenging arm of the all-powerful Soviet people. I demand that the accused Divnich be given, according to article 58-10 – ten years, according to article 58-4 – fifteen years, according to article 58-1A – twenty years, according to article 58-6 – twenty-five years imprisonment. In all, then (*to the secretary.*) you add it up!

He rushes off towards the left door, being muddled, then remembers and turns back towards the right door. Because of his running about, Stalin's statue begins to topple.

KASHEVAROV (*rising immediately at a sign from* KRIVOSHCHAP): Comrades, being an honest Soviet citizen, a true son of my Socialist Motherland, I have taken perforce the sad duty . . .

Stalin's statue falls down with a crash.

DIVNICH (*in an awe-inspiring voice*): Blind leaders of the blind! Who hath warned you to flee from the wrath to come? Verily, verily I say unto you, as the lightning cometh out of the east and shineth even unto the west . . .

Scene 10

A well-appointed drawing room, which has been turned into an office for the Head of Counter-Intelligence. There are Venetian

*ogival windows and to the right and to the left, oak double
doors. A long conference table is covered with a red cloth and at
a right angle there is the General's desk. There is a huge portrait
of Stalin and a smaller one of Beria.*[12] *The rest of the
furnishings remain as they were in the days of the landowners.
Slanting rays of the setting sun come through the windows and
shine on the ormolu. The* GENERAL *sits in front, without his
uniform jacket, in shirtsleeves, with a Turkish towel over his
knees.* GEORGE, *an efficient young batman in a well-fitting
uniform without epaulettes, is about to finish the General's toilet
and is massaging his neck and cheeks.* COLONEL
OKHREYANOV, *in a ceremonial uniform with all his medals,
stands looking cheerful. He is light on his feet.*

GENERAL: D'you know, Colonel, I'm never sick in a
'plane. And wasn't sick today either.

OKHREYANOV: You're very fit, sir.

GENERAL: But then, later, I feel so weak . . . so-o
weak . . .

OKHREYANOV: You're overtired.

GENERAL: Well, yes. We spent the whole night, last night,
at Beria's. Harder, George, harder.

There is a knock on the door on the left and RUBLYOV
enters. He is gloomy and he stoops.

RUBLYOV: May I? Good evening, Comrade General.

GENERAL: Good evening, Colonel. You look rather grey.

RUBLYOV: I'm ill, Comrade General, I'm very ill.

GENERAL (*carelessly*): As bad as that? Never mind, we'll get
you well again. We'll send you for a cure. We must look
after the old guard. Incidentally, I'm rather displeased
with you.

RUBLYOV: By what, precisely?

GENERAL: Well, listen, this incident today; the Colonel
here witnessed it: that shouting all over the yard, the
window panes breaking, "Help, they're killing me." If
you plan to kill, do it in secret, while there are thousands
of people in the yard here. What will the guards think?
Ours isn't a Nazi torture chamber. It shouldn't be

allowed. Kamchuzhnaya, was it? I shall have to punish
her.

RUBLYOV: She's a very able investigator. A bit over-
enthusiastic, being young. I've looked into it and . . .

GENERAL: For your sake I would have overlooked it, but
I'm afraid this time a punishment is due. What was I
talking about? . . .

OKHREYANOV: You spent the whole night at Beria's . . .

GENERAL: Yes, at Beria's till three in the morning and had
to be at the airport by seven . . .

RUBLYOV: Comrade General, permit me to sit down.

GENERAL: You're allowed to sit down, Colonel, do sit
down.

RUBLYOV *sits down.*

And just imagine, in the 'plane I was with Sergeyev
Artyom, Voroshilov's adopted son; what's more, he's
Svetlana Stalin's friend.

RUBLYOV *is glum, hardly listening.*

ADJUTANT (*entering from the left*): Permission to speak,
Comrade General. Following your instructions, the
members of the conference are now here.

GENERAL: Right. Let them wait. (*Exit the* ADJUTANT.)
He's a splendid fellow, about my age, twenty-four, he's a
Major-General, like me, but in the artillery. Not heard of
him? He's the one who had that famous contretemps
with Rokossovsky.

OKHREYANOV: I don't quite recollect, Comrade General . . .

GENERAL: Well now, that's something you must know
about, how he paid Rokossovsky back – the whole of the
First Byelorussian front line were killing themselves
laughing. In Moscow they appointed Artyom
Commander of the artillery brigade. However, its
tractors were not much good, so, through Voroshilov, he
managed to get a completely new set of tractors, which
were being transported by train. Artyom arrived ahead at
the headquarters of the front. And suddenly he's told
that it's not he but some old fogey who's been appointed.

Right! He phones Moscow, Moscow phones
Rokossovsky, who says, would you believe, that he
regrets, but the appointment cannot be changed: it's
been signed. (*His toilet is finished.*) "Is that so?!" He
issues an order: the train turns back. So the tractors left
for Moscow, away from the battle front. I tell you, they
all roared with laughter at the Byelorussian front.

OKHREYANOV (*laughing*): The train turned back.
Wonderful.

GENERAL: But what do you think of Rokossovsky! He
might be sorry! The shit! Has he forgotten . . . George,
you can go. (GEORGE *collects the toilet articles and loiters.*)
Has he forgotten the two occasions in 1938 when he was
taken out into the forest to be shot, to put the fear of
God into him? Incidentally, Lavrentiy Beria said
something – it's for your ears only – (*Exit* GEORGE
rapidly through the door on the right.) "If necessary, we'll
take him out for the third time and won't bring him
back; we must end these Zhukov habits!"

OKHREYANOV: End these Zhukov habits! That's right.
These Generals have been getting out of hand.

GENERAL: The Cossack host! These Partisans! . . . Yes.
Only, I must admit that at that point the battle front was
still at the Dniepr, so the whole thing is a bit of a
fiction. All right, Colonel. You can call them in. (*Exit
right.*)

OKHREYANOV *walks round to the back of the General's
desk and rings.*

ADJUTANT (*entering*): Yes, Comrade Colonel.

OKHREYANOV (*his demeanour completely changed. He is
taller, there is something steely in his immobility*): Let them
. . . ehm . . . come . . .

The ADJUTANT *salutes and exits.* OKHREYANOV,
indicating a place of honour.

OKHREYANOV: Change your place, Prokhor.

RUBLYOV (*sitting half-turned in a low armchair in front of the
conference table*): I'm all right here.

OKHREYANOV *sits down at the side of the General's desk. Members of the conference begin coming in from the left. They behave quietly. There are more than twenty of them, from the rank of Major upwards. Among them –* MORGOSLEPOV, KRIVOSHCHAP, SOPHIA LVOVA, *a tall, grey-haired medical officer,* OGNIDA, KAPUSTIN *and others. There is some awkward clearing of throats, a low hum of conversation. They settle down around the table and on divans along the walls.*

OKHREYANOV: Kapustin, why haven't you finished announcing the decrees of the Special Conference?

KAPUSTIN: I thought, Colonel . . . It was physically impossible.

OKHREYANOV: We've just locked up an astronomer, now there's a physicist here. (*Laughter.*) It's best not to think. A turkey died of thinking. (*He walks towards the door on the right. As he approaches it he begins to tiptoe. Peeps through it, then jumps away.*) Attention!
Everybody rises. The GENERAL *enters.*

GENERAL: All right. You may sit down.
Everybody sits. The GENERAL *walks briskly towards his desk and, still standing, sorts out his papers. There is a deathly hush.* OKHREYANOV *also sits down, having moved his chair completely silently.*

GENERAL: So . . . I've gathered you here, Comrades, I've gathered all of you who are in charge of those who work in our Counter-Intelligence, so as to outline most clearly, most precisely the basic problems facing us today. I have just returned from a Conference of the heads of the front line departments of SMERSH, as well as of the regional management of the N.K.G.B., which lasted three days and was under the chairmanship of Lavrentiy Beria. Yesterday it had the greatest honour and happiness of being visited personally by Comrade Stalin!
General applause, everybody rises, RUBLYOV *with difficulty. He is the first to sit down again.*

GENERAL: Comrades! I will not speak of that enormous

excitement, which took hold of me, when I saw the face so familiar and so dear to us all, the face of the greatest friend to Counter-Intelligence, of the fighter for the peace of the whole world, of our great Father, Friend, Mentor and Leader. Comrades, Comrade Stalin greatly appreciates the efforts of our Organs in defence of our country during the war. I shall repeat verbatim truly historic words, which were uttered yesterday by Comrade Stalin. He said: "It is now clear that without the Cheka we wouldn't have won the Civil War and without the N.K.V.D. we would not have won the Great Patriotic War." But, Comrades, is it typical of Bolsheviks to rest on their laurels? No, a hundred times no! The greatest danger now, is that we, the Cheka Officers, might relax, and say the war is over and we can slow down, etc. Yesterday, Joseph Vissarionovich made a joke. He said: "Your troops, Lavrentiy, spend the whole of the war in the Third Echelon and now want to push forward to the front." That is something we, each and every one of us, must understand and see where it is meant to lead us.

RUBLYOV: Comrade General, allow me to leave.

GENERAL: What's that? No. The war may be finished for the Army, but for us now it is the battle for Stalingrad, the major combat, the very peak of fighting. And our struggle is uneven, Comrades, numerically speaking. Our SMERSH management could be compared, say, to a select battalion of officers (without counting supervisory staff or the escort armies) who have to grind down whole divisions of the enemy – just look: they crowd our prison yards in whole divisions – do not count them as your compatriots, forget that they are Russians – they are a bitter, degenerate rabble who have breathed the poisoned air of Capitalist Europe. Today our responsibility is great. We, the Cheka officers, must be especially merciless, especially severe, so as to be able to fulfil the task of repatriation which has been entrusted to us by great Stalin. Read and re-read, Comrades, the amnesty which was published yesterday and which marks the fruits of our glorious Victory. Each and every one who deserted is forgiven by the Soviet government. Why is it so, Comrades? Because a deserter is nothing but a coward, he wants to save his own skin, but he is one of us, he is socially close to us, Comrades. But he who was not afraid of being in the front line, not afraid of dive bombers, not afraid of "Tigers", will not be afraid of turning the gun against us, and so forth. These decisive days what do we see among us, Comrades? On the one hand we record, we put up a roll of honour to our best workers: the President of our military tribunal Krivoshchap, our prosecutor Lieutenant-Colonel Morgoslepov, Major Ognida, Captain Mymra and so on and so forth. But, Comrades, we cannot and we must not cover up our deficiencies. I don't even want to mention that shameful case where we overlooked in our own ranks that double imperialist agent, the bourgeois degenerate Neklyuchimov. The responsibility for that lies on all our collective shoulders, but in the first instance, the responsibility is yours, Comrade Rublyov and yours, Comrade Okhreyanov. Let this be a lesson to you; the steely arm of the Cheka knows how mercilessly to eradicate even in its own back yard. But, Comrades, Comrade Stalin gave us a directive of genius, that our methods of investigation are still too liberal, that they are still in the rotten grip of juris*pru*dence and that using methods like these we will never solve the problems of today, of that enormous human flood which pours into this country from the West; we will never solve it on time. As always, Comrade Stalin has dialectically extracted the most important link of the chain, when he said all this must come to a stop. It's time to stop it, Comrades! Just examine the methods of our best front-runners, those of Comrade Krivoshchap or of Morgoslepov. It's harder for them, don't you think? There is a whole crowd of you interrogators, while they

are on their own and they are pressurised by various
social norms and forms; they, indeed, could have become
the bottleneck, but they have managed not to. Being
men of high social conscience, they know how to
organise their work so as to double, quadruple the
effectiveness of the Tribunal's output. It wasn't long ago
that we considered convicting forty people a day the
maximum we could manage and now we're convicting a
hundred and twenty and – the more the merrier. What,
in principle, is new about it? First, as a result of
Comrade Krivoshchap's initiative, we've got rid of the
so-called "discussion" room – and cigarette smoking now
takes place after work. In the first room, now, we listen
to the evidence, and we sentence in the second, then in
the first room we sentence and in the second we listen to
the evidence. Also, the sentencing department's work is
very precise and meticulously prepares all the sentences
no later than the day before the trial. Finally, owing to
Comrade Morgoslepov's initiative, we have a flow system
which enables us to have both sessions of the Tribunal
serviced simultaneously. The question is why such brave
innovatory methods, which have been borrowed from
industry, are not initiated among the investigators?

RUBLYOV (*rising. It has been obvious throughout that he has
been in great pain*): I . . . must go . . . (*He walks towards
the exit.*)

GENERAL (*looking him up and down, very perplexed*): . . .
Whose fault is it that the investigators are trailing
behind? It's the fault of the heads of department, yes!

RUBLYOV, *before reaching the door, sinks on to the parquet
floor.*

Confusion.

VOICES: What's wrong with him?
Sophia!
Why don't you lift him up?
Take him to the clinic!
Who's on duty there?

The doors are flung open. A couple of Lieutenants and a couple of Sergeants carry RUBLYOV *awkwardly out.* SOPHIA LVOVA *leaves behind them. The members of the conference settle down again. We can still hear:*

He's had it for a long time . . .

Cancer of the liver, or something.

I, too, have a terrible pain here . . .

GENERAL: Yes . . . Poor old thing's going down . . . Burnt himself out, working for the Cheka. I shall continue. It's you, you who are in charge of the workers, you've allowed this relaxed attitude, it's you who do not control the speed of investigations, it's you who allow the investigations to drag out for a month or more. That's quite insupportable! Your interrogators loll about in their armchairs as if they were at the barber's. Colonel Okhreyanov, you're to exchange them for hard chairs . . .

OKHREYANOV: . . . Yes, sir. Exchange for hard chairs. (*Makes a note with zeal.*)

GENERAL: . . . What is it that they twitter about with the prisoners, I'd like to know? Indeed, as I walk along the corridor – is there a raised voice, or a female scream? There isn't even a swear word, as if you're walking in a sanatorium and not Counter-Intelligence SMERSH. Last month I received only seventy-one notifications of increased physical pressure, which makes only one and a half per cent of all the cases investigated – what about the rest? Do they manage without? But where are the results? How many cases are being dealt with in one week? All of them must be finished! Our motto is: he who is arrested on Monday is to be tried on Saturday – that's all there is to it. (*Drinks some water.*) Also – I'm sorry Sophia Lvova has left – the health clinic gets in the way: out of seventy-one notifications three were objected to on the grounds, if you please, of the extreme physical weakness of the accused, so that I had to issue a second approval. This holds things up, after all! It's no accident

202

that owing to flabby and badly organised evidence the Tribunal is unable to bring out a verdict. As for the Special Conference Decree, the Tribunal comes up with an eight year sentence and even, in some cases – I was ashamed in front of Beria – a five year one. Where are we going, Comrades?! No, we must abandon this rotten practice. You're not making use of that brilliant advanced technology which the Soviet Government has provided for you. For instance, what prison cells are you making use of? You make use of ordinary ones, with wooden floors – grandfather's technology, early nineteenth century. Colonel Okhreyanov, you're to pull up the floor boards.

OKHREYANOV: . . . Yes, sir. Pull up the floor boards! (*Makes a note with zeal.*)

GENERAL: The majority, of course, are placed in damp ones with cement floors – that's all right as far as it goes. But I've brought with me permission to set up ten standing cells. A man is squeezed in by the door closing and there he is. If he tries to sit down, he's left hanging by his back and bent knees. Despair, of course; he can't tell if he's walled in for ever . . . You could even summon a plasterer and start a discussion in the corridor about plastering the door in . . . It is only for four hours in twenty-four that they push a rod through for him to lean on. It's a very ingenious construction. I've brought sample designs with me to show you. Apart from all this, for the most obstinate categories, I've Comrade Beria's permission to make use of the old and well-tried method of putting pressure on the genitals! (*Applause.*) That's the kind of lever which can . . . well, I don't know! While we spend our time force-feeding through a tube! . . .

Scene 11

*A sumptuous, gloomy study. On the back wall there is a large
map of Europe on which a red thread indicates the 1945
demarcation line. There is a large portrait of Stalin. All the
curtains are drawn. There is a large antique desk and another
one at right angles to it. Close to the door there is a small bare
table for the accused, and a stool. The middle of the study is
almost empty. The room is in half-darkness.* RUBLYOV *is lying
down on a couch. He half rises with an agonised groan and
lowers his feet. He is dressed.* SOPHIA LVOVA *enters without
knocking. She wears an overall on top of her uniform.*

SOPHIA: Colonel Rublyov, lie down. We'll give you another
injection in a minute.

RUBLYOV: Lieutenant-Colonel, stop pretending that you're
a sister of mercy. You're nothing but an old prison
doctor.

SOPHIA: A doctor's always a doctor.

RUBLYOV: Not always in a prison. You cannot help me,
you cannot save me, so let me die in peace. (SOPHIA
takes his pulse.) What are you doing? I have no pulse,
didn't you know? (*Pulls his hand away.*)

SOPHIA: You have, but it's very weak.

RUBLYOV: I'm one of those who hasn't got one. I quite
simply haven't got one! All that's invented for idiots.

SOPHIA (*anxiously*): You should be lying down. Drink this.
There'll be a 'plane tonight and we'll send you to a
Berlin clinic.

RUBLYOV: Why not to a Moscow one? Have the Germans
got all the answers? (*He drinks his medicine.*) Tell me,
why are the healthy so afraid of the dying? Why do they
lie? It's an hour since you said: a few days of suffering
and then death for sure. You said it, didn't you?

SOPHIA: Wh-who did I say it to?

RUBLYOV: You've been working in these departments for

years – and you ask – to whom? In front of whom? All
right, when the aeroplane comes, give me a ring. (*He
dials a number on his own telephone.*) Get Vorotyntsev here
from one hundred and twenty-five.

SOPHIA: Colonel Rublyov, after such an attack . . . (*As if
trying to prevent him telephoning.*)
A knock.

KAMCHUZHNAYA (*in the doorway*): May I come in,
Comrade Colonel?

SOPHIA: Captain Kamchuzhnaya, Colonel Rublyov is ill and
can't see anybody.

KAMCHUZHNAYA: Excuse me . . . (*To* RUBLYOV.) You
said at nine, but if you're ill . . .

RUBLYOV: Come in.

KAMCHUZHNAYA *enters.* SOPHIA *shrugs her shoulders and
leaves.*

KAMCHUZHNAYA: Comrade Colonel, I have two small
questions. The accused Rubin . . .

RUBLYOV: Well?

KAMCHUZHNAYA: According to the reports from cell 117
where he was held earlier, as well as now from 125, he
conducts himself in the cell arguments as a true loyal
Marxist, defending the Soviet Regime as well as the
organs of Security, although not with regard to himself.
During the investigations he continues to insist that the
case was cooked up against him and is due to a squabble
in the Army political section. This seems to me to be
correct. The Divisional Commander heard of Rubin's
arrest and sent a splendid character reference, which
contradicts the one from the Political Section. We've also
received, apart from that, references about his military
conduct from officers who are members of the Party and
who fought with him.

RUBLYOV: It's to be included in the surveillance file.

KAMCHUZHNAYA: Who, the officers? I've done that as a
matter of course.

RUBLYOV: The Divisional Commander as well.

KAMCHUZHNAYA (*surprised*): The Divisional Commander as well?

RUBLYOV: The motto is: the days of Zhukov are over.

KAMCHUZHNAYA: Ye-es. I un-der-stand. But I was talking about Rubin. He is sincerely devoted to the idea of Communism, he has two medals, been wounded twice . . .

RUBLYOV: So what?

KAMCHUZHNAYA: I understand, of course, that he can't be freed, you'd need the Minister's approval . . . But suppose he was freed on condition he works for us . . . as an informer? To deal with delicate matters to do with ideology. He's an educated person, used to teach Marxism-Leninism – which is important. Students after the war . . .

RUBLYOV: He's too complicated. He'll never become an informer. What are you so worried about? Who's the other one?

KAMCHUZHNAYA: Professor Mostovshchikov. Our scientific experts have confirmed that he's an outstanding specialist in atomic physics. In Europe he worked in . . .

RUBLYOV: Be brief.

KAMCHUZHNAYA: Maybe he shouldn't be in the general flow. A person like that might be needed, and probably soon.

RUBLYOV (*speaking with difficulty and some pauses*): "Soon" – nothing. He's to be in the general flow! In fact, I instruct you to see to it that he's sent off on a special Polar detachment intended for particularly heavy physical labour. Of course, we'll see to it that he doesn't die. When he gets to a certain point, he'll be yanked out, sent to Lubyanka; some respectable General would express his sincere regrets about not having known in time that such a great scientist was in need of help and defence and would respectfully *beg* the Professor to return to his scientific studies, but to overlook the inconvenience of the barbed wire around his laboratory.

Mostovshchikov, who until recently had been beaten over the neck by some miserable guard, would experience bliss, a renewal, and not to have to pick-axe the frozen soil of Siberia for an inch of butter for his breakfast, he would do more for us than for all the tea in China.

KAMCHUZHNAYA (*overwhelmed*): What a profound thought!

RUBLYOV: We've had some experience. Systems similar to this have been in operation for some fifteen years and with great success. That's how the best machines in our Air Force were made. You know, Kamchuzhnaya, that we're not rich, we have few resources. Instead of which we have to study the human psyche. Is that all?

KAMCHUZHNAYA: Yes, sir.

RUBLYOV (*approaching her*): Let me tell you something, Lydia. (*He puts his hand on the nape of her neck.*) You could have become a good investigator, a high flyer, but you take it too much to heart. You're too enthusiastic.

KAMCHUZHNAYA: Is that . . . a bad thing?

RUBLYOV: Nobody needs it any more. It was needed some time ago, long ago, when the wheel was being run in. It runs now, and all you have to do is give it a drop of oil. Keep your heart to yourself. This thing today, with the window being broken. I was trying to promote you to head of the department, but now Mymra's been appointed. Mymra would never let things get so public but all his papers would be duly signed. Why don't you become a Mymra? Or else leave the department altogether, eh?

KAMCHUZHNAYA: But I don't want to become a Mymra!

RUBLYOV: Then leave. You can't be all that fond of this work. I can't remember how you joined . . . Ah, yes. Through your husband. To whom you said: first, tell me all about it; then, let me come to the interrogation (I'll be behind the curtain), then you joined the courses . . .

KAMCHUZHNAYA (*with fervour*): Colonel. This is my kind

207

of work. I've a talent for it – I understand people, I
guess things quickly, I remember things . . . And you
tell me to give it up . . . (*With compassion.*) What's
wrong? You've never talked to me. You've always been
. . . I'm afraid to come close to you.

RUBLYOV (*thinking his own thoughts*): Drop it, Lydia . . .
Drop it and run . . .

KAMCHUZHNAYA: It so happens, I'm in terrible trouble
today. May I tell you? . . .

GUARD (*peeping through*): Comrade Colonel, excuse me.

RUBLYOV: Yes, yes.

> VOROTYNTSEV *enters; his hands are behind his back but
> he frees them as he comes into the study.* RUBLYOV
> *dismisses the guard with a nod.* KAMCHUZHNAYA,
> *annoyed, walks past* VOROTYNTSEV, *looking him up and
> down. She leaves.*

RUBLYOV: Well, Mr. Vorotyntsev, how are you? (*He
switches on the ceiling light.*)

VOROTYNTSEV: Better than you'd wish.

RUBLYOV: You didn't expect to be summoned?

VOROTYNTSEV: I did sign article 206, what else is needed?

RUBLYOV: The thing is . . . you know . . . in my private
capacity . . . I wanted to let you know that your case is
to be heard by the military tribunal – tomorrow.

VOROTYNTSEV: Did you have to take the trouble just for
that?

RUBLYOV: Apart from that . . . (*He suffers a sharp attack of
pain. He stumbles backwards, his head thrown back, across
the middle of the room. He knocks against an armchair and
sits down in it. Controlling himself.*) Apart from that, I
wanted to warn you about your fate . . .

VOROTYNTSEV: It was decided before the trial. I
understand that. As in every other case . . .

RUBLYOV: Decided, yes, but differently from all the others.

VOROTYNTSEV: I understand that too. I shall be shot.

RUBLYOV (*looks at him fixedly*): You're mistaken. You'll be
hanged.

VOROTYNTSEV (*takes it bravely*): And, of course, secretly. In a corner.

RUBLYOV: The day after tomorrow.

VOROTYNTSEV: I've worked that out. Is that all?

RUBLYOV: What else do you want?

VOROTYNTSEV: There's nothing else that I can expect from a Bolshevik Government. I know, it's the end. May I go?

RUBLYOV: Don't tell me, you're more comfortable there than here? The air is fresh here, there are comfortable armchairs here, instead of straw, slop buckets, stench.

VOROTYNTSEV: People are clean there.

RUBLYOV: Wait and you'll understand why I summoned you. Do sit down. No, not there – on the couch.
VOROTYNTSEV, *however, sits down by the empty table for the accused.* RUBLYOV *moves towards him, dragging his chair right up to the little table and sits down.*

RUBLYOV: Tell me, Colonel, how come you have such bright eyes? Your back is so straight – why? You hold your head up high – why? You've known for a long time that we would execute you, after all. You are going to die, die the day after tomorrow! Have you no fear of losing your life, tell me, Colonel? Maybe you have some secret . . . you know something? (*They stare at each other.*) I don't ask out of sheer curiosity. I'm also a condemned man. There's no salvation for me either. I have a terrible illness. Today is the 9th of July. By the 15th I'll no longer be here. Forget who I am. Today I'm no longer your enemy. I summoned you out of friendly feelings. Because now you're no longer an enemy of mine.

VOROTYNTSEV: I wish you *were* an enemy. As the saying goes, I respect courage even in a Tartar. But you're not an enemy. You're an executioner.

RUBLYOV: But your side – did you have no executioners? *Will* you not have any?

VOROTYNTSEV: Not the same quantity. Not the same quality.

RUBLYOV: Each party maintains three executioners for each "troubadour". How can you have a political party without executioners?

VOROTYNTSEV: We're not a party. Fortunately, or unfortunately, we never were a party. Otherwise, we might have won.

RUBLYOV: Lying on the couch just now in a cold sweat, in pain, I understood that I'm as lonely as a wolf; that *they* needed me while I held them together; while I pushed them on; but now that I'm a burden, they are in a hurry to get rid of me; they've found a replacement . . . And so I thought of you with gladness, of someone who's going the same way . . . Forget that I'm a Colonel in the N.K.G.B. In a few days these distinctions between us will disappear. So – man to man, a traveller to another traveller, can you help me?

VOROTYNTSEV: To be quite honest, having emerged from a cell and just one day from being hanged, I find it difficult to want to help you.

RUBLYOV: I understand, I know! But can't you rise above it? I've never been a coward, but I'm so frightened now. I used to be flint hard, so why am I crumbling now? I want to meet death with the same defiance shining in my eyes as in yours. Teach me the secret of your fortitude.

VOROTYNTSEV: There's no secret. I'm already 69 years old and I can see that I've followed the right path. Why should I lose courage?

RUBLYOV: How do you mean, the right path? What right path? You're a professional soldier. How many wars did you take part in?

VOROTYNTSEV: Five.

RUBLYOV: The Russo-Japanese? Which you lost. The Russo-German? You lost that too.

VOROTYNTSEV: We didn't lose it. It was because of you.

RUBLYOV: The Civil War? Lost again. The Second World War? Beaten again.

VOROTYNTSEV: You left out the Spanish Civil War.

RUBLYOV: For twenty-eight years we've been beating you in everything and everywhere, and today we've finally crushed you – and you say you have no reason to lose courage? The whole of your life is a road of utter defeat – and you consider it the right path?

VOROTYNTSEV: It was right, in the sense that I didn't make a mistake about whose side to be on. I always took the right side – *against you*. I never wavered, I never doubted, I never thought that truth was on your side. I never thought of joining you. However many your triumphs, I was always against you . . . One thing was certain: never to allow, never even to surmise that some tiny part of the truth was on your side – that was right! Yes, we've failed. But you haven't won either. That's why my eyes are bright. I've lived long enough to see that you haven't won either! That's why!

RUBLYOV: Today? You say that today. Are you quite sober?

VOROTYNTSEV: Yes, today, in the hour of your greatest outward victory, even in your prison and before my very death I've been given to see that you have lost utterly! That you're doomed! You persecuted our Monarchy, and look at the filth you established instead. You promised paradise on earth, and gave us Counter-Intelligence. What is especially cheering is that the more your ideas degenerate, the more obviously all your ideology collapses, the more hysterically you cling to it. That means you're finished. Without this pathetic ideology of yours you might have saved yourselves. With it – it's all up with you. For the last twenty-eight years Russia has never been quite so far from Bolshevism. In the Counter-Intelligence cell I saw it quite clearly – Russia does not belong *to you*, Comrades! The people in that cell are different from the ones you arrested in 1918. They do not wear signet rings on their white fingers, their forage caps still bear the marks of the five-cornered star. They're all young, brought up in *your* schools, not ours,

211

on your books, not ours, in your faith, not ours – but
they've grown up . . .

RUBLYOV (*nodding*): Not ours, but not yours either.

VOROTYNTSEV: A tiny whiff of freedom was enough to
blow away the black cloud of your magic from the youth
of Russia! You used to revile the first wave of émigrés,
you said that they were mercenary; that they didn't want
to understand progressive ideas. Maybe so. But where
does this *second* wave of émigrés come from – all those
millions of simple Russian lads who have tasted twenty-
four years of a new society and refuse to return home?

RUBLYOV: How do you mean, refuse? Where did you come
across them? In the cells? They came back, quite
voluntarily. They are coming back – that's the surprising
thing! But they'll be sent into camps – and your second
wave of émigrés will vanish!

VOROTYNTSEV: But then, how come they didn't
understand your progressive ideas? As far as I can see,
they reject your ideologists.

RUBLYOV: They reject your saints as well. They don't need
our ideas – they have their own: to do a bit of moon-
lighting, to pinch what is available, to spend it all on
drink, to have it off with a skirt.

VOROTYNTSEV: Natural demands, after all. What they
want is to live, let's face it.

RUBLYOV: Now, that's sensible. We agree at last . . . You,
on the other hand . . .

VOROTYNTSEV: But you prevent them living.

RUBLYOV: You, on the other hand, suffer from some kind
of blue-tinged enthusiasm. We prevent them living?
How, then, do you explain the way we've taken off? You
must look at facts, Colonel. The fact is, that Marxism
has not yet reached its centenary, but look at the size of
the continent we've acquired. (*He indicates the map.*) And
we're still growing. (*He is exhausted and sits down.*)

VOROTYNTSEV: Yes, I must say, there have been years
when one could have lost courage. I've been defeated

many times – however hard one worked, however hard one tried – it all vanished without trace. It seemed that even when no mistakes were made, there was one defeat after another. Why? I don't know. There seems to be some divine and limitless plan for Russia which unfolds itself slowly while our lives are so brief. There are moments when at some event one is even seized with mystical terror – and even asks oneself: why is everything so useless?! But don't keep on referring to your victories. Looking back, one can explain away each one of them, crack it open like a walnut. The Civil War? (*He rises and thereafter he paces about the room.*) Imagine you're an English Minister in 1917 and look at Russia from there. What a country! An ocean of pearly grain. Ancient, solid forests, the size of several Europes! The bowels of the earth bursting with whatever a human being needs on this planet. Hundreds of navigable rivers, swarming with fish and flowing into oceans, warm or cold, fresh water or salty. Within some paltry twenty years we developed oil fields, quarries, coal mines, factories, railways. Within some paltry ten years we had Stolypin[13] villages everywhere. Were you to give them liberty, we could have had a second America of prosperous farmers. Siberia, that frightening, impenetrable Siberia, the haunt of bears and vagrants, was on the point of becoming another Canada – four times as vast . . .

RUBLYOV: Don't go too far! Illusions again! And don't you steal *our* achievements!

VOROTYNTSEV: But what have you done to Siberia? Instead of filling in the marshes with wooden logs, you've filled them in with corpses. Along the wastes of the Yenisey river you put up barbed wire. Along the Arctic Ocean you've put up the fences and observation towers of the labour camps. One of your most arrogant myths is that you have developed Russian economy. But what you've done is to cripple its original thrust. A

213

factory is in the wrong place, approaches to it are from
the wrong end, any new building needs repairs within
three months. I've been watching you all these years with
all the attention of hatred and I haven't missed a thing!

RUBLYOV: Magnitogorsk. Turksib – I'm too lazy to
enumerate them all. Kuzbassk for coal . . .

VOROTYNTSEV: But the twentieth century is no longer the
stone age.

RUBLYOV: Balkhashsk for copper smelting . . .

VOROTYNTSEV: While the copper itself is a thousand miles
away. Just tell me, do you think that without you there
would have been no radio broadcasts, no electrified
railways? Don't pretend that progress is because of your
system. You're trailing behind the century and when you
have to fight, the trouble is you don't know which way
to turn and you foul it up . . . The Russian people used
to be hardworking . . .

RUBLYOV: . . . for the landowners . . .

VOROTYNTSEV: . . . good-natured . . .

RUBLYOV: . . . in front of the police . . .

VOROTYNTSEV: . . . adaptable, many-sided, exceptionally
gifted . . .

RUBLYOV: . . . but not allowed to go to school . . .

VOROTYNTSEV: That's another myth. As to you, what sort
of people did you condemn on political grounds? Read
your own trumped-up cases. Every one of them was at
the bottom of the heap. A nation, which was only just
beginning to become aware of itself, the immense powers
of which were still unfathomed, a nation of 170 million,
whose soldiers held up the Eastern Front of Europe . . .

RUBLYOV: . . . but lacking ammunition . . .

VOROTYNTSEV: They had ammunition! That's another
myth! I was in the trenches, I know. By 1917 we were
armed to the level of Verdun. Suppose there had been a
revolution in America in 1941 – you could have said with
assurance that they "had no Air Force" – but they built
it during the war!

RUBLYOV: So where were your arms?

VOROTYNTSEV: At the front! But it was you who gave
them away to the Germans after the peace treaty of
Brest. They were also in the rear, but for three years you
used them against us and later you used them to train
your Army . . . And it was to them that you were
prepared to give up the Straits. So as to have to face
their fleet in the Mediterranean? For a hundred years,
seven generations of English politicians, twenty-five
government administrations spent their time digging,
delving and building so as not to let the Germans
through, and you caved in. England fought against
Germany, but was equally afraid of Russia. But then
suddenly there emerged a handful of unknown rogues
from among "professional revolutionaries", that's to say,
from among those who chose destruction as their
profession, who had never in their lives created anything,
who were incapable of creating anything, people who
belonged to no nation, who had no experience of
practical life, irresponsible chatterers, who spent half
their lives in third-rate cafés . . .

RUBLYOV: That's what's known as self-criticism. Did you
reconstruct this from your experience of White émigrés?

VOROTYNTSEV: To some extent, yes . . . And it was that
handful of rogues that managed to decompose an Army
ten million strong, to take an unarmed Petrograd with
the bayonets of drunken sailors – so that the fields were
left unsown, factories grew silent, the mines were left to
silt up and Russians began to destroy Russians, breaking
their lances, not over Constantinople, but over
Novocherkassk. Tell me, sir, you English Minister, do
you like this Communist Party? Don't you think this
kind of Party suits you well? Don't you think this sort of
Party is quite exceptional? No Lawrence of Arabia, no
British Intelligence Service could have invented a better
one. There was no need to strangle it. (*Pause*.)

RUBLYOV: Well, from the English point of view . . .

VOROTYNTSEV: From the French point of view as well . . .
It's that that saved you. It wasn't Marti or the
International Proletariat. "Intervention", "the campaign
of fourteen states" – all rubbish. Two companies in
Odessa, a battalion in Archangel and disembarcation in
the Far East, but without any further movement – none
of them fought, there was no "campaign of the
fourteen", only Poland! Just remember, from your first
appearance, nobody abroad feared you or took you
seriously, considering – unfortunately without foundation
– that your whole enterprise was a circus.

RUBLYOV: What, even Hitler? Did he think it was a circus
when he had to retreat? Was he having fun when he
surrendered Berlin?

VOROTYNTSEV: Even Hitler – he more than anyone.
Mistake upon mistake. But what have you to be proud of
in your war with Hitler? A devastated country? The
blockade of Petrograd? Some fifteen million killed?
Drowning in blood and boasting of victory! Haven't you
been proclaiming for twenty-four years that you wouldn't
let anyone pass; that you could resist any alliance, that
you would fight on someone else's territory, that you
would shed hardly any blood, while Hitler, all on his
own, beat you as he pleased, where he pleased, with
lunch-breaks and rest days on Sundays. *We* didn't retreat
like that. We never surrendered even the tenth part of
what you had to give up. We didn't surrender Kiev or
Minsk, let alone the Caucasus or the Volga.

RUBLYOV: Well now, you argue against yourself. Strength,
then, lies in something else. You may not have
surrendered Kiev or Minsk, but you fluffed the war.

VOROTYNTSEV: I can now see all this clearly, with
hindsight – we didn't want to oppress our own kind;
unlike you, we didn't know how. We saw no point in it.
We didn't exile whole nations. We set up town councils
– it is they that ruined everything for us, those liberals.

RUBLYOV: While we retreated to the Volga, and still we

won . . . We have more backbone, wouldn't you say?

VOROTYNTSEV: Yes, all those conquerors are now in your
cells. If Hitler hadn't burnt their villages, they wouldn't
have destroyed his Imperial Chancellery. You've had
some help, from Western socialists, and from Churchill
and Roosevelt in particular. Even now, in Bavaria and
Austria, they've handed over excellent soldiers to you to
be destroyed. What is it but blindness? It must be
because to this day they haven't seen through your
crimes. But the day will come when they will wake up
and sort out your band of brigands properly for the first
time. And this first true test will . . .

RUBLYOV (*laughing*): Never in your life, Colonel! It is *we*
who will sort out their band of brigands so quickly that
they will only have time to snort, the weaklings. They're
as bad as Kerensky[14] in the Winter Palace!

VOROTYNTSEV: Never. This unstable world of ours will
still provide pockets of courage. You have no idea how
quickly weakness becomes strength, and how suddenly it
can blossom in its might. We did experience this – to our
own surprise.

RUBLYOV: What pockets of courage! Since you will not be
leaving here, I can tell you our secret. We shall (*he
approached the map, indicating*) bit by bit quietly swallow
them all. They will all become part of us. Just consider
your own experience. What happened to your brave
rulers? Where are they now? . . . You're silent. You
were all bankrupt, let me tell you. You were a generation
of bankrupts. Your Ministers, your military leaders, as
well as all the leaders of your political parties. Your
parties themselves were bankrupt!

VOROTYNTSEV: As to the *parties*, I don't hold myself
responsible.

RUBLYOV: All right, then. But you were not a small band.
There were millions, or at least hundreds of thousands of
you, of prosperous, well-heeled scoundrels, miserable
members of the gentry, who used to irritate the people

217

with your displays, your horse racing, your English
overcoats and condescending manners. But the moment
we appeared with our guns on the pavements – where
did all those millions of gentlemen disappear to? Did
they rush off to join General Denikin?[15] Oh no! Did they
shoot at us from their attics! No, again. They joined the
queues to give up their warm clothing to the Red Army.
There was an order, after all, to that effect, posted up on
the walls. Or else they exchanged it for lard in the
market. But that's not all they did. They played cards,
behind closed shutters. And they waited for the kindly,
bearded Ivan with a Tsarist insignia to turn up all the
way from the Don to liberate them. But who came to
visit them? The Cheka. (*He laughs.*) Isn't that so? (*He
roars with laughter.*) I'm talking to you like this only
because you yourself fought like a man. (*A pause. He sits
down.*) You won't find an answer to the puzzle of the
Revolution in London. Consider – there was this
prosperous mighty Empire and a handful of interlopers
came along, blew on it, and the Empire was no more –
things aren't as simple as that. The powerful army
disintegrates. That well-intentioned, hard-working nation
is led astray! With what power? With the power of our
ideas!

VOROTYNTSEV: In the first place, with the power of your
methods. And then, yes – with the power of your ideas.

RUBLYOV: That's just it. Go on beating your head against
that wall.

VOROTYNTSEV: As to the power of your methods. From
the very beginning your arsenal consisted of opportunist
insolence and consistent cruelty. You tried to strangle
your foster-brother, the Social Democrat, even while you
shared the same cradle. You stole the agrarian
programme from your cousin, the Social Revolutionary,
who was festooned with bombs. Who were you and what
did you signify when you crawled out of the woodwork
in the spring of 1917? The dummies of the Provisional

Government could have squashed you easily and silently
like a dry, anaemic bed-bug, if they hadn't been such
dummies. And you would have left no trace and no smell
in the annals of Russian history. But that couldn't be
done! In those heady days of spring everybody had to be
a European. Every opinion had a right to be heard. But
you weren't going to abide by such niceties. And above
all you disregarded other people's opinions. You moved
by night. With your curved Tartar sabre you chopped
down the cabbage heads of all those who opposed you, so
that there remained but one opinion – yours!

RUBLYOV: We never concealed this. Even our banners said:
"Dictatorship".

VOROTYNTSEV: That's just it, you didn't conceal it, while
we, asses that we were, never fully understood. But how
could one penetrate to the bottom of the abyss of your
souls? Our Gendarmes should have taken a few lessons
from your G.P.U.! Did they prosecute you in old Russia,
did they fight against you? They looked after you, they
nurtured you tenderly. Let's imagine a situation where
some snotty boy stuck an anti-government leaflet on a
fence and then got caught. According to the laws of the
Empire, his worst punishment would be three months'
imprisonment. A Lieutenant-Colonel in the Gendarmes,
fixing his golden pince-nez firmly on his nose, would
enquire politely: "Who are your fellow conspirators?
What is your secret address? Your printing press?" "I do
not wish to answer." "You don't wish to answer. Fine!
That's your right." Three months later the lad comes out
of prison and around his head there's a revolutionary
halo, the aureole of holy martyrdom. Elderly workmen
call him Mister, girls are proud to walk out on his arm,
his school fellows crowd respectfully behind him. And
everybody expects from him new heroic deeds, drawn
from Russian literature, fully available and free. So he
performs them. But look at you. Through hunger,
sleeplessness and beatings you extract from him a list of

219

fifty people who even in their dreams had never heard of the leaflet, who had never even walked along that street, but they are all seized and given ten years, while he is given twenty-five. They all go to die in Norilsk, while their surviving contemporaries remain, numb at the disappearance without trace of their friend. His sister is summoned to the Komsomol regional committee to sign her renunciation of her brother, while his father and mother, pretending to be cheerful, insist to their neighbours that their boy's gone to work in Kazakhstan. Otherwise, they will lose their flat as well as their job. Had you been treated like that, where would you be now?

RUBLYOV: To treat people like that you need a steely faith. You have always been tortured by your conscience, because you thought you had stolen something from the people.

VOROTYNTSEV: True enough. You, on the other hand, aren't tortured by it. The old Russia held twenty thousand political prisoners. They, out of fastidiousness, refused to eat their three pounds of bread, and organised university classes in their cells. Basking in the sun of Stalin's Constitution there are twenty million political prisoners. They crawl in search of herring scales in the rubbish dumps of labour camps and as to books – they might as well forget they exist. Such is the power of your methods!

RUBLYOV: Yes, I must say! We *were* tenderly nurtured . . . When I was fourteen, in 1905, my father Daniel Rublyov, a railway coupler on the Moscow–Kazan line, was killed by a humane punitive detachment of your just Tsarist government.

VOROTYNTSEV: But how many were shot during that revolution? Altogether? I read somewhere that only twenty were in Kolomna.

RUBLYOV: You think that's nothing? Nothing? It was my *father* who was among them!

VOROTYNTSEV: But those were the days of the revolution, of a rebellion. While you, when the revolution was over, shot thousands upon thousands right across the country – and in secret. That's the power of your method. Now let's talk about the power of your ideas. There was a time when your ideas had strength. They consisted of: grab what you can! You demanded nothing, you just gave away: peace, land, factories, houses. That was a convenient idea and it wasn't damaging: after all, you were distributing what didn't belong to you . . .

RUBLYOV: . . . created with our hands . . . To that extent it belonged to us.

VOROTYNTSEV: Created with whose hands? The one who came flying in from Geneva? You awakened in millions of Russian souls the instinct of greed, of easy acquisition. And for a brief moment you were transformed from a handful into a mass movement. But before very long you had squandered Mother's inheritance and your ideas changed. Now you say: give! In other words, *they* must give everything to *you*. It's over twenty-five years since you stopped giving and started demanding. Taking: muscles, nerves, sleep, family happiness, life. So that once again, you've been transformed from a mass movement into a handful. Why is it that you're not now offering – you don't say: grab what you can?

RUBLYOV (*emerging from a bout of pain, speaking slowly*): I must admit that when I summoned you I thought you'd be talking to me . . . (*a pause*) about something else . . . (*a pause*). About that . . . (*a pause;* VOROTYNTSEV *looks fixedly at* RUBLYOV) migration of souls . . . about God . . .

VOROTYNTSEV: Whenever death is near, you all want to grasp at God.

RUBLYOV: That's because, probably . . . Because . . . (*He can't find the right word. Pulls himself together.*) All in all, Colonel, your arguments are weak, weak! You're 69 years old, but you're as naïve as a young man. You

refuse to weigh up either the overpowering might of our
army or the tenacity of our centralising apparatus. You
speak of handfuls and of the people. All *that* has grown
together long ago like that (*he intertwines his fingers*) and
it's not in human power to separate it without killing it.
To shake off Bolshevism is not possible any more – you
can only pull it up and half the nation with it. (*He dials
a number on his telephone.*) Do you still believe in the
importance of the pulse? . . . Hallo. Supper, first class,
in my study.

VOROTYNTSEV: What are you talking about?

RUBLYOV: Well, a doctor – was it in Chekhov? – a doctor
arrives from town to examine a patient and he then
summons the local medical assistant to a neighbouring
room, for a consultation, so as not to hurt him.
Colleague, he says, I'm a bit worried about our patient's
pulse – it's very weak. The medic, glancing at the door,
says: Doctor, since we're alone, you can speak freely,
you and I know that the "pulse" doesn't exist . . . I had
to put collectivisation through; I'm not boasting – I had
to face a crowd with stakes, while I had no arms. I
would shout loudly – you can tear me to pieces, but we'll
achieve what we want! . . . But years passed and I
became dimly aware that, however hard we tried,
rushing from region to region, some stupid, cruel power
emanating from Moscow was simply forcing us to do
things in ways that were more and more painful. In 1933
they clobbered us with a wheat procurement plan on
such a scale that even with the aid of the G.P.U. we
could only gather forty per cent, and had to stop.
Impossible to get more! Another twenty per cent, and all
the peasants would have died. The President of the
Inspection Committee, as well as the Secretary of the
Regional Committee, wrote a report and . . . of course a
month later they were both shot for being reactionary.

VOROTYNTSEV: I don't mind hearing this.

RUBLYOV: It was just at that time that an invitation came

into our regional executive committee for a representative
to attend a celebration of the 15th anniversary of the
local Infantry Division, which was formed in our area
during the Civil War. I was chosen to go. Two hotels
were allocated for the guests. Carpets, ormolu. At every
turn there were officers with attendants, clanking their
spurs, their leather belts creaking. The doors to the
banquet were flung open: "You're invited to come in" –
they nearly added: "Officers and Gentlemen". There
were guests from Moscow, four top brass among them.
Crystal glass. Silver. Exotic wines. Pastry as light as air.
Silent footmen. Well, well, I thought to myself, that's
after fifteen years. What will it be like after thirty?

VOROTYNTSEV: Most amusing.

RUBLYOV: After supper, there was a dance in the ballroom
of the former Club of the Nobility. Invitation by ticket
only, of course. Motor cars drove up to the entrance, *hoi
polloi* rubber-necking, the militia dispersing the crowd.
(*He sighs.*) It was then that I saw the medic was right –
there is no pulse . . . And the enemy, where is he? We
used to think that you were the enemy. But those who
sent us directives, who are they? There I sat in all the
glitter, thinking of our starving little villages, who never
delivered sufficient grain – I thought of Cherepinikha, of
Kvasnikovka . . .

VOROTYNTSEV (*gently*): Why then, after that evening,
didn't you try to stand up for Kvasnikovka . . .

RUBLYOV: How was one to do it? Write a report to the
Central Committee? That meant – to get arrested and to
shoot oneself. As I said, some did and they were
liquidated . . . It was after that evening that I decided to
flee the villages.

VOROTYNTSEV: Into the "Organisations".

RUBLYOV: The "Organisations" turned up. (*A pause.*) I'm
no saint. My arms aren't strong enough to protect
everybody.

VOROTYNTSEV: That's a pity. I too . . . well, all of us,

while we were in clover, argued like that and, while we argued like that, God took our souls away. You were asking about my secret. I'm going to give it to you. Stop being an executioner, lose everything and your eyes will begin to shine.

RUBLYOV: Is that all?

VOROTYNTSEV: That is all.

RUBLYOV: A bit too late to start now. And I'm not altogether convinced . . .

VOROTYNTSEV: It may not be too late.

RUBLYOV: Yes, I see, you're about to start your sermon: give up your last shirt, turn the other cheek . . . (*Reviving.*) Do you really think that I will concede that those who made the Revolution were rogues? You never saw those people, but I knew them personally. What right have you to call them that? The famous Muralov was the secretary of the Party Committee in the Temiryaz Academy. He was among the leaders. Ten years after the Revolution I visited him in his flat – all he had was ten square metres. The maximum allowed by the Party. And not a penny from anywhere.

VOROTYNTSEV: But the official distributors must have seen to it that he had ten times more than a worker, surely?

RUBLYOV: There was a threadbare and heavily darned tablecloth and jacket potatoes for supper. Just tell me, did your miserable Nicholas have ministers of such moral purity? At a Party discussion, Muralov spoke up for the Trotsky opposition. The regional committee instructed us to heckle, to stop him speaking. We were in the majority. But we listened to him for two hours in silence, out of sheer sympathy towards him personally, out of acute pain on his behalf. Oh dear! Did we get into trouble after that! . . . Going into exile, he took nothing with him – there was nothing to take, except a shotgun and a dog. Let me tell you something nobody else knows. I went to say goodbye to him. "Keep your head high, Prokhor," he told me. "A forest doesn't weep over

224

one tree. If people like you begin to droop – there'll be
no one left. We started it, it's up to you to carry it
through. Look after the Party! Take care of the
Revolution!"

VOROTYNTSEV: You've achieved that all right, thanks very
much! You've undermined it to an extent that no so-
called reaction could have managed in twenty years.
Someone once said that you need a Revolution to kill off
revolutionaries.

RUBLYOV: You seem to have learnt a thing or two, now.
But, earlier on, if it weren't for the Revolution, how
could one have got through to the thick skulls of the
ultra-reactionaries. How else could we have penetrated
the minds of your Rodziankos[16] or Tereshchenkos[17] and
proved to them that the time's come to give in?
A knock on the door.

WAITRESS (*in the doorway*): Permission to enter, Comrade
Colonel?
RUBLYOV *nods. A number of girls, wearing aprons, enter.*
The first one spreads a tablecloth and takes trays from the
hands of others. There is wine. They go out silently during
VOROTYNTSEV'*s speech. It is obvious that the smell of food*
is unpleasant for RUBLYOV.

VOROTYNTSEV: As for that rotter Tereshchenko, I'm no
more enamoured of the man than you are. You, with
your Soviet mentality, lump together everybody who's
not a Bolshevik. You could have learnt a thing or two by
now. As to "giving in" – you're quite right. The whole
of world history would have been different had people
learnt this one thing – how to give in from time to time.
Would you like me to make a funeral oration over your
Revolution? Seriously. The Revolution was very useful to
the whole of humanity. Those in power, the rich, are
very prone to forget some things. It reminded them that
an *abyss* exists. Even in the West they've grasped this.
Just look how many socialisms have cropped up: Social-
Fascism, National-Socialism, Social-Falangism, Radical-

Socialism, Social-Catholicism – enough to get your
tongue twisted. The only party in the world, don't you
see, that dares to call itself conservative, is the party of
Churchill. The great multitude of others elbow each
other out in order to prove that they are for Progress, for
Democracy, for the rights of the ordinary man. Whatever
could be sweetened, has been sweetened: wherever they
could give in, they did so. Who won? The French, and
the Americans, the Greeks and the Italians, the Indians
and the Zulus – you can cheer up – everybody won, with
the exception of the Russian people. Having once
shielded Europe with their flesh and blood from the
Mongol whirlwind, they have done so for the second
time from the hurricane of Communism. Cheer, Colonel
Rublyov, why don't you cheer?

RUBLYOV: I'm quite cheerful. I'm happy, can't you see? It
was I, after all, who invited you to this cheerful supper
for the dying. We will uncork a bottle and drink a few
carefree toasts.

VOROTYNTSEV: The horror is that you grieve over the fate
of a few hundred Party dogmatists, but you care nothing
about twelve million hapless peasants, ruined and exiled
into the Tundra. The flower, the spirit of an annihilated
nation do not exude curses on your conscience. You lose
no sleep over the hatred which you have inflamed against
the Russians in the Baltic provinces, on the Oder, the
Visla and the Danube!

RUBLYOV: You'd have made an excellent Prosecutor! I will
drop everything and write at once to petition the Appeal
Court, Devil take it. You never know, they might even
pardon you. (*He is all contorted by pain. Eventually he
straightens up.*) I would like to have seen you dealing with
this cursed job, these superhuman duties, had you got as
far as my office. There's a very fine dividing line between
a hero and a prison warder. Today your eyes shine and
you are walking nobly out to your death for the sake of a
lost cause, but had history developed differently, it

would have been my eyes that would have shone and I would have called you an executioner with some justification, while you'd have said – fifteen days' solitary. True, isn't it?

VOROTYNTSEV: You are blinded by your own myths. Our Government never had anything approaching your Counter-Intelligence.

RUBLYOV (*pouring wine into glasses*): Well, all right. You will have supper with me?

VOROTYNTSEV (*shying away*): Not for anything in the world!

RUBLYOV: What Asiatic barbarism! And it's you who accuse us of Party narrow-mindedness! This duck isn't to blame, just because it was roasted by our cook and not yours. You've been starving for half a year. Do sit down.

VOROTYNTSEV: I wasn't starving on my own.

RUBLYOV: Well, I can't feed the lot.

VOROTYNTSEV: Such old arguments. Will you let me go back to my cell?

RUBLYOV: Oh do sit down! (*He offers him a phial.*) Can you read Latin?

VOROTYNTSEV (*reading*): *Venenum.* A poison. (*He returns it.*)

RUBLYOV: Death by hanging is a terrible thing! Have you ever seen it? The hanged man is convulsed for a long time, as if dancing, his arms separately, his legs separately, after which each muscle, each sinew, contracts all on its own. You're a soldier, of course. There's little difference. (*He pours the poison into both glasses.*) Let's share it. There's enough for two. (VOROTYNTSEV *hesitates.*) Let's go, the pair of us. To the other side! (*He moves the glasses nearer to himself and to* VOROTYNTSEV. VOROTYNTSEV *sits at the table holding his glass and is silent.* RUBLYOV *speaks very simply.*) To be honest, I'm frightened to do it by myself. Frightened. While together – it's not so bad. We'll be gazing at each other as we drink. It'll burn inside for a few minutes and . . . Why drag it out? (*He attempts to clink glasses.* VOROTYNTSEV *remains silent.*) Let's clink glasses and we'll crawl under the table on all fours. Afraid as well? Or are you thinking you might get a pardon?

VOROTYNTSEV: No. I'm not thinking that.

RUBLYOV: Then, consider. Is it better to have your head put through a noose? . . . Death makes us equal. Courage! Your health, Colonel! (*He lifts his glass.*)

VOROTYNTSEV: It's a strange thing. You've caught me unawares. I was prepared for anything, but not this . . . A pardon? No, I'm not expecting that. I know I'll be executed.

RUBLYOV: Maybe you're thinking that in a couple of days there'll be a change, is that it? That we will be overturned?

VOROTYNTSEV: Alas, no! It is now entrenched for a long time. The only chance we had, the Second World War, we let slip. Now, you'll be on our backs for at least another twenty-five years. Europe is laid so low, it'll be a long time before it will rise again. It was weak towards you as far back as 1919. (*A pause.*) I don't understand it myself. Why is it that I'm prepared and yet not prepared? When I was being taken prisoner, if I'd had my gun – the English tricked me into giving it up – I could have finished it all. And I would have done so unhesitatingly. So why not now? (*He strides about the room, talking mainly to himself.*) Is there someone I haven't said goodbye to? My family? Long ago. To the inmates? Have I failed to say something that matters? That could . . . for somebody, later on . . . It looks as if being in prison brings its own new obligations. (*More loudly.*) Do you know, each extra day during which I can be of service . . . do some Good . . .

RUBLYOV (*still sitting in the same place*): There you go again, like a schoolboy. Good and Evil. Black and White. Grey-brown-purple! You can't grasp them; you can't see them.

It's all twisted up and nobody can disentangle it. You're
scared, eh? Why don't you admit it. It would seem,
then, that I'm braver, after all.

VOROTYNTSEV (*hesitating again*): I'm . . . not . . . sure . . .

RUBLYOV: I'm younger, you know. It's more bitter for me
to die. But I don't want to go on suffering . . . It would
have been a good end, eh, Colonel?

VOROTYNTSEV (*looking at him, at the table, at the poison,
with renewed surprise*): It's a very strange thing, ye-es. It
can't be out of religious considerations: after all, I was
quite prepared to shoot myself. And if death is so close
. . . why not a little sooner? No. I can't do it. I refuse.
(*A pause.*) Perhaps it's this: you kidnapped Kutepov[18] –
so what have you done with him? You've probably
hanged him. And Kutepov was a friend of mine. Well,
then, hang me too. Just wait, it'll be your turn for the
noose soon enough.

RUBLYOV (*reaching for his telephone*): Hullo. Take him away
from here into one hundred and twenty-five. (*He replaces
the receiver.*) First you were in charge; then we were; a
third lot will come along – and the people will remain
dissatisfied and oppressed: nothing go-od will ever
happen!

VOROTYNTSEV: Do you know, many years ago in
Manchuria an old Chinaman predicted that I would die a
soldier's death in 1945. I remembered it all this time. It
helped me to be more courageous in previous wars. But
as this one was coming to its end, I expected to die every
day, but I lived on. The war ended. But now I'm faced
with death from an enemy *after* the war. I suppose it's
also a soldier's death. It's from an enemy hand. But –
self-inflicted? No, that lacks dignity. That's not soldierly.
That, indeed, would be cowardly. And then, why relieve
you of one more murder? Why take it upon myself? No,
let this, too, be your responsibility.

A guard appears in the doorway. With a wave of his hand
RUBLYOV *indicates that* VOROTYNTSEV *should be*

*removed. Straightening himself up as an officer, his hands
behind his back,* VOROTYNTSEV *leaves.* RUBLYOV,
*holding his glass of poison, tries, in a croaking voice, to sing
the International.*

RUBLYOV: Upon us too the sun will shine.
          Its brilliant warming rays . . .

Scene 12

*Before the curtain rises, one can hear soft singing, in harmony,
from the stage.*
Ding-dong, ding-dong, that's the clang of fetters,
Ding-dong, ding-dong, chain-gangs march and clatter . . .
*The curtain rises. It is evening, the window in the cell is dark.
A smoky oil lamp on a little shelf is about to go out.*
MEDNIKOV *is asleep by the slop bucket. Next to him,*
BOLOSNIN *and* GAI *are talking. Further back,*
MOSTOVSHCHIKOV *is telling something to a group around him,
consisting of* PRYANCHIKOV *and two newcomers: a*
PRISONER IN HORN-RIMMED SPECTACLES *and a*
PRISONER WITH A GOATEE BEARD. *To the right,
downstage,* KULYBYSHEV, KLIMOV *and* PECHKUROV, *sit
with their legs tucked under them and sing under* RUBIN's
direction. There is no one else in the cell.
   RUBIN's *choir sings:*
Ding-dong, ding-dong, we march to labour camps
Ding-dong, ding-dong, we're wretched lonely tramps
They continue singing, but soundlessly.
(The rest of the scene, in the original Russian, is in verse.)
MOSTOVSHCHIKOV: Whether we fuse the light elements, or
   split heavy uranium, bombs will soon throw the crust of
   continents upwards in the form of fountains ten
   kilometres high. But even that does not transgress the
   limits, compared to what we would do if we allowed the
   chain reaction to escape, like a fairy-tale dragon from its

230

cave. It will be too late, when we break through the
atmosphere or crack the earth's crust. The moment we
disturb the all-pervading nitrogen or upset the peaceful
stillness of silicon, we shall be unable, like Goethe's
sorcerer's apprentice, to contain the cataclysm.

PRYANCHIKOV (*jumping up*): No need to worry,
gentlemen. There won't be time to blow up our planet.
Did you know that our Sun is a "new star"? That means
that the Sun's yellow ball can explode in the twinkling of
an eye and a fireball of a hundred thousand degrees will
burn up both freedom in the West and the labour camps
in the East!

MOSTOVSHCHIKOV: Hasn't the time come for us,
scientists, to form a World Government? Can't you see
how, like Hamlet and Laertes, East and West have
exchanged swords? After so many centuries, humanity
should not be condemned to living in hovels. But the
White House will strike the Bolsheviks with the sword
poisoned by the venom of the International. And the
crazed, wild Soviets, summoning us back to the Dark
Ages, into forests and animal skins, cling all the same to
the broken edifice of Sovereignty. Thus, in a couple of
decades, the culmination of centuries . . .
The hatch is being opened.

8TH SUPERVISOR: Mednikov. Without belongings!
There is a momentary silence in the cell. MEDNIKOV
*shudders, lifts his head, looks around, dazed. There is a
movement in the cell, an offer of help, as it were. The door
is already open.* MEDNIKOV *rises to his knees uncertainly.
Leaning on* BOLOSNIN *and* GAI, *he gets up and, with his
hands behind his back, moves submissively into the corridor.*

RUBIN's *choir sings:*
Ding-dong, ding-dong, that's the clang of fetters,
Ding-dong, ding-dong, chain-gangs march and clatter.

Ding-dong, ding-dong, we march to labour camps,
Ding-dong, ding-dong, we're wretched lonely tramps.

Prisoners

The door is shut behind MEDNIKOV. *The group at the back of the stage has broken up.* MOSTOVSHCHIKOV *and the* PRISONER WITH A GOATEE BEARD *are standing and try to walk about the cell.*

MOSTOVSHCHIKOV: You wake up in the morning, sluggish from the straw, the stench, the numbness. The brain seizes up from a depressing lack of sleep. But towards the evening you get flashes of thought; your imagination is fired, you feel light, weightless, some kind of Nirvana, you know . . . It's strange.

PRISONER WITH A GOATEE BEARD: You find it strange. Not at all. The human spirit is not to be claimed by the flesh. Mahatma Gandhi fasted for ninety days! We get our rations, our prison soup, after all. We may occasionally become despondent, we may droop, and lose our faith and not know what to do, and yet our vitality, our spiritual strength, which gives us wing, is inexhaustible! I used to live full of pride and self-admiration, as if drunk with the love of life; and it is only the nocturnal shadows of prison that have revealed to me the true meaning of life . . . In freedom we are far too well fed, we are too greedy, too noisy, too quick . . . We learn the flavour of life for the first time only when we get thin prison soup and sleep on rotten straw.

BOLOSNIN (*to* GAI): We were the only ones who could have stood up in defence of a tired Europe, but in their mad ignorance they sold us – not for material gain, not for barter – but to appease Stalin's insatiable maw. The Americans sold us in Bavaria, and the English this very May hurried to betray us on the Danube. In the Russian Liberation Army there were splendid fighters, the Russian Corps, and those Cossacks after Cossacks . . . They'd seen it all in the war, they'd read all the propaganda and they'd reached the end of the line, the limit of their trust; they were ready to go anywhere – to the Devil himself, to Venus, to Caledonia, to become galley slaves – so long as it wasn't the Soviet Union!!!

. . . And those Britons, who "never, never shall be slaves" didn't overlook us. They lured our arms out of us and issued an order: all the officers are to attend a conference in Judenburg, in the English zone. I don't think that even the Ottoman Turks would have fed Christians to the dogs. Not suspecting a thing, we went trustingly, while the English left quietly by night! . . .

RUBIN (*humming to himself*): "Night is black, night is black Like a treacherous deed,
Like a tyrant's untrustworthy soul . . ."

PECHKUROV: What sort of song is that? Let's belt it out.

RUBIN: I don't feel up to it, friends. Tomorrow . . . Even the lamp is going out.

The lamp flickers. The scene is now dimly lit by arc lights.

KLIMOV (*patting* RUBIN *on the shoulder*): It hurts me to listen to you, Major. You keep on saying you're a Communist – the Devil you are! You quarrel with the bastards and are quite cheerful when you are with us . . .

RUBIN: I'd rather not have such praise, Peter . . . (*He stretches out on the straw, motionless.*)

BOLOSNIN: Leafy suburbs . . . Acacia in white cascades . . . A bridge over the river. We drove up. Half-surrounded by tommy-guns. Red stars on their caps . . . Friends! We've been betrayed . . . Give us our arms! Return our arms to us! Ill-fated Russians, accursed Russian fate. Shoot oneself – there's nothing to shoot oneself with . . . It's all over . . . Pushed back as through a funnel, but they call out our names from a list . . . And someone, in his despair, jumps off the parapet on to the stones below.

The door opens with a crash. VOROTYNTSEV *enters, holding himself very erect, very solemn.*

KLIMOV: Oh Colonel!

PECHKUROV: Who did you have to see?

VOROTYNTSEV (*after a pause*): This, my sons, is our last evening. The tribunal is tomorrow. (*A pause. He embraces* KLIMOV *and* PECHKUROV, *who have come up to him.*) Days pass and everyone's turn comes. We were close, but they will scatter us far and wide . . . A new lot will be pushed in here . . .

PRISONER WITH HORN-RIMMED SPECTACLES: A holy place is never empty.

The lamp has finally gone out. The corners of the cell are quite black. People are lit dimly.

VOROTYNTSEV: Before winter comes, where will we all be? In which lairs to hide from freezing snowstorms? Will we be cutting up pine logs in Pechora? Or transporting the produce of the Kolyma?

BOLOSNIN (*standing up*): I will not believe that all that's left of us in this world is the dignified acceptance of hard labour in the depths of Siberian mines. Perhaps, if our great grandfathers' lives ended in Siberia, their great-grandsons will start theirs there.

VOROTYNTSEV: This belief must give you strength, yes! And, Friends, do not expect any help from the West. Prosperous countries have no will to resist, they have no strength, no conception, no understanding, no . . . even when disaster stares them in the face. The hope of the world lies with you, the convicts. All of it is up to you! Maybe Russia, that has borne so much, has been waiting for people like you.

The arc lights which have been spotlighting the prisoners become gradually bronze in colour. Each prisoner, either speaking for the last time, or in silence, moves to form a group sculpture. RUBIN, *who is lying down leaning on one arm, and* MOSTOVSHCHIKOV, *who is leaning against the wall, are also motionless.*

KULYBYSHEV: Ten years. Fifteen. Twenty-five.

PRISONER WITH A GOATEE BEARD: We're strong because we've nothing to lose.

PECHKUROV: Because, one way or another, we must all die.

GAI: But should we rebel – there's a noose. There's no turning back.

Scene 12

KLIMOV: There will not be an angrier soldier against Stalin.

VOROTYNTSEV: Not to have to bear the shameful
disgrace . . .

BOLOSNIN: Of a labour-camp brand of slavery.

KLIMOV: Come on, snow-covered Pechora, let's feel your
breath!

GAI: And you, Kolyma, straighten your shoulders!

*The bronze light gradually fades. The sculptured group is
motionless. Somewhere near, just beyond the window, there is
the mournful howling of guard dogs, which was heard at the
beginning of the play. Both the stage and the auditorium
grow dark.*

PECHKUROV'S VOICE: Every midnight, howling, howling
of the dogs. Who are they howling for?

VOROTYNTSEV'S VOICE: "Never send to know for whom
the dogs howl; they howl for thee."

The disjointed howling of the dogs grows ever louder.

1952–1953
Ekibastuz, Kok-Terek
during *gang-work*
orally

TRANSLATORS' NOTES

1. Supervisors were, and still are, part of the complex and oppressive Soviet system of supervision.
2. Stalin.
3. "Decembrists" who rebelled in 1825 and were sent to Siberia.
4. Ivan Susanin: a peasant who, in 1612, saved the life of the newly elected Tsar Michael Romanov; hero of Glinka's opera *A Life for the Tsar*.
5. A reference to Pushkin's poem *The Bronze Horseman*.
6. "The Bell": a periodical edited by Herzen and Ogaryov, in London, then in Geneva, 1857–67. "It was the first systematic instrument of revolutionary propaganda directed against the Russian autocracy written with knowledge, sincerity and mordant eloquence." Professor Sir Isaiah Berlin.
7. Batiy: Tatar Kahn who, in 1252, subjugated South Russia and set up his "Golden Horde".
8. A. A. Vlasov: General in the Red Army, taken prisoner by the Germans in 1942. Agreed to head the Russian Liberation Army (*c.* one-million-strong). Executed as a traitor by the Russians in 1946.
9. Russian Liberation Army: set up under the aegis of the Wehrmacht, headed by General Vlasov and consisting of Soviet prisoners of war and White émigrés in the hope of liberating Russia from Bolshevik rule.
10. Taborites=Hussites.
11. Vyshinsky (1883–1954): Foreign Minister, U.N. Delegate.
12. Beria (1899–?): Commissar for Internal Affairs, Deputy Prime Minister, disappeared after 1953 (the year of Stalin's death).
13. Stolypin, P. A. (1863–1911): Minister of Internal Affairs. Introduced agricultural reforms to help the peasantry.

14. Kerensky, A. F. (1881–1970): Member of the Fourth Duma, Premier of the Provisional Government.
15. Denikin, A. I. (1872–1947): Lieutenant-General, Commander of the White Army's South-Western Front in 1917.
16. Rodzianko, M. V. (1859–1924): President of the Third and Fourth Dumas.
17. Tereshchenko, M. I. (1888–1958): Minister of Finance and Foreign Affairs in the Provisional Government.
18. Kutepov (1882–?): Emigré White General allegedly kidnapped by the Soviets in Paris in the thirties.

THE LOVE-GIRL AND
THE INNOCENT

Translated from the Russian
by Nicholas Bethell and David Burg

DRAMATIS PERSONAE

Prisoners

RODION NEMOV, recently an officer in the front line
PAVEL GAI, another officer, gang leader of the bricklayers
LYUBA NYEGNEVITSKAYA
GRANYA (AGRAFENA) ZYBINA
BORIS KHOMICH
TIMOFEY MERESHCHUN, doctor in the camp living area
NIKOLAY YAKHIMCHUK ⎫
MAKAR MUNITSA   ⎬ foundrymen
GRISHKA CHEGENYOV ⎭
DIMKA, fourteen years old
CHMUTA, gang leader of the plasterers
KOSTYA, work allocator
POSOSHKOV, prisoner in charge of the camp living area
BELOBOTNIKOV, a clerk
DOROFEYEV, rate-fixer for prisoners' productivity
ZINA, a typist, Pososhkov's camp "wife"
CAMILLE GONTOIR, a Belgian
SHUROCHKA SOYMINA
BELLA
1ST GIRL STUDENT
2ND GIRL STUDENT
GOLDTOOTH ⎫
GEORGIE   ⎬ professional crooks
LENNIE   ⎭
ZHENKA, who sings tenor
VITKA, the compère
AGA-MIRZA, doctor's assistant in the camp living area
ANGEL, orderly working in the works and planning
    department
BATH ORDERLY
HEAD COOK, working in the camp living area

241

1ST, 2ND, 3RD, and 4TH WOMEN FROM THE NEW
    TRANSPORT
1ST, 2ND, 3RD and 4TH BRICKLAYERS
1ST, 2ND and 3RD GANG LEADERS
FIRST "GONER"
A "GONER" who carries a mess-tin
A "DRUDGE" PRISONER, from Chmuta's gang

Free Men

KAPLYUZHNIKOV, chief engineer in the camp complex
ARNOLD YEFIMOVICH GURVICH, senior works manager at
    the construction site
VASILI ONUFREVICH BRYLOV, foundry manager
FOMIN, a foreman
1ST and 2ND FOREMEN
SENIOR FOREMAN, in the machine-shop
SMITH FOREMAN

Camp Guards

LIEUTENANT OVCHUKHOV, the camp commandant
JUNIOR SERGEANT KOLODEY, a senior warder
A WARDRESS, with a long mane of hair
VISITING WARDER, from the timber-felling camp
ESCORT-GUARD SERGEANT

Other Characters

"Drudge" prisoners. Gang leaders. "Skivers". Actors from
the camp's Culture and Education Department. Warders.
Check-point guards. Escort-guards. Watch-tower sentries.

*The action of the play takes place in the autumn of 1945. An
interval of a few days is presumed to have elapsed between each
act.*

The audience will walk from a brightly lit foyer into the darkened auditorium. In here the only light comes from a number of tinplate hooded lanterns which are placed, almost like crowns, on a semicircle of posts right along the edge of the orchestra pit. The posts are quite low, so as not to interfere with the audience's view of the stage. They are wrapped with barbed wire which vanishes down into the orchestra pit. The centre post carries an indicator to mark the dividing point in the field of observation from the two nearest watch-towers.

There are two camp watch-towers standing to the right and to the left of the arch of the stage. Throughout the play the towers are manned by sentries.

The curtain rises. It is an ordinary theatre curtain, but is not used again until the end of the play. Behind it there is a second curtain – a length of fabric crudely painted with a poster-like industrial landscape, depicting cheerful, apple-cheeked, muscular men and women working away quite effortlessly. In one corner of the curtain a joyful procession is in progress complete with flowers, children and a portrait of Stalin.

To start the show a loudspeaker plays a lively melody from a concertina. It is the march from the film "The Jolly Fellows".

As the curtain is raised the melody is taken up by an actual concertina-player, sitting quite far back in the stage by the camp gates.

Behind the curtain one can hear the harsh sound of a crowbar banged against a metal rail.

The camp zone lanterns go out. They are not re-lit until the last scene of the play.

ACT I

Scene 1

Work Parade

It is morning. The sun is about to rise. White autumn hoar frost is gleaming on the roofs of the prisoners' barrack huts.

The front of the stage shows part of the camp zone, the inside area of the camp. Further back stage there is a barbed wire barrier where the camp zone becomes the forward zone. There are two gates in it: a high gate in the camp zone barrier, a low gate in the forward zone barrier. To the right of the gate there is a sentry-box made of wooden planks, which is a check-point. Further back still behind the barrier, there is a work area. There is a tall brick building still under construction with a "pioneer"-type crane towering over it, and some portable scaffolding used by the plasterers. There are also a smithy, a foundry with smoke coming out of its chimney and various other auxiliary buildings.

On the left is the work-detail parade area, crossing the stage diagonally towards the check-point box. The area is full of prisoners, both men and women, wearing ragged, dirty jackets. Some of the women are wearing skirts over their quilted trousers. On one side of the gate stands the check-point guard, while on the other side stands KOSTYA, *the work allocator, an apple-cheeked man who looks like a prize fighter. They are letting the prisoners out in ranks of five, tapping the last in each group on the back with a hardboard plank they use for counting. The work detail looks almost like a military parade, with the gang leaders reporting the numbers of gangs and the numbers of people in them when their names are called by the work allocator. Once out of the gate, the formation breaks up into disorder and conversation. Everyone looks sluggish and depressed. The only thing that happens is a bit of horse-play between* CHEGENYOV

and DIMKA. *One prisoner bends down to tie up his shoes,
another takes a final bite of his morning bread ration, a third
huddles himself up with cold. Right at the end of the queue come
production department "skivers". They stand out from the others
because they are more neatly dressed. Among them are* ZINA, *the
typist, in a chic dress, and* DOROFEYEV, *the rate-fixer, who is
squat and fat. The concertina-player is sitting on a stool by the
gate, all the time playing the march from the film "The Jolly
Fellows", lazily and with interruptions. On one side of the
queue stands* AGA-MIRZA, *the swarthy doctor's assistant,
wearing a white coat. On the ground at his feet sits the* FIRST
"GONER". *A "goner" is a man whom camp life has brought to
the end of his tether.*

*To the right of the stage there is one corner of a standard
barrack-hut, its length disappearing into the wings. At the side of
the hut stands a post, a metal rail hanging from it on a wire.
Beside the post stand* KOLODEY, *a squat warder, and* NEMOV,
*a tall man wearing high boots and a long officer's greatcoat, still
new but without badges of rank. Both men are watching the
parade.*

*On the left of the stage the corner of another hut juts out from
the wings. In its front wall is a small door with a pair of steps
leading down towards the audience. Further forward still there is
a carefully painted box made of wooden boards, marked
"Garbage" and covered with a lid.*

*On the walls of the huts as well as on hoardings scattered over
the camp zone there are posters with such slogans as "Work
ennobles man", "Instead of the onerous burden it was under
Capitalism, work has become a matter of honour, of glory, of
valour and heroism – Stalin", "He who does not work does not
eat".*

*One sees the gangs in the work area dispersing as soon as they
pass through the gates. Towards the end of the scene they start
their work.*

CHECK-POINT GUARD: Join arms! (*Counts the ranks of
    five.*) One! Two! Three!

KOSTYA (*loudly*): Come on, number five hut, wake your

ideas up! I haven't taken my stick to you lately, have I? Don't worry, I'll be there!

More "drudge" prisoners rush out towards the parade area.

YAKHIMCHUK: (*He is at the check-point. He has a slight foreign accent.*) Chegenyov! You crook!

CHEGENYOV (*he wears his cap on one side, like a hooligan*): Yessir! Crook reporting, sir! (*Hurries to catch up with his work gang.*)

YAKHIMCHUK: Short-arse!

DIMKA: Sir! Short-arse on parade, sir! (*Catches the others up.*)

DOROFEYEV (*leaves formation and comes up to* NEMOV): Nemov, I want to talk to you . . .

KOLODEY: Hey you! Were you in the army?

DOROFEYEV: Come on, sergeant, we're not in the army now . . .

KOLODEY: Shut your mouth! In here's *smarter* than in the army. Get your hat off!

DOROFEYEV (*bares his bald head*): Citizen senior warder junior sergeant Kolodey! Request permission to address production chief prisoner Nemov, sir!

KOLODEY: Tha-at's better, do it like that next time. Permission refused!

DOROFEYEV *walks away.* NEMOV *follows him towards the formations, where they talk.*

AGA-MIRZA: Let's have it then.

FIRST "GONER" *has a thermometer under his arm.*

FIRST "GONER": It's supposed to stay in ten minutes, doctor.

AGA-MIRZA: Wise guy! You know your rights, do you? How long have you been like that? (*Takes the thermometer.*) Normal. Get out and work!

FIRST "GONER" (*does not get up off the ground*): Please, doctor, I spent all night in the latrines . . .

AGA-MIRZA: And before that all evening in the kitchen, isn't that so? Think I'm soft, do you? Bastard! (*Makes as if to strike him. The other gets up hurriedly.*) Sergeant! I've

247

got a shirker here, says he won't work. What do I do
with him?

KOLODEY: Put him in the cooler, what do you think?

*AGA-MIRZA gives the "goner" a kick. He limps off after
his work gang. Another check-point guard calls* KOLODEY
to the right. Exit KOLODEY. *By the gates a concertina is
still lazily sighing. Voices emerge from the queue of men and
women going out to work.*

VOICE: Look at Zinka's new skirt. Whore! That's
Maruska's skirt. The head prisoner took it off her when
she was posted.

VOICE: That's it, girls. Shacking up with the boss, that's
what I call life. (*She sings.*)

> I loved a gang leader,
> The camp boss liked me best,
> I slept with the work-clerk
> to feather my nest!

VOICE: Well, that's that, that's our rations for today.

VOICE: Minimum issue, that won't go far. Bloody gang
leader took a whole kilo for him and his girl. Little tart,
wiggling her bottom.

VOICE: Hey, boss, my shoes are bust. Look, they're bust.
What do I wear to work?

VOICE: I'll see you get some horseshoes tomorrow. Best
tyre rubber.

The work detail is coming to an end. MERESHCHUN, *a
fat, thick-set fellow, comes out on to the steps of the front
hut, stretching himself. He is still only half dressed.* AGA-
MIRZA *comes up to him.*

AGA-MIRZA: Good morning, doctor, sir.

MERESHCHUN: O-o-h! God knows why I woke up so early
this morning. I can't sleep without a woman.

AGA-MIRZA: You did it yourself, sir. You told her to get
lost.

MERESHCHUN: I'd had enough of her, the shit-bag. Well,
what's new in the hospital? Have they scrubbed the
floors?

AGA-MIRZA: I had the men up all night polishing them.
They're like a new pin.

MERESHCHUN: They'd better be! And another thing: I
don't wan't to find any crumbs in the bedside tables . . .
don't say I didn't warn you.

AGA-MIRZA: Valka's going to die today.

MERESHCHUN: What about Matveyev?

AGA-MIRZA: He turned his toes up. He's in the morgue.

MERESHCHUN: No wonder, falling from a height like that
. . . And mind you make sure all the sheets are tucked
in. (*He looks over to the right.*) Now what's going on? A
new transport?

*Behind their backs from the left enter the "goner" with a
mess-tin, making his way stealthily towards the dustbin. He
is wearing a jacket cut out of an army greatcoat, tied round
with a piece of rope. Behind him a German soldier's mess-tin
hangs lidless from the rope by the handle. The "goner" opens
the dustbin, rummages around in it, picks out some food and
puts it in the tin.*

    *The work parade is now finished, the gates have been
closed. The dawn sun is playing against the upper brickwork
of the construction site. The work allocator and check-point
guard check the count, each with his own counting board.
The allocator is explaining something to the guard. From the
right enter* KOLODEY, *in his hand a couple of pieces of
paper, behind him the chugging noise of a lorry approaching.*

KOLODEY: Hello! Anyone around! Production chief
Nemov, over here! (*To someone or other.*) Get the head
prisoner and the . . . what's he called? . . . the bath
orderly.

The prisoner he was addressing runs off.

Here now . . . read this. (*He hands* NEMOV *the papers.*)
There's a new transport.

NEMOV: How many? (*He is reading.*)

KOLODEY: Four lorry-loads. Here comes number one.

*A high-sided three-ton lorry backs slowly from the right on to
the stage. It looks empty except for two machine-gunners who*

249

*are standing inside the lorry, towards the front of it,
separated off by a grill. They jump down from the lorry and
walk off.*

NEMOV: Here's their ration order. They've had their rations
up to the eighteenth of the month.

KOLODEY: That's today. Good! We don't have to feed
them. What else?

NEMOV: We might give them some soup . . .

KOLODEY: Soup? What do you mean? Soup costs money.
Make sure they go out to work, though.

NEMOV: Today?

KOLODEY: Yes, today. They can chip in and help our
figures.
*The driver opens the back flap of the lorry. The escort-guard
sergeant emerges from the cab carrying a stack of prisoners'
files.*

NEMOV: But citizen commander, first we have to sort them
out: list them by professions, assign them to gangs. Then
there are more lists of . . .

KOLODEY: Look, don't be a fool. They're here in the
morning, right? But by evening they may be out in the
forest chopping trees. Let them do their stint while
they're here. I'm not like your other guards, there's no
skiving when I'm on duty. Get twenty prisoners
together, one man in charge, and quick march, left right!
Otherwise the commandant'll be back and he'll have your
guts for garters. (*Walks up to the lorry.*) Get out, you lot.
*The prisoners begin to rise to their feet. They have been
sitting on the floor and therefore invisible, concealed by the
high sides of the lorry. Carrying their belongings, they jump
down to the ground and walk about to stretch their legs.*
Stop walking! Sit down!
SHUROCHKA, *a young lady wearing a bright city hat, sits
down on her suitcase instead of on the ground like the rest of
the prisoners. She towers over them. Suddenly* KOLODEY
comes alive, runs up to her and kicks a hole in her suitcase.
Sit down!

SHUROCHKA *sits down on the ground. The bath orderly appears from the left. He is a well-fed red-faced man.*

BATH ORDERLY: Citizen commander, bath orderly reporting, sir.

KOLODEY: Good, now let's see. I suppose there's no underwear, is there?

BATH ORDERLY (*in amazement*): Underwear?

KOLODEY: What about soap?

BATH ORDERLY: They never brought it.

KOLODEY: There *is* water, isn't there?

BATH ORDERLY: Water? Who says there's water? It's turned off at the main.

KOLODEY: Hm-mmm.

AGA-MIRZA: So much the better, citizen sergeant. Won't take so long to wash them.

KOLODEY: You're right there. (*To the bath orderly.*) Just stoke up the hot-house, right? Stoke it up hot. How about that, doctor? It doesn't matter if there's no water, does it?

MERESHCHUN: No—oo. (*To the prisoners.*) How many days' journey?

VOICE: Over a week.

MERESHCHUN: No, that's all right, don't bother.
The bath orderly has trotted off. About thirty prisoners are now on stage from off the lorry, which has been driven away to the right.

NEMOV (*looking carefully at the new arrivals*): What's your name?

KHOMICH:(*Gets to his feet. He is wearing a bright red jumper.*) Engineer Khomich.

NEMOV: Engineer – I thought so. You'll be prisoner in charge of the men's gang. Make a list of names and give it to me.

KHOMICH: Yes, sir.

NEMOV (*inspecting the women equally attentively*): What's *your* name?

GRANYA (*she sits up*): Zybina.

NEMOV: You're in charge of the women. (*Murmuring among the women.*) What's the matter?

A WOMAN: He's got X-ray eyes.

2ND WOMAN: She was gang leader back in the old camp.

NEMOV: Why, are you all from the same place?

KHOMICH: Just outside Moscow. They brought in the Jerry P.O.W.s, so we had to be shifted.

The work allocator and the check-point guard have finished counting with the aid of their counting boards. The work allocator now approaches. Enter POSOSHKOV from behind the hut on the left. He is small and volatile, and wears a large cap.

POSOSHKOV (*greets them all*): I'm Pososhkov. Ten foot tall and ten inches long . . .

KOLODEY (*laughing*): Show-off! . . . All right, head prisoner, this is the way we'll do it. We'll call the names out from the file, and you and the clerk frisk them at the same time. I'm trusting you, see. Only make sure it's a proper rummage.

POSOSHKOV (*shouts*): All women strip to the waist!

Laughter among the prisoners.

ESCORT-GUARD SERGEANT: O.K., read the names.

KOLODEY: I'm no reader. You read the names.

MERESHCHUN is watching from the door of his hut. The head prisoner and work allocator stand with their backs to him facing the newly arrived prisoners. Behind them all the "goner" with the mess-tin is still rummaging around in the garbage. NEMOV stands next to KOLODEY. The sergeant calls the prisoners' names out, and they are searched. Then they move over to the left of the stage.

ESCORT-GUARD SERGEANT: Nye-gne . . . Nye-gne . . .

LYUBA: Nyegnevitskaya?

ESCORT-GUARD SERGEANT: Bloody awful name . . .

LYUBA: Nyegnevitskaya, Lyubov Stefanovna, born 1923, convicted Article 58, paragraph ten, eight years.

KOLODEY (*in a hostile voice*): Anti-Soviet agitation, eh?

LYUBA (*to POSOSHKOV, who has grabbed her by the breast*

while searching her): Get off! You can't afford it!

ESCORT-GUARD SERGEANT: Soykina.

SHUROCHKA: Soykina, Alexandra Pavlovna, born 1917, Article 58, paragraph twelve, ten years.

KOLODEY (*grimly*): Failure to inform.

ESCORT-GUARD SERGEANT: Zybina.

GRANYA: Agrafena Mikhailovna, born 1920, Article 136, ten years.

KOLODEY (*nodding his head*): Murder.

ESCORT-GUARD SERGEANT: Khom . . . Khomich.

KHOMICH: Khomich, Boris Alexandrovich, born 1920, Special Law seven eight, ten years.

KOLODEY (*grinning broadly*): How much did you get away with?

KHOMICH (*as he is being frisked*): Enough to keep me in parcels, sergeant.

KOLODEY: That's my boy.

POSOSHKOV (*takes* GRANYA *by the breast*): What you got stuffed up here?

GRANYA *gives him a sharp blow with her elbow, which sends him staggering. She moves on and the roll call continues in silence.*

MERESHCHUN (*to* LYUBA, *who is sitting on her bag of belongings not far away from him*): Hey you! Little girl!

LYUBA: What?

MERESHCHUN: How long have you been inside?

LYUBA: Long enough.

MERESHCHUN: Why don't we, sort of, get married?

LYUBA: Just like that?

MERESHCHUN: Why waste time?

LYUBA: You think I'm a cheap lay?

MERESHCHUN: I'm not trying to get you on the cheap. This is where I live – my own cabin. Just thought I'd let you know.

LYUBA: All right, live there.

MERESHCHUN: It's boring.

LYUBA: You've got the nurses. Aren't they enough? (*She*

turns away. MERESHCHUN *watches her for a moment, then notices* KHOMICH.)

ESCORT-GUARD SERGEANT (*straining to read a name*): Gop- . . . Bloody hell, where do they get a name like that? Gop- . . .

GONTOIR (*an old man, broad-shouldered with silvery hair, short cropped*): Gontoir, Camille Leopoldovich, born 1890, Article 58, paragraph one A stroke nineteen, ten years.

MERESHCHUN (*to* KHOMICH): That's a great sweater you've got. Look at the colour.

KHOMICH (*he hasn't yet got his clothes back on after being searched*): Yeah, it doesn't fade. Can you imagine that? Feel the material. (*Gives* MERESHCHUN *a bit to feel.*) It's foreign. You know who used to wear it? The son of a Swedish millionaire.

MERESHCHUN: I don't believe you.

KHOMICH: I'll tell you, it's an interesting story. We were in transit prison in Kuybyshev. It was sweltering, and a hundred of us in one cell. All I had was a pair of shorts. He had woollen trousers and this sweater. "I'm stifling," he said. "Where in the Soviet Union can I get myself a pair of shorts?" I told him that for a millionaire's son I had a spare pair, a bit torn, but would he like to swap them for the sweater, a blind swap? So we swapped. Try it on. See how warm and soft it is.

MERESHCHUN: I'll try it on. Interesting. A millionaire's son . . . (*He puts it on.*)

ESCORT-GUARD SERGEANT: Semyonov. (*Silence.*) Semyonov!

GOLDTOOTH (*he is wearing gay, brightly coloured clothes. He has no luggage. He gets up and approaches the sergeant with a slow, swinging gait*): Do you mean me?

ESCORT-GUARD SERGEANT: Alias?

GOLDTOOTH: Makarov.

ESCORT-GUARD SERGEANT: Alias?

GOLDTOOTH: Baltrushaitis.

ESCORT-GUARD SERGEANT: Alias?

GOLDTOOTH: Pribylenko.

ESCORT-GUARD SERGEANT: Convictions?

GOLDTOOTH: Article 162, Article 165, Article 136, Article 59 stroke three.

ESCORT-GUARD SERGEANT: Sentence?

GOLDTOOTH: Five years.

KOLODEY: Are you going to work?

GOLDTOOTH (*drawling in a sing-song voice*): Yeah, I don't mind working – in the parcels room. You know the score, sarge, we don't work on Saturdays. And for us professionals, every day's Saturday.

NEMOV (*in a commanding tone*): No need to ask questions, he'll work all right. What else can he do?

GOLDTOOTH *turns to* NEMOV *and looks at him in silence, then moves towards the work allocator.*

POSOSHKOV (*shaking the contents of* GONTOIR's *suitcase out on to the ground*): Citizen commander! Look at this! Books and papers, what's the form? Is he going to work or what?

KOLODEY *joins* POSOSHKOV, *and together they inspect the books.*

GOLDTOOTH (*to the work allocator, who is about to frisk him*): Who the hell are you? A screw-lover or something? (*Pause.*)

KOSTYA: "Professional", are you? All right. (*Motions him to pass without being searched.*)

KHOMICH: Poor old millionaire's son, it shook him, that transit prison. It's an interesting story. They tried to change his attitudes, make him renounce the western world, and his bloodsucker of a father . . .

KOLODEY (*flipping through a book*): It's all in funny letters. You're not a spy, are you?

GONTOIR: I'm a war invalid. I was in two world wars.

KOLODEY: You're German?

GONTOIR: German? I don't even know the word "German". They burnt my town. "Boches", that's what I call them, "Boches"!

KOLODEY: God knows what he's on about. If they burnt your place there must have been a reason . . . (*Thinks.*)

KHOMICH (*to* MERESHCHUN): No, don't take the sweater off, keep it. I've got enough rags as it is.

KOLODEY: Why do you say you're a war invalid? You won't get off work that way, you know. When I was in Spasski camp they used to get one-armed men together, four of them two right arms, two left arms, and make them carry barrowfuls of stones. Worked like a charm.

MERESHCHUN: It's a beautiful sweater. Thank you. What did you say your name was?

KHOMICH: Khomich. Boris Khomich.

MERESHCHUN: Come and see me in my cabin this evening, we'll have a talk. We'll fix you up.

KHOMICH (*lightly*): Thank you. You see, I don't complain. If a man's got talent, he won't go far wrong.

GOLDTOOTH (*to the "goner" with the mess-tin*): You! (*The "goner" carries on rummaging in the dustbin.*) Yes, you! (*The "goner" carries on as before.*) Listen, I said you! (*The "goner" turns round.*) Who's the guy in the greatcoat? The one who thinks he's a field-marshal?

"GONER": He's just come. About a week ago.

GOLDTOOTH: Is he on the staff?

"GONER": Staff? No, he's a prisoner. (*Goes on rummaging.*)

GOLDTOOTH (*looking at* NEMOV): Prisoner, eh? (*Makes a threatening gesture at him.* NEMOV *sees it.*) Fascist! I'll have your eyes out!

CHMUTA (*shouting from the other side of the gate*): Production chief! There's not enough work! Men standing idle again!
NEMOV *hurries across into the work area.*

BATH ORDERLY: (*Enters from the left in front of the hut. Gives the "goner" a kick.*) Scrounging as usual? Bastard! (*The "goner" falls over after being kicked, then limps away.*) Comrades, thieves and gentlemen fascists! To the delousing chamber – quick march!
Movement. Prisoners begin to exit left, carrying their belongings.

GONTOIR: What's wrong with having books? Books are
allowed, aren't they?
KOLODEY: What do you mean, "books are allowed"? Who
said books are allowed?
The painted curtain falls.

Scene 2

The Foundry

*A foundry with a high ceiling. A melting cycle is about to end.
Piles of burnt earth are strewn over most of the floor, making it
difficult to see the finished machine parts. A light greyish smoke
rises out of the casts. A steady drone comes from the fan tube just
under the ceiling.*

*On the right and to the back of the stage is a round, rust-red,
cupola-shaped furnace disappearing into an opening in the iron
ceiling. A bit closer to the audience and facing it there is an
unplastered brick dryer with an iron door. On the flat roof of the
dryer all kinds of rubbish are scattered: wires, used moulds,
buckets with holes in them and torn felt boots. In front of the
dryer is a door leading out to the right.*

*There are more doors: on the left, the way out into the yard;
in the centre at the back, a door leading into the coke and cast-
iron store. When this door is open you can see a staircase leading
up to the top of the furnace.*

On a low bench next to the dryer sits BRYLOV, *chain-
smoking cigarettes which he rolls himself. He is wearing a bluish
military jacket and a well-worn winter hat with ear-flaps. The
workers in the foundry are* YAKHIMCHUK, *enormous and bald,*
MUNITSA, *fat and squat,* CHEGENYOV, *quick-moving and
supple, and* DIMKA, *who is still a boy. As a team they work
briskly and need no words to understand one another. They move
from place to place quickly but without fuss. Their shovels,*

crowbars and scrubbers are all over the place, but each thing has its proper position and everyone knows where that is. They are all naked to the waist, wearing only a pair of torn canvas trousers.

On CHEGENYOV's *head is a torn old cap, set cheekily on one side.*

As the curtain rises YAKHIMCHUK *is using a large crowbar as a lance to open up a hole in the stoppered furnace. Cast-iron pours in a fiery stream out of the furnace along a chute and into a bucket. When the bucket is full* YAKHIMCHUK *uses another lance to stopper the hole.* CHEGENYOV *scrubs off the slag with a scrubber. They lift the bucket by the ends of a long pole with a* U-*shape in the middle and carry it towards the moulds. When the casts are ready* MUNITSA *strikes them out of the moulds.* DIMKA *carries the moulds away and piles them up. The second mould into which metal is poured after the curtain rises boils up, and metal splashes out.* MUNITSA *puts a shovel up in front of* YAKHIMCHUK's *face.* DIMKA *does the same for* CHEGENYOV. BRYLOV *shouts something inaudible over the roar of the metal, waves his arms and gets to his feet, swaying slightly.*

Enter GURVICH *quickly through the door on the left. He is dark and well-built, his raincoat trailing behind him. After him comes* NEMOV, *walking wearily. The metal stops splashing. The prisoners fill the mould up to the brim and carry the bucket away.*

MUNITSA: (*Swearing at the mould. He has a strong foreign accent.*) She boil over once more, yes? Damn her eyes!

YAKHIMCHUK: (*Shouting over the roar. He also has a foreign accent, but not such a strong one.*) I told you cones were wet.

MUNITSA: No, they no wet! They no wet!

YAKHIMCHUK: How come it happened then? How come?

MUNITSA: How the hell do I know?

GURVICH *makes a sign for the fan to be switched off.*

CHEGENYOV: Don't argue, Munitsa, it's your own fault. The boss said give the cones another day to dry.

BRYLOV (*to* CHEGENYOV): Save your breath. Munitsa's
right even when he's wrong.

MUNITSA (*in a temper*): I say so all along. I say long girders
like this, they want more air, more vapour.

GURVICH: Well, why didn't you do it, eh? Why didn't
you? Who's foreman, I'd like to know. You, Brylov,
what do you think you are, a piece of furniture?

BRYLOV: I do things my own way. I'm in charge here.

GURVICH: Looks like you've over-fulfilled your drinking
quota. You've downed a couple of bottles, isn't that
right?

BRYLOV: So what? You don't pay for it.

GURVICH (*examining the shop-floor carefully*): *I* see, been
making sewing machines again, have you? And what
about those pressing irons?

MUNITSA (*vehemently*): No, we no make irons.

GURVICH: Don't worry, I'll check it. What's this then?
(*Points to a mould which has been filled but not emptied.*)

MUNITSA: Rollers.

GURVICH: And this?

MUNITSA: Base-plates.

GURVICH: All right, empty this one. Go on, empty it! (*To*
NEMOV.) Look, you, what's your name, production
chief! You're always fiddling work orders and getting in
my hair; why don't you get a grip of these foundrymen
for a change. Load of well-fed crooks! Every time they
do a job for the state they make things to sell on the
side.

NEMOV (*with restraint*): All right, I'll look into it.

BRYLOV: You've never caught us, have you? You've never
caught us once. That's a fine way to talk. You're a
cunning one, Gurvich. You're too clever for us and that's
a fact.
Carefully MUNITSA *knocks off the moulds and uses a poker
to extract the metal objects, which are still red, from the
earth. They are rollers and thin base-plates.*

BRYLOV: All right, what about that? Thought you'd got us,

did you? (GURVICH *says nothing.*) Why get at us when
you don't know what you're talking about? You keep out
of it. I'm in charge here. I'll see everything's in order.

GURVICH: Huh! I know you, drunk for a month and on
your feet for twenty-four hours. If your foundrymen
aren't making them, how come every house in town has
got an iron? They're all over the place.

BRYLOV: Improvement in the retail supply system. Why not?
Maybe the factory shop brought some in. Or the co-op.

GURVICH: Co-op? That'll be the day!

A PRISONER (*in the doorway*): Boss. Telephone for you.
Head office.

GURVICH *departs swiftly, his raincoat flying after him.
Once more* YAKHIMCHUK *opens up a hole in the furnace,
but this time only a thin trickle of metal comes out and it
soon stops.*

YAKHIMCHUK: Well, that's the lot, not enough to go
round. (*Points to some moulds.*) Those'll have to wait.

BRYLOV (*after* GURVICH): Stupid jerk, thinks he's going to
boss me around does he? This is my shop, I do what I
want here. (*To* NEMOV.) You see what a reputation
we've got in the foundry? Imagine, me, Brylov, letting
my boys make things to sell on the side. Never in a
million years. We'd all end up in the dock.

YAKHIMCHUK (*to* NEMOV): Let's go and inspect our so-
called safety arrangements, chief. Tons of cast-iron
pulled up by hand in that bucket to a height of fifteen
feet. There'll be a hole in someone's head one day. (*He
takes* NEMOV *out through the back door.*)

BRYLOV (*as soon as they are out, agitatedly, to* MUNITSA): I
tell you, that Gurvich, he's a bloodhound! He's got a
nose and a half, smelt a rat straight away . . .

MUNITSA (*laughs*): He's too young to catch Munitsa.
Dimka, you keep *cave*. Chegenyov!

DIMKA *runs out through the door on the left.* CHEGENYOV
opens the dryer door with a clatter. MUNITSA *and he dig
frantically into the earth and discover a second hidden layer*

of moulds, right under the spot where GURVICH *had
pointed. From the moulds they take out some lace-like pieces
of metal which make up the frame of a treadle sewing
machine, also two steam irons and several ordinary irons.
They use hooks and pokers to push the metal parts quickly
into the gaping darkness of the dryer. They close it,*
CHEGENYOV *whistles and* DIMKA *returns. He busies
himself around a pot in which he has something cooking on
top of a freshly moulded piece of metal.* MUNITSA *sits down
next to* BRYLOV.

MUNITSA: He won't catch me, not in my shop. He's not
born yet, the guy who's going to catch *me* red-handed.
BRYLOV: How's the sewing machine?
MUNITSA: First-class! I fix mould. I, Munitsa!
BRYLOV: That one'll be collected tonight. There, the
painted one. This one's to be ready by Saturday. Now,
how much do I owe you? Forty roubles. And for the
three irons . . .?
CHEGENYOV: We'd like some butter, and some meal.
BRYLOV: There's only linseed oil now, boys. How do you
think things are in town? Bugger all, same as here.
Vodka and matches – that's all you'll find in the shops.
And the matches don't light. What the hell do they make
them out of?
CHEGENYOV: What about meal? You can get us some meal?
BRYLOV: Yeah, I'll fix that. Just as soon as it arrives. I'll
send my old woman to queue for it. But what about that
new production chief? Nemov? Who does he think he is,
Queen of the May?
DIMKA: He'll get over it.

He turns on the fan. CHEGENYOV *washes himself from a
barrel at the back of the stage.* NEMOV *and*
YAKHIMCHUK *return from the back room. Enter*
GURVICH *from the door on the left, very quickly, as before.
They come together near the dryer, but their conversation
becomes audible only after* DIMKA *switches off the fan,
obeying a signal from one of the others.*

BRYLOV: You see, there's nothing to melt the bronze in. We've got some black-lead crucibles left over from the English concession, but they're no good now, they're full of holes. The welded ones leak . . .

GURVICH: So what's to be done? Our excavators are standing idle. The front bushes are cracked.

BRYLOV: What do you expect me to do? Make crucibles out of thin air? You might send me on a trip to the Urals. I might be able to organise some.

GURVICH: Send *you* on a business trip? Five roubles expenses and you'd spend the lot on vodka . . .

BRYLOV: All right, fill in a form, fill in an indent and see where it gets you. The crucibles'll arrive just about now, only *next year* . . .

NEMOV: Citizen foreman, I'd like to draw your attention . . .

GURVICH (*taking* BRYLOV *on one side*): Look here, Brylov, you're a parasite, you realise that, do you? You're a lousy parasite. You get fifteen hundred for running this shop, and you grab two and a half thousand selling things on the side. You think you deserve it?

BRYLOV: Some cats are jealous even of a dog's life . . .

GURVICH: You don't do any moulding or smelting, the boys do the lot. Don't you have the time to show a little interest? You don't give a damn about production.

BRYLOV: It's my stomach, Mister Gurvich, that's what it is. The other day I had this terrible dream . . .

GURVICH: To hell with your dream, you're a . . .

NEMOV (*going up to them*): Citizen foreman, I really must draw your attention to the mediaeval methods being used in lifting metal in this shop. One broken bucket, with pieces of metal falling out when it's pulled up into the air. You think prisoners aren't human beings?

GURVICH: Look, you'd better stop that bellyaching. Don't lecture *me*, do you hear? I've been on this job three years . . .

NEMOV: That makes it worse!

GURVICH: . . . You've been here three days, so don't teach
   your grandmother to suck eggs. Your job is to *help*, not
   put a spanner in the works. Get up there and check the
   construction gangs – up on the roof! Sons of bitches,
   they just lie around, don't do a stroke. That's your job.
   We don't need you here.

NEMOV: I'll certainly go up on the roof . . .

GURVICH: Go on then, get up there now.

NEMOV: But I'm not going to stand by and see things going
   on like this. I'll draw up a report and close the foundry.

MUNITSA (*exploding*): Hey, just a minute. (*Pause.*) What
   about us? You close shop, they send us out with shovel
   to dig ditch. What about my twelve hundred grammes?

CHEGENYOV (*still washing himself at the barrel*): That's
   Munitsa's signature tune! Twelve hundred grammes and
   two extra helpings.

BRYLOV (*to* NEMOV): Close the foundry? What sort of
   production chief does a thing like that?

GURVICH: To hell with the lot of you! *Before* you get your
   report in I'll write my memorandum, and by *tomorrow*
   you'll be out in the forest cutting down trees! Here am I,
   my excavators at a standstill, and you moan about a
   bucket! (*To the foundrymen.*) What do *you* think about it,
   eh? What do you want to do?

   NEMOV *is puzzled by the unanimous rebuff he has received.
   For a few moments he stands there in silence. Then he walks
   hesitantly towards the exit. He changes his mind and walks
   out through the back door.*

MUNITSA: When Rumanians in my country, our factory
   make furnace for bronze. We run on fuel oil. We smelt
   hundred kilogramme in two hour.

GURVICH: That's it! That's a wonderful idea! You mean
   you can make us a furnace for bronze? 'Course you can,
   you wouldn't be Munitsa if you couldn't. You'll make us
   a furnace, right?

MUNITSA: Yeah, why not? I do it.

GURVICH: You'll get a bonus, Munitsa, a big bonus.

BRYLOV: Are you sure you can? You name it, he'll try it. Isn't that right, Munitsa? I've never seen a furnace like that, and I've been in charge of foundries a long time.

GURVICH: Now look, you're supposed to run this place, aren't you? What do you think you're doing, sapping the man's initiative? You keep at it, Munitsa, right?

MUNITSA: All right, all right. I make furnace. I make.

GURVICH: Where'll we put it? Over there. (*Points.*)

Enter GAI. *He is short but powerful-looking. Like* NEMOV, *he is still in his old military uniform, with breeches and high boots, but it is all worn and dirty.*

GAI: Cement-mixer's stopped again, Comrade Gurvich. I can't do . . .

GURVICH: What d'you mean, "stopped"? Why has it stopped? (*Rushes towards the exit.*) You keep at it, Munitsa. You'll get a bonus.

GAI *moves off after* GURVICH, *but* CHEGENYOV *whistles to halt him in his tracks. They come forward together.*

CHEGENYOV: We're in contact with old Igor.

GAI: Where is he? In the cooler?

CHEGENYOV: Solitary confinement. I've got a pal on duty there today. He says . . .

GAI: We'll have to get him some bread.

CHEGENYOV: We've done that. Pencil and paper too. He asked for that.

GAI: What's their plan? To get him another sentence?

CHEGENYOV: That's right.

GAI: Who shopped him? Have you found out?

CHEGENYOV: Doctor's assistant, Aga-Mirza. Found something under his pillow in the hospital and took it to security.

GAI: He's got T.B.! You mean they took him out of hospital and threw him in the cellar?

CHEGENYOV: Pososhkov's giving evidence as well.

GAI: Bastard! They're all around us, Grishka. These bastards are all over.

CHEGENYOV: Old Igor isn't going to last. He's written a letter home. To say goodbye.

GAI: To his wife?

CHEGENYOV: No, his sister. He didn't have time to get himself a wife. They shot his father in '37. His mother died in the camps. They've got us by the throat. What are we going to do?

GAI: What can we do? Remember – that's all.

CHEGENYOV: I've got his letter. I'll see it gets off.
Exit GAI. CHEGENYOV *climbs numbly on to the dryer and rummages around up there.*

MUNITSA (*to* YAKHIMCHUK): So what about it, Nikolay? We build yes? We build it fast?

YAKHIMCHUK: You make the promise, you build it. I don't want nothing to do with it. I don't want no bonus.
CHEGENYOV *gets out the envelope he had hidden on top of the dryer and jumps to the ground.*

BRYLOV: You know, Munitsa, I can't make you out. It's right what they say – stupidity can kill. Look, boys, it's not a bad life, now, is it? I fix your quotas so you're best of the bunch. I've worked fifteen years in the camps. I've built eleven new foundries and I've always got on well with the prisoners. Tell me one thing you haven't got? Your bread ration's best in the camp. You've got double porridge, double soup. We make irons to sell on the side, and as for your uniforms, I'll sell them for you any time you want. Any time you want to mail a letter, just give it to me. Any time. Right now if you want to.
(CHEGENYOV *hands him the envelope, which he puts in his pocket.*) There, you see what I mean. You've got your work, and there's enough left over for me. Enough to wet my whistle.

CHEGENYOV: Munitsa's going for a Stalin Prize.

BRYLOV: Honestly, boys, I mean it. I built one foundry on the Igarka and another in Taishet. We've been all right up to now. If there's no crucibles, there's nothing they can make us do. As long as there's coke, we can make a little cast-iron, enough for you and for me. You don't get whipped if you lie down. But once the furnace is ready and the bronze starts flowing, that Gurvich'll be on our backs all day long, wanting more and more. Take my word for it, boys, I know! You'll have to smelt five times a week – bushes today, some other damn thing tomorrow. Everything upside down and no percentage for exceeding the quota . . .

DIMKA *sets a sort of stand up in the middle of the floor to serve as a table, and around it some moulds to serve as chairs*

CHEGENYOV: 'Course there won't be any percentage. They'll pay for the bronze like they now pay for the cast-iron – by weight. An iron girder weighs half a ton, a wheel-bush weighs half a kilo. Your furnace'll be the death of us, Munitsa. Forget about it.

BRYLOV: I never saw a furnace like that, and I remember the real craftsmen, back in the old days. Babushkin, for instance, may he rest in peace. You don't see his sort nowadays. Back in '23 he threw me out of his foundry for breaking up the old women's Easter cakes. Working-class for generations, he was, and he wasn't afraid of anything. (*He coughs violently.*) I'm sorry, boys, last night I had a bad dream . . .

YAKHIMCHUK: You go and get some sleep, boss. Maybe you'll have a nice dream this time.

BRYLOV: Yeah, I'd better go. (*Gets to his feet.*)

YAKHIMCHUK: So what about the butter?

BRYLOV: You'll get it. I told you, you'll get it. Word of honour! Brylov always keeps his word. If Gurvich wants to know where I am, tell him I'm over at construction site number one . . . or number two . . .

YAKHIMCHUK: I'll say the trade-union committee wanted you. (*Exit* BRYLOV.) We aren't finishing any sewing machines today, boys. We're going to take our time. For some reason Brylov's keeping us waiting with the money.

DIMKA: That was a stinking lot of meal he brought. Must have been meant for the pigs.

Enter NEMOV *from the back. He looks depressed and walks indecisively towards the exit.* DIMKA *takes the pot into the middle of the room.*

YAKHIMCHUK: What's wrong, chief ?

NEMOV: Comrade Yakhimchuk, I . . . I don't know. I really don't know. (*Puts his head in his hands.*) We were better off in the trenches, fighting in the front line . . .

DIMKA: O.K., family, porridge ready!

NEMOV: Family? What family?

DIMKA: He's daddy (*Pointing to* MUNITSA.) and he's mummy (*Pointing to* CHEGENYOV.) and this is big brother. How about that?

YAKHIMCHUK: Sit down and have some porridge with us.

NEMOV: No thank you. I don't think . . .

YAKHIMCHUK: What do you mean? Everyone's hungry in the camps. (*Takes him by the shoulder.*) Sit down. We don't mind. We've got enough, we manage.

NEMOV *almost sits down on a slab of hot metal.*

DIMKA: Look out! You'll burn your pants!

They all sit down except MUNITSA, *who stands there examining the spot where his furnace is going to be.*

YAKHIMCHUK: Munitsa, sit down! Lovely yellow gruel, just like the grits mother makes.

MUNITSA (*does not move*): You never tasted real stuff – back home in Moldavia. You should taste the way we make it . . .

CHEGENYOV (*to* NEMOV): Are you straight from the front line?

NEMOV: That's right.

CHEGENYOV: What did they get you for? Speaking out of turn?

NEMOV: That's what they said.

CHEGENYOV: Yackety-yak. Anti-Soviet agitation, right?

NEMOV: I didn't think so, but they did.

YAKHIMCHUK: All right, Munitsa, we're starting without you.

MUNITSA: What you mean, start without me? What you mean?

Sits down. They all start spooning the porridge into their mouths in regular time. NEMOV *eats with difficulty.*

YAKHIMCHUK: Go on, eat up. Don't think too much. You think too much, you won't live out your ten years.

NEMOV (*drops his spoon*): How can a man live out his sentence in this place? How can a man *live* in this place? (*He sits there, paralysed. The foundrymen continue spooning the porridge regularly into their mouths as the painted curtain falls.*)

Scene 3

The Ash Tree

A remote corner of the construction zone. On the left is a brick building under construction, standing at a slight angle across the stage. As yet there is no sign of woodwork or carpentry in the windows or doorways. It is the same building that the audience saw from a different side in scene one. It is now very close and more than three storeys high, at which point it vanishes into the heights above the stage. From time to time the flashes of an electrical welder can be seen through the windows of the first floor.

At the back of the stage there are posts and lines of barbed wire marking the inner and outer camp zones. At the corner where the fence changes direction stands an ugly-looking watch-tower made of wooden boards, the same as the one on the audience's side of the stage. Further on, past all the barbed wire, the bare steppe extends as far as the eye can see. Over it hang a few clouds, high in the sky. Somewhere in the distance an excavator is at work. The characteristic screeching sound it makes can be clearly heard.

On the left by the building itself there is a large pile of

*construction debris. Nearer the audience are about ten women
from the new transport sitting on a low heap of wooden blocks.
They have already changed into rough working clothes. On the
right is a pile of logs on which a couple of dozen men from the
new transport are lolling in a state of exhaustion. In the middle
of the stage is a large bucket which looks as if it belongs to an
excavator. It is rusty and overgrown with grass.*

*It is an October afternoon, quite hot. The sun is shining down
from the right.*

LYUBA (*as the curtain rises she is singing a sad song*):
    There across the roadway, there beyond the river,
    There beyond the river stands a lonely oak-tree.
    Why can't we two join, be oak and ash together?
    There would be no need for me to shake or tremble.

THE WOMEN (*following her lead. Without rising or moving
    from their places*):
    I would move and so entwine our slender branches,
    Day and night my leaves with his would softly whisper,
    But the ash and oak can never join each other,
    So I must remain alone, unloved for ever.

A WOMAN: I thought . . . I thought it was the cranes
    flying. But it was only the excavators making cooing
    noises.

2ND WOMAN: It might be the cranes. Winter's on its way,
    girls. Warm clothes, that's what we need.

SHUROCHKA (*to no one in particular*): This is the third camp
    I've been in. It's always this first day that's the most
    terrible. It's not a day, it's a year. No strength
    to move.

3RD WOMAN: It's a long way they've brought us, a long
    way.

2ND WOMAN: This isn't far. Potatoes grow in the ground,
    no one can call this remote. There's a railway. Parcels
    arrive all year round. Visitors can come. You wait till
    they send you up to Norilsk. Six months in the year the
    boats can get in. The other six you're on your own.

GRANYA (*to* LYUBA, *continuing her story*): . . . I never even

finished primary school, but he was a man of *education*, a
senior lecturer. Funny sort of thing he taught – all about
Egyptian pots and vases. We even had quite a few of
them in our home. He was so sweet and kind. But what
was I? A little girl from the village.

LYUBA: Stuff it, there's no man who's sweet and kind.
They're all the same, they're only after one thing . . .

GRANYA: Don't say that, Lyuba. You had bad luck, that's
all. The war started, everything turned upside down. My
husband wasn't called up, but I was. I was a young
communist and an auxiliary and a dead shot, so they
took me. I did two years. You should have seen the
letters he wrote to me – thousands of them!

LYUBA: What did you do?

GRANYA: I was a sniper. Then they made me platoon
commander, junior lieutenant.

LYUBA: Out in the front line – all those men . . .

GRANYA: No, that's the point. I didn't. Not once.

LYUBA: I don't believe you!

GRANYA: You see, I realised I'd never be so happy again,
never for the rest of my life . . . Then suddenly out of
the blue I got a letter from one of the neighbours to say
he was having an affair with some slut from the operetta.
It was as if a red-hot iron was pressed against my brain.
I didn't believe it. The C.O. gave me leave, I took the
next 'plane to Moscow. I got there, it was very early, the
sun was just rising. I broke open the door and went in.
There he was, lying with her on *my bed*. I didn't have
time to think. I took out my TT gun and plugged him.
Right there on the pillow.

LYUBA: Dead?

GRANYA: He lived five minutes.

LYUBA: I wouldn't have done that. I'd have shot *her*!

GRANYA: No, it had to be him. You see, he didn't
understand. Only now I'm sorry. He never treated me
badly – except that one morning.

LYUBA: It's like I said. They're only after one thing.

Act I, Scene 3

GRANYA: It's not true. It can't be!

Enter from the left GURVICH, *striding swiftly, his raincoat flying after him;* FOMIN *the foreman, a little old man with a big moustache; and* KHOMICH. *After them comes* NEMOV *in his army greatcoat.*

GURVICH: Fomin, why are these prisoners doing nothing? Haven't they got work to do? I told you, put them to work!

FOMIN: What work?

GURVICH: I don't know. Digging ditches, for example.

FOMIN: I sent ten of them out. There weren't any more shovels.

GURVICH: Funny! Why weren't there?

FOMIN: It'd be funnier if there were any. There'll be five more soon, they're putting handles on.

NEMOV (*he sounds depressed and forces the words out*): Comrade works manager, what quota rate shall I put down for these people? If there's no work for them, I ought to make out a report.

GURVICH (*sharply*): Make your report and stuff it up your arse, I won't sign it. We never applied for extra personnel, did we?

NEMOV: They've come anyway . . .

GURVICH: What's that got to do with me? We didn't ask for them. You listen to me, Nemov. Barrack-room lawyers like you don't last long in the camps. Fomin, get that rubbish moved . . . (*Looks around.*) . . . There! Over there! (*Points to the far right-hand corner of the stage.*) Get these women to work on it.

FOMIN: The bricklayers have all the barrows.

GURVICH: Well, aren't there any spare ones?

FOMIN: You should have given me some more wood. Getting planks out of you's like getting blood out of a stone.

GURVICH: It's the book-keepers who are stingy. It's not my fault. Go and get four from the bricklayers.

FOMIN: What'll they carry the bricks in, then?

271

GURVICH *waves him away. Exeunt* FOMIN, GRANYA
and two other women.

GURVICH: Who's in charge of the men's team? You?

KHOMICH: That's right, sir. Engineer Khomich.

GURVICH: Engineer.

KHOMICH: Civil engineer.

GURVICH: Fine, only I've got engineers here digging
ditches. What can I do? We even had a member of the
Academy of Sciences. He went sick on me.

NEMOV: He went dead.

GURVICH: I don't know about that. Get your men together
and take them over there. (*Points to the left.*) Go on, off
you go. We'll find you work. Every man'll get his
job.

KHOMICH (*in a shrill voice of command*): Hey, you clowns!
You think this is a holiday camp? Get on with the job!
The men rise heavily to their feet.

1ST VOICE: What about our three days' quarantine?

2ND VOICE: We're not supposed to go out to work.
All the male prisoners and NEMOV *leave the stage.*

GURVICH (*he has been walking round the excavator bucket,
examining the scene carefully*): Hey you, girl! Come here!
(LYUBA *comes up to him.*) Are you from the new
transport?

LYUBA: Just arrived, yes.

GURVICH: You've got . . . er, a good pair of legs?

LYUBA: Exactly what do you mean?

GURVICH: I need a messenger in my office. You'll have to
run up and down all over the building, all over the area.
Clean my room and cook my lunch. I don't have time to
get home for lunch. Can you manage it?

LYUBA: I can manage anything.

GURVICH: I like the look of you. Let's go, I'll show you
what you have to do.
Enter CHMUTA *and* FOMIN *quickly from the left.*

CHMUTA (*shouting*): I will *not* put that plaster on again!
We've done it twice. And we scraped the old stuff off.

272

FOMIN: Come on now, don't exaggerate; you didn't scrape anything off.

CHMUTA (*more loudly*): What do you mean, "didn't scrape"? I demand a quality check.

GURVICH: What's this, then? You keep your mouth shut.

CHMUTA (*even louder*): I will not keep my mouth shut! I will stand up for my men. (*Quietly and calmly.*) Give me a cigarette, will you, foreman?

FOMIN (*gives him one*): What the hell does the chief electrician think he's doing? His fittings are late, and now his men are here cutting grooves in the plaster for their damn wires. They've scratched all the door panels, just newly painted . . .

CHMUTA (*heatedly*): We painted them twice!

FOMIN (*waving him away*): You painted them once!

CHMUTA (*shouting*): You know what this place is? A shit-bin! I know what'll happen – the sanitary inspectors'll be in next, moving the batteries, drilling holes in the walls . . .

GURVICH (*to* LYUBA): Go and get Kuznetsov. Now!

LYUBA (*instantly assuming her new role, she runs off shouting loudly*): Kuznetsov!

GURVICH: They're completely out of hand. They're a lot of drunks. (*He strides swiftly out, followed by* FOMIN.)

4TH WOMAN (*jumping to her feet*): Boss! Let me finish your cigarette! (CHMUTA *takes a final drag, gives her the cigarette, slaps her on the rump and leaves.*)

SHUROCHKA: Pig! God protect us from a man like that! Says he'll stand up for his men – huh! Did you see him this morning? Knocked one of them down, kicked him around.

2ND WOMAN: How do you think these gang leaders last fifteen years in the camps? Riding on our backs, that's how.

1ST WOMAN: Lyuba's the lucky one. What a job! All the grub she wants, no work, just twiddling her thumbs.

273

4TH WOMAN: You call it luck? Why didn't he pick you, I wonder? (*Smirks.*)

3RD WOMAN: They won't look at her either in a year or two, the way she lives.

4TH WOMAN: Two years is all she's got left – winter-summer, winter-summer, and that's it.

3RD WOMAN: What'll she do then, outside?

1ST WOMAN: Stupid question! Get out first, then wonder what you're going to do.

4TH WOMAN: She'll find her way around, that woman, inside or outside. That's the way it goes. There aren't many men around now after the war, but it's always the same: either you have men up to here (*Places one hand across her throat, palm downwards.*) or else you don't get a touch.

GRANYA *returns with two women. They are pushing three barrows, one wooden shovel and one scoop shovel.*)

GRANYA: All right, girls, we've got till this evening, so let's spin this job out – two loading, six on the barrows. Who's missing?

3RD WOMAN: Lyuba. The works manager took her to his office.

GRANYA: What for?

2ND WOMAN: What do you think?

The women sort themselves out and begin carrying away the rubbish little by little. They move slowly as if at a funeral, taking long breaks at the points where they load and unload. At the beginning their conversation can still be heard.

A WOMAN: Look, what do I do with this spade, it won't cut into the pile?

GRANYA (*sitting down next to the excavator bucket*): To hell with it, just do what you can. Everyone takes their turn digging. Just get a bit on the corner.

1ST WOMAN: Is it true, girls, we don't get any supper?

SHUROCHKA: Of course not. You heard what the guard said. We've had our rations for today. It's down in black and white in the Movement Order.

274

1ST WOMAN: It's not fair! They didn't give us a thing!

2ND WOMAN: You stay inside a bit longer, you'll learn.

4TH WOMAN: They treat us anyhow they want in the camps.

3RD WOMAN: I hope they choke to death on their salt herring.

Enter KHOMICH. *He comes up to* GRANYA *who is sitting thinking and sits down not far from her.*

KHOMICH: Well, Granya, how do you like our little camp? (GRANYA *says nothing.*) Real "Gonersville", isn't it? But you know what they say? If you need a spoon to eat your porridge, it's a good camp. Gonersville's when it's so runny you can tip your tin and drink it over the edge. (GRANYA *says nothing.*) This new transport's really screwed us up. I've gone over the whole work area and I still can't find anything to do. We'll have to think something up back inside the zone. I've got the doctor on the end of a string, that's a start.

GRANYA: Why are you telling me this?

KHOMICH: Who else is there to tell it to? (*Pause.*) Four years I've been in the camps, and not one single day on general duties. So I'm not going to start now. I'll fix myself up even if I have to mow down the lot of them.

GRANYA: I'm sure you will.

KHOMICH: You sound like you disapprove. You must have more on your conscience than I do.

GRANYA: Maybe so. But then maybe not. It's different somehow, I can't explain . . .

KHOMICH: It's the same as it was in your blasted war. Prejudice, that's all it is. You've shot dozens of people. You've got medals all over your chest. You went round like a general, didn't you? Then you go and knock someone off on your own, and boom! Ten years! (*Heatedly, not allowing her to interrupt.*) For God's sake get rid of that damn honesty of yours! No honest man lives to see the end of his sentence. It's your first year, you haven't realised yet. You'll see, I don't waste time, I'll start tonight. I do anything for my own people!

GRANYA: Fine, do it. Only keep it to yourself.

KHOMICH: I'll make this camp so nice and cosy for you, you won't even notice the barbed wire. You've got ten more years to do, Granya. Think about it. If we were on the outside I'd be the sort of man who had his own car. I'd whizz past leaving you gaping. I'm an engineer, I've got talent. I'm concentrated energy, *and* I'm a good talker, do you see that? God knows what I'd be if I hadn't been pinched.

GRANYA: What do I care about your brains? What do I care?

KHOMICH: Forget about the war. And forget the outside world. Life has different laws in here. This is Campland, an invisible country. It's not in the geography books, or the psychology books or the history books. This is the famous country where ninety-nine men weep while one man laughs. I'd rather be the one who laughs.

GRANYA: I just don't feel like laughing.

KHOMICH (*stroking her hand*): I'll be sorry to let you go. But I'll manage. What about you, though? Up to now you've been gang leader, you haven't had a taste of general duties. It won't take you long to lose that pride and those rosy cheeks. Then you'll jump at the chance of going to bed with some bum for five hundred grammes of sticky bread . . . Granya!

GRANYA (*takes her hand away*): All right. I'll drop dead under a pine tree. You've made me all confused. I can't . . . I can't make anything out . . . Please, go away. Go away!

KHOMICH *gets to his feet, stands there for a moment, then walks slowly away.* GRANYA *sinks her head in her hands. The women are still carrying their barrowfuls of rubbish, in slow funeral time. The painted curtains falls.*

Scene 4

Works and Planning Department

A small bare room in a barrack-type building. There is only one window, in the back wall, and it is covered with a net curtain. On the right is a door made of new unpainted hardboard. One table is set diagonally across the left-hand corner of the room. A sign reading "Works Manager" hangs over it on the wall. A second table stands by the back wall, a sign over it reading "Work Allocator". There are two or three stools, and a bench which stands awkwardly in the middle of the room. It is dark outside and the electric light is on. At the table on the left sits NEMOV, *wearing a woollen field shirt, together with a visiting warder, an old man in a worn greatcoat with blue shoulder-pieces, bearing the insignia of a sergeant. At the right-hand table sits* KOSTYA *the work allocator, also in a new officer's field shirt with a broad officer's belt. He is never without a cigarette sticking out of his mouth and he looks like the poet Mayakovsky.*

WARDER: Look, can't you? Look! I want short-term prisoners, do you understand? You must know the situation, I'm not giving away official secrets. We're in a remote area deep in the forest. There aren't many guards and they're all like me, disabled, you see? We can't wait to be demobbed. I'm not taking any ten-year men.

NEMOV (*irritably*): But sergeant, where do you expect me to find them? It's not my fault, it's the courts'. Nowadays they never give less than ten. Ah, here's one. Eight years. Do you want her? (*He looks through a list.*)

WARDER: All right, I'll have her.

NEMOV (*writing*): Kalashnikova, Akulina Demyanovna.

WARDER: What's her trade?

NEMOV: No trade, she's a housewife. You don't need a trade to chop down trees.

WARDER (*sighs*): An old woman, I suppose?

277

NEMOV: Born 1900. Forty-five years old. (*Writes.*) Article
58, paragraph eight . . .

WARDER (*animatedly*): What's that? Terrorist?

NEMOV: That's right, but its sub-section nineteen –
intention only. She must have blabbed something out at
the market.

WARDER (*stretches out a finger to stop* NEMOV *writing*): No, I
can't take terrorists. Cross her out.

NEMOV: Well, I can't take much more either, sergeant. I'll
be all night sorting this new transport into gangs. I've
got to send orders to the catering department and find
jobs for them in the morning. Where have I got time to
fool around with you? Choose your own people. (*Pushes
list over to him.*)

WARDER: Look, I can't see without my glasses. Anyway,
I never learnt to read, did I? I'll ask the work
allocator . . .

NEMOV: He's busy, leave him alone.

WARDER: There's something else, I need a barber. We had
a very good barber once, a deserter from Georgia, God
bless him. But there was an amnesty and they let him
go. It's been two months now and we're like a lot of
shaggy dogs, guards as well as the prisoners.

KOSTYA: Barber? Let's see . . . (*He comes up to him and
takes the list.*) Now you run along to the guard-room.
There'll be people coming back from work soon, gang
bosses all over the place, you should hear the noise they
make. I'll come and see you in half an hour and we'll
sort them out, O.K.? I'll want something for it though.
Two packets of "king-size".

WARDER: "Ordinary size".

KOSTYA: Two packets of "ordinary size"? For sixty
workers?

WARDER: You'll get me a barber?

KOSTYA: Only for another packet of best smokes. Don't be
such a Scrooge, you can nick them out of the
parcels.

WARDER: All right, but hurry up. The lorries are on their way to . . . (*Exit.*)

NEMOV: For God's sake, Kostya, why get tied up with him? Haven't we got enough work with the new transport?

KOSTYA: Look, you're still . . . a mug, an innocent! You don't understand. I'll see he gets all the "goners", ours and the new ones, every single no-good in the place. Then when winter comes they'll all be in hospital, flat on their backs. In for the duration, take my word for it. Let him have them. (*He claps his hands and shouts.*) Angel!

ANGEL *appears in the doorway. He is a young prison orderly with one arm.*

NEMOV: Why do they call him Angel?

KOSTYA: He flies all over the camp, waving his empty sleeve like a wing. Isn't that right, Angel? Go and get me that girl from the new transport. (*Looks down at the list.*) . . . Nyegnevitskaya. Lyuba they call her. Quick as a flash!

ANGEL: Yes sir! Lyuba Nyegnevitskaya. Quick as a flash, sir! (*Runs out.*)

KOSTYA: She's the barber. And I'm off. (*Winks at him in the doorway.*) It's going to be smokes all round.

Enter BELOBOTNIKOV, *a clerk, a lame old man in felt boots. He bumps into* KOSTYA *in the doorway and before closing the door says in a loud voice* . . .

BELOBOTNIKOV: Papers for you to sign, Comrade Nemov. (*Having closed the door he limps over towards the table, looks back over his shoulder and speaks in a low voice.*) Comrade Nemov, there's a plot against you. I'll tell you who they are – Solomon, Titok, that storekeeper, Rubyan, Pososhkov – he's head prisoner – and what's-his-name, that one from the cultural section. I'm disabled, you see, they can't send me out on general duties. But it makes me sick, Comrade Nemov, I don't mind telling you. I sit there in the office, I hear everything they say. They're only waiting for the

commandant to come back, then they'll shit on you. I'll
give you a bit of advice: get that camp order book away
from Solomon, get it away from him! And don't trust
that work allocator, Kostya. (*Points at door.*) He's no
good. He works for both sides.

NEMOV (*coming to life*): Thanks, Grandad, thank you very
much. I'll deal with them. I'll roll over them like a tank!
I wasn't in the cavalry for nothing . . .

BELOBOTNIKOV: But be careful. They're clever bastards,
they might even try and get you a second term. You
know, that's one thing they're generous about in this
camp, the way they hand out second terms . . . (*Shakes
his head warningly.* NEMOV *becomes more subdued.*)
Enter BELLA, *a plump, oriental-looking woman.*

BELLA: Excuse me, could you spare a moment?
(BELOBOTNIKOV *limps away.*) How do you do? (*She
stretches out her hand and* NEMOV *shakes it.*) My name is
Bella. (*She sits down with dignity.*)

NEMOV (*nervously, still huddled over his papers*): As you can
see, I'm very busy . . .

BELLA (*taking her time*): You cannot imagine how delighted
I am to see this job held by a man of education, by an
intellectual, not some labour-camp lout. The best people
in the camp were thrilled to hear of your appointment.

NEMOV: I'm no intellectual! I served four years in the
army, and now I'm a prisoner.

BELLA: Oh, that makes no difference at all. I can tell an
educated man when I see one. I'm from a very good
family myself . . .

NEMOV: Can I ask you please to come to the . . .

BELLA: The first thing you must do is get your own people
into key positions. Otherwise you'll have no power. To
be more specific, I would like to mention the matter of
bread-cutting. I used to work there, but they threw me
out and put me on general duties because of some
ludicrous accusation that I was giving short measure. You
can rely on me completely. If I get a job in the bread-

cutting room, you will have a minimum of three kilos a day, all to yourself.

NEMOV: Listen, I personally couldn't . . .

BELLA: No, it's not for you, not for you *personally*. Of course, there's no reason why *you* should eat black bread. But you can sell it. Or exchange it for vodka. Or give someone a bonus, so to speak. You see, you'll have to *pay* the people who work for you. There's no other way. You haven't been in the camps long, have you? You'll learn.

NEMOV: What are you in here for, if you don't mind my asking?

BELLA: What's that got to do with it? Article 107.

NEMOV: Black-marketeering?

BELLA: What *are* you talking about? I sold penicillin and gramophone needles. Very profitable. Absolutely fair and above board. (*She puts on* NEMOV's *table a parcel wrapped in paper.*)

NEMOV: What's this?

BELLA: It's just . . . a little something . . . to start you off. Half a piece.

NEMOV (*without unwrapping it*): Half a piece of what?

BELLA: Good heavens, I said a piece! Don't you know what a "piece" is? A thousand roubles!

NEMOV: Certainly not! Not in a thousand years! Take it away this minute! (*Forces her to take it back. A knock on the door.*) Yes, come in.
Enter timidly two girl students. They are still quite decently dressed.

BOTH GIRLS: Comrade director, may we come in?

1ST STUDENT: There's something we very much want you to do for us . . .

2ND STUDENT: We've just arrived. They brought us here today . . .

1ST STUDENT: There are rumours they're going to send us on somewhere else.

NEMOV: That's right, they are.

1ST STUDENT: There's something we very much want you to do for us. Allow us to stay here.

2ND STUDENT: But the most important thing is – we mustn't be separated.

Exit BELLA *with dignity.*

NEMOV: What are you in for?

2ND STUDENT: Article 58, of course.

NEMOV: I see, all right, you can stay. By the way, who are you?

1ST STUDENT: We're students.

NEMOV: Where?

1ST STUDENT: The High School of History, Philosophy and Literature. Afterwards it was merged with . . .

NEMOV: Yes, I know. A real nest of free-thinkers! Did you know Herman Mednoborov?

1ST STUDENT: Oh yes, he used to lecture to us.

2ND STUDENT: What a coincidence! Were you in the . . .?

1ST STUDENT: There were so many students arrested after the war . . .

NEMOV: Sshhh! You *must* be careful what you say, even in here. How long have you got? Ten years?

BOTH GIRLS (*together*): No, five.

NEMOV: Then you should be all the more careful. They'd get you on another charge just like that! (*Snaps his fingers.*)

LYUBA (*entering quickly*): You sent for me?

NEMOV: Name?

LYUBA: Lyuba Nyegnevitskaya.

NEMOV: Yes, I did. All right, girls, we'll have another talk later.

BOTH GIRLS (*together*): Thank you! Thank you very much! (*They leave.*)

NEMOV: Now you are . . . (*Forgets what he wanted to say.*)

LYUBA: I'm . . .

NEMOV: The barber?

LYUBA: The watchmaker.

NEMOV: Is that right? It says here in the lists . . .

(*Rummages around.*) Damn, they've taken the lists. It says in the lists that you're a barber.

LYUBA (*keenly trying to guess his intention*): Well, I'm . . . I'm a barber too.

NEMOV: Good Lord, you're a jack of all trades.

LYUBA: But we already have a barber, don't we?

NEMOV: We don't need one for here. It's for the tree-felling site out in the forest.

LYUBA (*hastily*): You see, I'm not really a barber. I'm a theatrical wig-maker.

NEMOV: Theatrical? Who are you then? Nyegnevitskaya . . . are you Polish?

LYUBA: No, I'm practically Russian. Except for my great-grandfather. He was in the Polish uprising. They exiled him to Siberia. Please don't send me away.

NEMOV: My dear, I would gladly send no one away. I feel sorry for everyone. Only someone's got to go.

CHMUTA (*bursts in dragging behind him a "drudge" prisoner, a "goner"*): Now look, boss, what sort of a place is this? I'm sick and tired of this crap. They just sit around warming their arses . . .

NEMOV: Sshhh, calm down! What's the matter?

CHMUTA (*shouting as before*): They sent us a consignment of boots, but the quartermasters aren't issuing them. Look what the "drudges" have to wear. Go on, show him! (*The prisoner lifts one foot, then the other, flapping the soles of his shoes. They are home-made out of old car tyres and almost completely torn off. Meanwhile* LYUBA *withdraws.*) That bastard in the clerks' office, I'll break his abacus over his head. You know who'll get the boots, those skivers of theirs. And what I want to know is, whose side are you on?

NEMOV (*ordering him*): Sit down, Chmuta. (*Claps his hands.*) Angel! (*The duty prisoner appears in the doorway.*) Get me the head clerk. Now! (ANGEL *disappears.* CHMUTA *sits down.*) How many pairs arrived? Do you know the figure?

CHMUTA (*not shouting any more*): Fifteen pairs.

The door opens slightly and swings to and fro a bit. Shouts of "Get in the queue!" and "Stop jumping the queue!"

KHOMICH: Shut up! (*Closes the door behind him and walks in jauntily.*) What a miserable little office you've got. You've got your own builders, haven't you? Why don't you get them to polish it up a bit? (*Sits down.*) I've come to introduce myself. Have a cigarette. They're "Kazbek", the best in Russia. (NEMOV *takes a cigarette and lights it. Without getting up* KHOMICH *makes a slight movement with the box and offers it to* CHMUTA.) Do you want one, gang leader?

CHMUTA (*without moving*): Get it, Ivan.

The "drudge" walks over to KHOMICH, *takes one cigarette and carries it across to his gang leader.*

ANGEL: (*Entering.*) Comrade director! The head clerk says he's busy, sir.

NEMOV (*leaning forward and speaking in an angry tone of command*): I said, go and get the head clerk!

ANGEL *disappears.*

KHOMICH: How long have you been in the camps?

NEMOV: This one? Four days. What about you?

KHOMICH: It's my fifth year inside. When did they pick you up?

NEMOV: Last summer.

KHOMICH: P.O.W.?

NEMOV: No, they took me out of the front line. What about you?

KHOMICH: It was worse than the front line where I was. I was in one of the Ministries in Moscow in '41. Those bombs! It was a nightmare. What rank were you?

NEMOV: Captain. What are you in for?

KHOMICH: Special paragraph seven stroke eight. A lorry-load of sugar.

NEMOV: You had an exemption from the army?

KHOMICH: That's right. You see, it was an interesting situation. They exiled my wife way out in the Narym

284

country. I stayed in Moscow. If I'd gone and joined her,
I'd have lost my exemption and been called up.
Whatever happened we wouldn't be together. So I didn't
go.

NEMOV: What was she in for? Article 58?

KHOMICH: Strictly speaking, Article 7, paragraph thirty-
five. "Socially dangerous element". Her father worked
for the Chinese Far-Eastern Railway, so she was brought
up abroad. The security boys warned me. "Young man,"
they said, "do you love her very much? Your record's as
clean as a whistle so far. We must advise you against
marrying her." I should have listened to them, but you
know what a pretty girl can do to a gentleman . . . Now
she's out there with our child. He got badly bitten by
some Eskimos' dogs. Nothing but tundra for hundreds of
miles. No doctors . . .

CHMUTA (*raising his voice again*): Listen to me, production
chief. Are you the boss here or aren't you?

NEMOV *makes as if to rush out of the room, but at that
moment* SOLOMON, *the head clerk, enters with great
dignity, wearing a new cotton overall, smart by camp
standards.*

SOLOMON: What's happened? The world come to an end?

NEMOV: I'll tell you what's happened. In the first place, if
you want to keep your job as head clerk you will come
when I call you. In the second place, how many pairs of
boots have you just received, and why weren't they
reported?

SOLOMON (*very slowly*): We haven't entered them in the
books yet.

CHMUTA: Don't shoot the shit with me, Solomon! One
pair's gone to the bath orderly, another pair to the
dentist . . .

NEMOV: How many pairs did you get?

SOLOMON: Twelve.

NEMOV (*sharply*): Fifteen! I'm not playing games, you
understand? You will go immediately and get those boots

back from your skivers. In ten minutes I'll send you a
distribution order for the boots and you will obey it.

SOLOMON: You've got no right to do things like that. You
can't take things away from people!

CHMUTA: Those skivers? They're not people!

SOLOMON: First of all you cut the office's extra rations,
now you want to hand out fifteen pairs of boots among
five hundred people. They're a drop in the ocean! The
camp commandant can give them out himself when he
gets back.

NEMOV: The commandant left *me* in charge!

SOLOMON (*restraining himself*): Comrade Nemov, you're no
fool. If a bath orderly wears them they won't tear. If an
ordinary working prisoner wears them they'll be finished
in three days.

CHMUTA (*shouting*): That's what boots are for, to get torn.

SOLOMON (*pointing to the rubber "shoes" which the prisoner is
wearing*): You mean get torn the way he's torn those? He
did it himself on the way here, isn't that right?

CHMUTA (*more coolly*): You watch it, Solomon. You're too
clever by half.

SOLOMON (*to* NEMOV): It's not winter yet. When the snow
starts we'll give them the boots.

NEMOV: The "drudges" will all have caught colds by then.
Today's October 18th. It's not summer any more. That's
all I've got to say.

SOLOMON (*calmly*): You're being completely unreasonable,
and you'll have to answer to the commandant. Some of
us have been here for years. You've been here a week
and want to turn everything upside down.

NEMOV (*shouting*): I'll have you out on general duties!

SOLOMON (*quite unperturbed, to* KHOMICH): Are those
cigarettes "Kazbek"?

KHOMICH (*stands up and offers him the box*): Oh yes, help
yourself. There is one thing I want to ask you . . . (*He
catches him up and walks out of the room behind him.*)

NEMOV: (*He spends a moment watching them leave. Then he

tears off a sheet of paper and writes some words on it.) All right, Chmuta, two pairs for you.

Enter YAKHIMCHUK, *large and dignified, his bald head shining.*

CHMUTA (*in a hostile voice*): Boss, be reasonable . . .

NEMOV: How many "professionals" will your gang take?

CHMUTA: I don't want any of your crooks! There isn't enough food to feed my own people . . .

NEMOV: You'll get two pairs of boots, that's all. You can go.

CHMUTA: Look, you think you're tough, but watch out. They'll break you. Come on, Ivan. Two pairs of boots among thirty-five men. It's ridiculous. (*He and the "drudge" prisoner walk out.*)

NEMOV: Sit down, Yakhimchuk. Tell me something. You're an old lag. All those years we were in the war, defending Russia, was it as bad as this in the camps?

YAKHIMCHUK *sits down.*

YAKHIMCHUK: It was much worse. We had no bread – just grain. You mixed it with snow and that was your soup for the day. During morning parade they'd read out lists of prisoners who'd been shot the day before. It's like a holiday camp now. (*Pause.*)

NEMOV: Will you take one "professional"? Just one?

YAKHIMCHUK: Those crooks have never done any work, not since the camp started. Gang foremen, work allocators – they just kill them . . .

NEMOV: I've had a taste of them already.

YAKHIMCHUK: They can do anything they want. Stalin likes them. They're what he calls "social allies".

NEMOV: Why are they "social allies"?

YAKHIMCHUK: That's what it says in the register. We're social enemies, so they must be social allies. It's been like that since the 'twenties.

NEMOV (*he is quite upset*): That's wonderful! You run away from the front line, become a deserter, there's a special Stalin amnesty and you're forgiven. You don't run away,

287

you fight and get captured by the Germans, and you're an enemy. I spent four years in the front line fighting the fascists, and now here I am, a fascist, while the ones who stayed in the rear thieving and murdering are called "social allies". Is that right? Our writers like the "professionals" too. They're always noble at heart, they always turn out right in the end. (*Makes a note on the paper.*) One pair of boots for you. Yours is a small gang.

YAKHIMCHUK: It's because Chmuta shouts at you and I don't, isn't it? In our foundry boots burn away, literally burn away. Bits of molten metal fly through the air and burn right through them. You stand on something hot, and your sole's burnt right through. We do our quota two hundred per cent, we're Stakhanovites. Give us four pairs for the foundry and the smithy.

NEMOV: Four pairs! What *do* you mean? I gave Chmuta two. All right, I'll give *you* two. (*Notes it down.*)

YAKHIMCHUK: Fine, you won't regret it. (*He walks towards the door, then comes back.*) Look, I'll tell you something. You stay here as production boss, that's all right by me. But if they sling you out, I'll take you into the foundry. So you needn't be afraid.

NEMOV: Thank you, Nikolay. I'll stick where I am for the moment. (*Exit* YAKHIMCHUK. NEMOV *is alone.*) For the moment . . . I must be out of my mind. It's like a bad dream. What did I want to go and become one of the bosses for? I thought it was like the army -- Officer! On the command, left, right! Or was it just fear of general duties? General duties -- it's horrible, it's as good as a death sentence (*Pause.*) Only being a boss here is worse than death . . .

Repeated knocking on the door. Finally NEMOV *hears it.*)
Come in!

Enter SHUROCHKA, *as usual in a fashionable hat and a brightly coloured overcoat.*

SHUROCHKA: Good evening. May I? I'm sorry to disturb you . . .

288

NEMOV: What can I do for you? You want to stay here?

SHUROCHKA: Why, are they going to send some of us on?

NEMOV: Of course. What would we do with the lot of you?

SHUROCHKA: Then I want to stay! I must stay! They've taken us far enough already – me who spent my whole life in Moscow.

NEMOV: What are you in for?

SHUROCHKA: Article 58, of course. Same as everyone else.

NEMOV: A girl like you getting mixed up in politics?

SHUROCHKA: Oh no, it wasn't true! I'm a theatre-lover, I prefer the world of elegance . . . I heard a conversation and didn't report it . . . Couldn't you fix me some sort of . . . some sort of office job?

NEMOV: There's nothing like that.

SHUROCHKA: I used to work as a secretary – typing and book work. My name's Shurochka.

NEMOV (*he nods*): I can imagine. You used to rush up to the stage shouting "bravo", carrying your handbag, cheering your favourite tragic actor. You saved your money for weeks to buy tickets, because it *had* to be the first night. You bought them from the touts at the door . . . I'm sorry, you see, I've only been here a few days, I can hardly . . . Why don't you go to the culture office or the clerk's room? Maybe if one of the men there liked the look of you . . .

SHUROCHKA: The look of me. Are you suggesting that . . .

NEMOV (*sadly*): I'm not suggesting anything. Only that's the way it is . . .

SHUROCHKA (*with passion*): Tell me, what is it that makes people in the camps so horrible? Were they different outside? Or were they just lying low?

Enter the visiting warder.

WARDER: All right, Nemov, what about this barber?

NEMOV: We've got one. Except that it's a woman. Except that her job's making theatrical wigs.

WARDER: This one? (SHUROCHKA *blushes and walks*

289

away.) All right, so long as she's strong enough not to
drop the scissors.

NEMOV: Where is she? (*Claps his hands*.) Angel! (ANGEL
appears in the doorway.) Remember that first girl you
went and got? The cheeky one? Go and get her. (*Exit*
ANGEL.) Have you picked your people for the transport?
Knock on the door. Enter the two girl students.

WARDER: I suppose so. It's just a lucky dip -- no time to
look them over. The lorries are waiting at the
check-point.

1ST STUDENT: Comrade director . . .

2ND STUDENT: Excuse me . . .

NEMOV: What's the matter now?

1ST STUDENT: We want to go. We've heard it's a good
transport.

WARDER: That's right, it's wonderful. Of course it's a good
transport. We're out in the woods. You should smell the
trees during the summer. It's like a holiday in the
country.

NEMOV: It's nearly winter!

WARDER: It's all right in winter too. You see, there aren't
enough guards, so we can't take the prisoners out to
work. They just lie on their bunks! Go on, write them
down! (*He shoves the list in front of* NEMOV.)

NEMOV: You'll regret it, girls.

BOTH GIRLS: Oh no, we won't. Go on, write us down.
NEMOV *writes them in.*

WARDER: Hurry up and get your things. Meet me at the
check-point. Go on, quickly! (*The students run off
chattering excitedly*.) Stupid little things! Swamps,
mosquitoes, tree-felling – what use will they be? Unless
our lieutenant takes a fancy to one of them, that's their
only hope. He's crazy about women and we haven't got a
single one. He's starving! I'll take that barber too. He'll
be beside himself!

Enter LYUBA.

NEMOV: Well, where were you? Don't you think I'm busy

enough without chasing you? (*To the warder.*) Here she is.

LYUBA: I don't know if I'll be right for the job.

WARDER: You'll be fine, just fine, a sharp little girl like you.

> LYUBA *comes closer and stretches out her hands. Her palms and the backs of her hands are covered in black blisters.*

NEMOV: What's wrong with them?

LYUBA: I don't know. They didn't tell me. I'm getting treatment. Maybe its infectious . . .

WARDER: Maybe it'll go away . . .

LYUBA: I've had it more than a year. It's torment!

WARDER: What a nuisance – a lovely girl like you. So what now? If our hair grows any longer we'll weave it into felt and make boots out of it. All right, off you go. We don't even have a surgery out there.

> *Exit* LYUBA.

NEMOV: How do you manage without a surgery?

WARDER: Oh, we manage. When here's no doctor somehow no one gets ill. They just live on and on until one day they're dead. No problem. (*He leaves. Enter* GAI. NEMOV *stands up and shakes his hand.* GAI *sits down.*)

NEMOV: Look here, Gai, we've got four professional crooks. What do we do with them?

GAI: Four's a lot. But you can give me two. If you must.

NEMOV: They'll refuse to work.

GAI: They'll work all right in my gang.

NEMOV (*writing them in*): You're a bit of a hero, Gai, isn't that so? What did you do in the war?

GAI: You mean, what didn't I do? Gun-aimer in an anti-aircraft unit. Then I was in a punishment battalion, then an artillery platoon commander. I shot down two Messerschmidts. (*Retreat is sounded outside.*)

NEMOV: I wish there was more time to talk and sort things out.

GAI: It makes me furious. I remember when counter-intelligence had me inside near the front line. They were tigers – the ones in the cell with me, tigers! We heard

stories about the camps and the political prisoners and
we thought it must be their own fault – big-headed
softies. We thought, just wait till we get to the camps,
we'll sort it all out. But now we're here – I don't know.
I'm stuck like an axe in the dough.

NEMOV: What are we to do, Gai? How can anyone explain it?

KOSTYA (*appears in the doorway and shouts at the prisoners
standing in line outside*): All right, everyone dismiss!
Retreat's sounded, office hours are over. Production
chief's busy. (*Dissatisfied murmurings.*) Angel, don't let
anyone else in, right? (*Enters.*) Well, that's better, they're
on their way. That's a couple of dozen cripples off our
hands.

NEMOV: I'm giving Gai two professional crooks. (GAI *shakes
hands with them both to bid goodbye.*)

KOSTYA: That's fine. (*Exit* GAI. KOSTYA *puts down a
packet of cigarettes in front of* NEMOV.) These are yours.
(*Claps his hands.*) Angel! (ANGEL *appears.*) Run over to
the cookhouse and get them to do us some rissoles or
something, enough for two.

NEMOV: Just a minute, Kostya. Hold it. Is this for us?

KOSTYA: Who do you think it's for?

NEMOV: O.K., Angel. Forget it. (*Exit* ANGEL, *looking very
disappointed.*) Kostya, you know I like you but . . . but
it's quite out of the question.

KOSTYA: You're a natural, aren't you? A real mug, green as
grass! How do you expect to live in this place? On prison
soup?

NEMOV: I'll live the same way the others do.

KOSTYA: Then you'll drop dead in a week.

NEMOV: Others don't . . .

KOSTYA: Oh yes they do! They're dropping like flies. I
write the registers, I see them being whisked off to
central hospital or else dumped straight in a mass grave.
You might as well listen. You've got a good job now,
and you might as well listen to what I'm saying.
Otherwise out you go on general duties . . .

NEMOV: To hell with your general duties . . .

KOSTYA: Now that's more like it. (*He takes from his pocket a bottle of vodka. Standing with his back to the door, he pours it into an earthenware mug.*) Look what I brought – a dozen drops each, enough to rinse our mouths out. But what shall we do for a chaser?

NEMOV: You know your way around, don't you? Where did you get it from? (*Drinks.*) I mean, it's not allowed inside is it?

KOSTYA: You bum, inside's where a man can *really drink*. (*He drinks up the vodka and puts the empty bottle back inside a drawer in his table.*) Aha! I'd forgotten. I've got a nice piece of salt fat. Here, have a bit as a chaser. (*Cuts off a bit and gives it to* NEMOV.) I got it from a Lithuanian for moving him to another gang.

NEMOV: Just imagine, I had a whole barrel of this when I was at the front. It was war booty. I used to give the boys a nip every day. I never drank it myself. But now I'm in here I like it.

KOSTYA: You're a tricky customer, Nemov.

NEMOV: Look, when are we going to allocate the new transport?

KOSTYA: We'll do it. The night is long.

NEMOV (*he is getting a bit tipsy*): I gave two of the crooks to Gai. Did I tell you that? . . . Kostya, forgive my asking . . . you're a bit of a crook yourself, isn't that right?

KOSTYA: Do I look like one?

NEMOV: Ye-es. You do a bit.

KOSTYA: I'm what they call a bitch.

NEMOV: What did you say?

KOSTYA: A bitch, that's what I said, a bitch.

NEMOV: What does it mean?

KOSTYA: It means I used to be a "professional" but I gave it up. I "bitched out" – that's what they say. We get jobs as work allocators or gang bosses or head prisoners. We help the administration. The "professionals" aren't allowed to do that. Any time there are three bitches and

293

one crook together in a room, we cut his throat. Three
crooks and one bitch – they cut our throats. That's the
way we get by.

NEMOV: What about me? What's the camp slang for what I
am?

KOSTYA: You? I've already told you what you are, you're a
mug. Little Lord Fauntleroy, that's what you are. I've
no time for people like you. But you put the boot in
those skivers, that's why I took a liking to you. They're
thick as thieves, those skivers, they're a closed shop, like
this. (*Holds up his hands with the fingers interwoven.*) Mind
you, I'm one of them. But there was a woman Rubyan
the storekeeper and I both wanted. So either I get him
sent out to cut trees, or else he gets me sent. That's why
I can go along with you. We can work together. Don't
worry, I'm reliable. "Mutual aid in action" – that's what
they teach you in the navy. What do we do next?

NEMOV (*by now quite drunk*): That's right, what do we do
next?

KOSTYA: Kitchen: the head cook's one of my men, so that's
all right. (*Crooks one finger, counting.*) Bread-cutting
room: we must have our own bread-cutter. That's
number two. And our own quartermaster – number three
. . . (*Crooks another finger.*)

The painted curtain falls.

*During the interval, though not immediately after the end of
the act, there is a change of sentries on the towers at the side
of the stage. Having relieved one sentry, the guard party
marches down into the stalls and across the auditorium in
front of the first row. If members of the audience are in their
way, the officer shouts at them rudely, "Get back from the
wire! Stop crowding!" then they relieve the other sentry.*

ACT II

Scene 1

The Camp Commandant

The spacious office of the camp commandant. The middle of the room is empty except for a strip of red carpet. A dozen chairs in a row with their backs to the left-hand wall. Further back is a door, and behind it in the corner a large bust of Stalin on a pedestal. At the back there is a wooden-plank partition with an opening and a pair of parted curtains on either side. Through it a bed can be seen. On the right are two windows which provide the only light in the room. Outside the weather is overcast. Also on the right is a writing desk, and on it a tall inkstand in the form of a Kremlin tower. There are also some shelves with a radio set on them, and a sofa.

It is quiet. The sound of rain falling into the drainpipes can be heard quite distinctly.

From behind the partition comes a heavy groaning noise, after which a pair of boots are lowered from the bed on to the floor. Lieutenant OVCHUKHOV *comes out into the room carrying his officer's tunic and wanders about.*

OVCHUKHOV: Blast the damn thing, where the hell is it?
    Bloody nuisance! God knows why they issue the things.
    We're not in the front line, are we? I haven't cleaned it
    for three years . . . If I report it I'm sunk, if I don't I'm
    sunk even deeper. (*Comes up to the window.*) It's been
    pouring for nearly three days now. (*Walks up to the desk.
    Without sitting down he rummages around in the papers.*)
    Look at this letter! I've only been back a few hours and
    it's here already. Do they drop it out of an aeroplane or
    something? I suppose they've got so many typists in
    Head Office now, they've got to justify their wages. (*He*

295

switches on the table lamp and tears open an envelope.)
Listen to this: Decision passed by full staff conference
. . . Point 34: "To warn Comrade Lieutenant
Ovchukhov that unless he achieves a sharp rise in
productivity he will be transferred to a labour camp in
the remote north of the country." They want to exile
me, somewhere up in Kolyma. They're tightening the
screws, they really are. (*He sits down at the desk.*) There's
only one way out. I'll have to report it. I'll tell them I've
lost my revolver. All right, let them throw me out of the
Service. I can find myself a job, can't I? Only not one
with thousands of roubles a month and food from the
camp store. No, I don't think so . . . Or they might put
me on trial. No, they won't throw me out. They'll put
me in, blow me up sky-high, but they won't throw me
out. (*Rings the bell.* ANGEL *appears in the doorway.*)

ANGEL: Welcome home, citizen commandant. Would you
care to order your breakfast?

OVCHUKHOV: Yes, go and get it. And send for that . . .
that production chief, what's his name?

ANGEL: He's out on the site, sir.

OVCHUKHOV: Well, go and get him.

ANGEL: Yes, sir. (*He leaves.* OVCHUKHOV *sits at the desk,
head in hands. A knock at the door.*)

OVCHUKHOV: Come in. (*Enter* SOLOMON. *He is very neatly
dressed.*)

SOLOMON: May I come in? Good morning, citizen
commandant. Welcome home! (OVCHUKHOV *mumbles
something in reply.*) Citizen commandant, this is for your
breakfast. (*Puts a bottle of vodka on the desk under the
lamp.*)

OVCHUKHOV: Solomon, where *do* you get these things
from?

SOLOMON: We do our little best, sir.

OVCHUKHOV (*pointing to behind the partition*): There's a
glass over there, pour me one. (SOLOMON *goes behind the
partition.*) Turn on the light.

A bright light is switched on. A knock at the door. Enter the head cook dressed in white carrying a tray covered with a muslin cloth. He closes the door skilfully behind him with his foot.

COOK (*putting tray down on desk*): Welcome home, sir.

OVCHUKHOV: To hell with you all, is this a conspiracy or what? Don't you know any other words?

COOK (*lifting the cloth*): It's *boeuf strogan*, sir.

OVCHUKHOV (*points*): And what's that?

COOK: Rice rissoles. *Sauce de plume.*

OVCHUKHOV: *Plume?* That sounds good. You're a good cook, aren't you? If you weren't I'd have had you on general duties long ago.

COOK (*indignantly*): Sir! What for?

OVCHUKHOV (*slyly*): You know what for. Now scram. (COOK *leaves.* SOLOMON *creeps up and presents the commandant with the glass. He drinks and starts to eat his breakfast.*) Hmm, good meat this. Not from the general kitchen, I hope? Trouble is, we feed you prisoners too well. What's the meat quota these days?

SOLOMON: Half-ounce basic ration. But if it's third-category offal – gullet, say, or lungs or oxtail – then they get more. Or sometimes we substitute fish or peas.

OVCHUKHOV: It's very good meat indeed! Go on, pour me another. (SOLOMON *presents him with another glass.*) Well, what's new? Let's have your report. This new production chief, how's he managing? What are you grinning about?

SOLOMON: Well, sir, you chose him, you appointed him, he must be all right.

OVCHUKHOV: Of course. I appointed him, which means he's all right. I understand about people. (*Pause.*) What are you getting at?

SOLOMON: Sir, he behaves like some king, like God Almighty. Like your deputy!

OVCHUKHOV: He's quite right. That's what I told him to be when I left him in my place.

297

SOLOMON: I couldn't agree with you more, sir. But being in your place doesn't mean he has to go against your wishes and countermand your orders . . .

OVCHUKHOV: What's that?

SOLOMON: For instance, the other day he re-distributed the extra rations. Then he really let himself go. He put the dentist on general duties. He's been tightening up on camp personnel . . .

OVCHUKHOV: Camp personnel needs more than tightening up. I'd like to send them *all* on general duties. I've had enough of our production figures dropping. All right, you're the clerk, you can stay; the cook too, he can stay. But as for all these quartermasters and barbers and deputy head prisoners, they can get out and do a day's work. I'm not getting posted to the North Pole on *your* account.

SOLOMON: Citizen director, you only have to say the word. If you say, "Solomon, during the day you will work in your office, during the night you will dig holes in the ground," I'll go straight out and get my pick-axe. But that Nemov – I'm not so sure about him. Another thing: the new boots – he just gave them out to anyone he felt like. He didn't get your permission.

OVCHUKHOV: He shouldn't have done that.

SOLOMON: I told him to wait till you got back, but no, he wouldn't. He's taken bribes from the new prisoners over who to send out on tree-felling.

OVCHUKHOV: Takes hands-outs, does he? Good for him. He'd be a fool if he didn't.

SOLOMON: Well, yes, I agree. But quite frankly, sir, he's not the sort of man we need here to raise our productivity. There's one man in the new transport, an engineer, talented, keen as mustard. Now he *knows* about productivity . . .

OVCHUKHOV: What does "talented" mean, I'd like to know? What is he, an opera singer? (*Reaction.*) I'll deal with your men of talent, Solomon . . . (*Knock on door.*) Come in!

Enter NEMOV. *His clothes are all wet.*

NEMOV: Citizen director! Production chief Nemov reporting as per instructions, sir!

OVCHUKHOV: You can see he's been in the army, can't you? Well, Solomon, what about your complaints? Where's he gone wrong?

SOLOMON: I've no complaints, sir.

OVCHUKHOV: Well, if you've no complaints you can go. (*Exit* SOLOMON.) And what have *you* been up to while I've been away? Bossing everyone around?

NEMOV (*speaking as if he was making a report to his superior officer*): Sir, I have acted strictly according to your instructions: productivity to be raised by all available means.

OVCHUKHOV: How much has it gone up, then?

NEMOV: During the past ten days productivity has been increased by eight per cent, sir.

OVCHUKHOV: That's magnificent! How did you manage it?

NEMOV: In the first place by investigating the quota office. I discovered the works department are swindling us. Sometimes they write an incomplete description of the assigned work. Sometimes they falsify the quotas.

OVCHUKHOV: Why wasn't Dorofeyev keeping his eye open for that? The bald son of a bitch! I'll send him on general duties. He's our man, from our camp. He ought to stand up for *us*, not the works department.

NEMOV: Citizen director, Dorofeyev's the one person who can't do a thing. He works for Gurvich. It won't help us if Gurvich throws him out after one day protecting our interests.

OVCHUKHOV: You know, I always felt the works department were screwing us. How much did you say you've upped production?

NEMOV: Eight per cent.

OVCHUKHOV: That's not enough, not nearly enough. It needs upping by *fifty*-eight per cent! No, not fifty-eight, sixty! Fifty-eight's something else. I'll have to see you get a few lessons, you haven't got the experience, you don't know your onions yet. (*Very distinctly.*) The prisoners have to be made to *work*! Today, for instance, it's raining. Have you been out and checked? I bet none of the outside workers are doing a stroke. You must go and drive them out. They aren't putting their *souls* into the work, that's the trouble. These prisoners are lazy bastards, they'd rather give up their bread ration and starve than get off their backs. It's your job to get them by the scruff of the neck. And if you have to clip them one round the ear in the process, that's fine by me. (NEMOV *says nothing.*) Now look at this. (*He picks up a piece of paper off the table and throws it at* NEMOV.) Here you are bellyaching to Gurvich about safety regulations. It's a lot of crap, and none of your business. Now, have you collected anything nice off the new transport?

NEMOV: I don't understand.

OVCHUKHOV: I mean jumpers, leather coats, silk skirts . . . Or do you want to pinch the lot for yourself?

NEMOV: I don't understand. (*Pause.*) Why should I take other people's belongings?

OVCHUKHOV: To *live*, you idiot! Rule number one in the camps! "You drop dead today, I'll drop dead tomorrow" – haven't you heard that? When you fought in the war you took booty, didn't you?

NEMOV (*embarrassed*): Yes, I did . . .

OVCHUKHOV: It's the same thing, Little Lord Fauntleroy . . . I'm sorry, Nemov, I'm not trying to insult you, but you'll never survive in the camps this way. You won't. You know what you should have done just now? Brought me something useful. "Here's a new skirt for your wife" or something, you should have said. And I'd have loved you for it.

NEMOV (*very depressed*): Sir, when we first met I told you I'd been an officer in the front line, that I had experience of leadership and that I would try to sort out our production. I didn't promise anything else.

OVCHUKHOV: All right, you raise productivity by sixty per
cent and I'll love you all the same. You step on the gas
and I'll back you up.

NEMOV: Very well, sir. I should like to suggest that we
halve the administrative personnel, get rid of those
hangers-on. There are too many people wandering about
inside the camp while others are outside working – for
example, in the book-keeping office and in the kitchen.
We seem to have two bread-cutters, three bath orderlies,
even though the bath-house never seems to be working,
and a million other people. There's the dentist, and I
know for a fact he hasn't crowned one single tooth. And
there are all those nurses in the hospital . . .
Knock on the door. Enter MERESHCHUN *without waiting
for an answer. He is fresh-looking, clean-shaven and thick-
set. Under his white coat we can see he is wearing*
KHOMICH's *bright red sweater.*

MERESHCHUN: Good morning, citizen commandant. (*He
walks across the room and sits down at* OVCHUKHOV's
desk. NEMOV *remains standing throughout.*)

OVCHUKHOV: Hullo, doctor. Production chief here's been
telling me you've got too many nurses. He says we ought
to cut down.

MERESHCHUN: He needn't be jealous. All he has to do is
to come and tell me who he wants. Manya? Clara?
Certainly, take your pick! (OVCHUKHOV *roars with
laughter.*) I've got two nurses on my staff, one for day-
duty, one for night-duty. I've got six others, but they
come under "patients", they're not mine. Production
chief ought to realise that.

NEMOV: In other words every day six people who are ill
have to go out to work instead of going into sick-bay? I
suppose this is to justify your nurses?

OVCHUKHOV (*waves him away*): You watch your tongue,
Nemov. So what if a few extra people go out to work,
the State doesn't lose anything, does it? (*To*
MERESHCHUN.) But it doesn't mean I don't love him,

so long as he raises productivity. (*To* NEMOV.) O.K., off
you go. Step on it and tighten the screws! I'll back you
up. (NEMOV *does a smart about-turn and leaves*.) That's a
very nice red sweater you're wearing . . .

MERESHCHUN: Just a minute! You're the one who owes *me*
a favour, not the other way round. (*Pause*.) I believe
you've lost something!

OVCHUKHOV (*startled*): What have I lost?

MERESHCHUN: You're sure you haven't lost anything?

OVCHUKHOV: You've found it? (MERESHCHUN *takes a
small packet out of his pocket.* OVCHUKHOV *quickly
unwraps it, finds the gun, waves it over his head and
embraces* MERESHCHUN *impulsively*.) You've done it,
you wonderful man! You've saved my life! Where was it?

MERESHCHUN (*relishing the situation*): Do you remember,
before your trip to Head Office? You came from the
guardroom and called on me in my hut.

OVCHUKHOV: That's right.

MERESHCHUN: And you had a drink . . .

OVCHUKHOV: A large drink.

MERESHCHUN: And then you fell asleep . . .

OVCHUKHOV: That's what happened.

MERESHCHUN: When did you get up, in the morning? I
didn't hear you, I slept through it. Then I went over to
your bed and on it was lying . . .

OVCHUKHOV: Must have fallen out of the holster. Little
darling! (*Fondles the gun*.)

MERESHCHUN: I rushed to your study, then I rushed to
the guardroom. They said you'd gone.

OVCHUKHOV: I searched high and low. I searched the
ground all the way back.

MERESHCHUN: I was terrified. There's always a search
before October Revolution Day. I couldn't keep it in the
hut, so I wrapped it in a bit of cloth and hid it under the
steps. So here we are!

OVCHUKHOV: That's superb. Thank you, Mereshchun. I
was scared they'd throw me out of Security. I'd decided

302

not to own up till next pay-day. Well, what do you
want? Half my kingdom is yours! Only there's nothing
you need, is there? You live better here than you would
outside. You turn your nose up at the cookhouse rations,
you've got as many women as you want, and as for
vodka, *you're* the one who brings it to *me*. So what's it to
be? You want to go into town for a week without escort?
Now there's an offer! You're an Article 58 man, you
know what that means?

MERESHCHUN: A trip to town? Now that's a possibility.

OVCHUKHOV: It's not a possibility at all, it's absolutely
impossible. But I'll do it! I know you'll be back, you
won't find a better paradise than here. What else do you
want?

MERESHCHUN: Thank you, sir, don't think there's
anything else. Except perhaps . . . I'd like to help
you . . .

OVCHUKHOV: Go on, go on . . .

MERESHCHUN: Why was it they called you to Head Office?
They're leaning on you to achieve higher productivity?
(*Pause.*) Aren't they?

OVCHUKHOV: It's not a matter of leaning on me, they're
squeezing hell out of me. I can hear my bones crack!
They said, "We shall be forced to send you to the Arctic
Circle." I've got a flat here and a family, I've started
building a house . . . Well, at least the gun's been found.

MERESHCHUN: Listen, if you want to increase
productivity, I've found just the man. He's perfect. He'd
send his own father out into the forest if it would help
his production figures.

OVCHUKHOV: Is that so? He sounds ideal. Where did you
find him?

MERESHCHUN: (*Rings the little bell.* ANGEL *runs in.*) Go
and get engineer Khomich. He's staying in camp today,
he's off sick. (ANGEL *runs out.*) He's efficient, he's
demanding, and he knows productivity inside out. He'll
fix it for you just like that.

OVCHUKHOV: Hmm . . . It would mean I'd have to sack this one.

MERESHCHUN: Which one? The Marshal? The "professionals" call him "The Marshal".

OVCHUKHOV (*laughs*): That's good . . .

MERESHCHUN: I was an officer myself, I can see he's the sort of man who might be used *in the army*. But he's no good here. You have to understand the *soul* of a prisoner in the camps. Five hundred grammes of black bread a day – they built the White Sea Canal on that. (*Knock at door.*)

OVCHUKHOV: The soul . . . Yes, you're right. Come in. (*Enter* KHOMICH.)

KHOMICH: Engineer Khomich reporting, sir.

OVCHUKHOV: What sort of engineer? Civil engineer?

KHOMICH: Yes, sir.

OVCHUKHOV: What about mechanics!

KHOMICH: I'm an engineer of that too.

OVCHUKHOV: Electrical work?

KHOMICH: I spent three years on it.

OVCHUKHOV: Sanitary installation?

KHOMICH: Yes, I know a bit about that.

OVCHUKHOV: Good heavens, the man's a miracle.

MERESHCHUN: There's one speciality he hasn't told you about – he's an engineer in human souls.

OVCHUKHOV: Is he now? Well, we'll check that right away. Suppose I make you production chief and say to you, "Increase productivity!" Where would you start?

KHOMICH: I'd start with the bread. For example, I'd issue the minimum bread guarantee for one hundred and one per cent norm fulfilment, not for one hundred as it is now. Then all those who work by the hour would switch over to piece work. It would work out in our favour. Next, I'd lower the scale for those who qualify for top rations . . .

OVCHUKHOV: Just a minute. That scale's been laid down by Camp Central Office. We can't . . .

KHOMICH: We can! Don't worry, no one's going to get into

304

trouble. I used that dodge in my last camp. I was work superintendent. Brilliant results!

OVCHUKHOV: It's certainly a stroke of imagination.

KHOMICH: Next, we must change the scale for the porridge issues. We must make them over-fulfil their quota more and more to get an extra bowl of porridge.

OVCHUKHOV: We thought that one out ourselves. We've upped the quotas as much as we dared. If we go any higher we'll drive them over the limit. They'll turn "goner" on us.

MERESHCHUN: No, they won't. As a doctor I'm telling you they will not turn "goner".

KHOMICH: Thirdly, meetings between men and women will be allowed only for one hundred and fifty per cent norm fulfilment. Night meetings: two hundred and one per cent qualifies for one night together, two hundred and fifty per cent for two nights. Fourthly, food parcels for prisoners who fulfil their quota by less than one hundred and twenty per cent will not be accepted from the post office.

OVCHUKHOV: Do we have the right to do that?

KHOMICH: Listen, by the time the relatives have worked things out, written complaints and sent them to Moscow, and Moscow sends them on to us, we'll have had three months to get a grip on the prisoners who live off their own food, the ones who don't need the cookhouse food. They'll realise: either work like an ox or drop dead. A very important lesson! Number five – fixing the rates. I'll manage that myself. Number six . . .

OVCHUKHOV: This is excellent stuff. How many more points?

KHOMICH: About fifteen.

OVCHUKHOV: All right, what's the sixteenth?

KHOMICH: Number sixteen – thanks to a general increase in productivity we shall be able to detail a construction team to work on your own house and finish it by the anniversary of the October Revolution!

OVCHUKHOV: That's right. That's the answer I wanted! There's carpentry to be done and painting and . . .

KHOMICH: I know, I know.

MERESHCHUN: Sixteen points altogether.

OVCHUKHOV: That's what I call efficiency – and experience. (*Rings the bell. Enter* SOLOMON, *hands behind his back.*) How did you guess it was you I was ringing for?

SOLOMON: Angel had to go out for a minute, sir. I came in so that you wouldn't be kept waiting.

OVCHUKHOV: Go and get me the order book.

SOLOMON (*producing the book from behind his back*): Right here, sir.

OVCHUKHOV (*quite amazed*): You're as wise as old King Solomon! How did you guess I wanted the order book?

SOLOMON: It's my job to guess your thoughts, sir.

OVCHUKHOV: Marvellous staff I've got, marvellous! I know how to choose the right people, that's what it is. Comrade Stalin was quite right. He said, "Personnel selection is decisive. People are our most valuable capital." I want that slogan up in the camp yard!

SOLOMON: It's hanging in the canteen, sir.

OVCHUKHOV: They're a lot of fools in the culture office. All they know about is pinching wood from the construction site. I meant to tell them, "He who does not work does not eat" should be hung in the canteen. "Valuable capital" should be hung outside.

SOLOMON: I'll tell them, sir.

OVCHUKHOV: Sit down and write what I say. (SOLOMON *sits down and puts on his glasses*.) Order number . . . What's the number?

SOLOMON: Two hundred and thirty-six.

OVCHUKHOV: Right. Paragraph one. Prisoner . . . What's his name . . .?

MERESHCHUN: Nemov . . .

KHOMICH: Prisoner Nemov, for his failure to guarantee a sharp increase in productivity, is to be dismissed from his post as . . .

SOLOMON: May I suggest, sir? It might look better if we put "for permitting a decrease in productivity"?

OVCHUKHOV: Fine, go ahead. "For permitting a decrease in productivity . . ."

MERESHCHUN: Hadn't we better say "for permitting a sharp decrease in productivity . . ."?

OVCHUKHOV: . . . is hereby dismissed for permitting a sharp decrease in productivity and output. Paragraph two. In his place I hereby appoint to the post of production chief prisoner . . .

MERESHCHUN: Prisoner Engineer Khomich!
Painted curtain falls.

Scene 2

The Rate-fixing Office

*A spacious high-ceilinged room, crudely plastered, in a building which is still under construction. By the left-hand wall is a huge awkward looking table. Further along the same wall there is a door with a plate on it reading "*SENIOR WORK SUPER-INTENDENT*". In the back wall there is a door leading into the kitchen where* LYUBA *is cooking, and another door leading on to the staircase. The right-hand wall has two windows.* DOROFEYEV, *with a towel wrapped round his bald head and forehead, is sitting at the table surrounded by handbooks and papers. In the middle and towards the front of the stage there is another table belonging to no one in particular. A few roughly planed benches and stools, some broken, some in one piece.*

It is the day when percentages are calculated to determine the fulfilment of norms. The office is buzzing with various foremen filling in work order-forms, and gang bosses arguing with them. Their clothes and footwear show that it is raining and muddy. People come in and go out, writing things down either standing

*up or sitting down wherever they can find a place. They keep
grabbing forms from the rate-fixer and spoiling them, pestering
the exhausted* DOROFEYEV *and taking books from the table.*
NEMOV *too takes a lively part in the discussions.*

*The room is dark, untidy, full of cigarette smoke and stuffy.
Amid the hubbub various remarks can be heard.*

GAI: What about the mortar preparation?

FOMIN: It's included in the bricklaying rate. You don't do
it by hand, do you? You do it with a mixer.

CHMUTA (*shouting at* FOMIN): It's a double-cross on good,
honest folk, do you hear? What the hell use is your
mixer when it works one hour and then the current fails
for the whole day?

KHOMICH *comes out of the work superintendent's room. He
walks slowly across to the table at the front and sits down on
it, his back to the audience.*

1ST FOREMAN: These figures aren't written with a pen,
they're piled up with a shovel. You can't do a hundred
and twenty per cent, it'd kill you, you'd be down
crawling on all fours.

1ST GANG LEADER: What do you mean, only eighteen
kopecks a hole? This is marking and boring, I have to
use a vertical milling machine.

DOROFEYEV: My dear boy, these are norms, it's the
standard rate approved by the State. It doesn't say
anything about the machine you use.

2ND GANG LEADER: Plan? It's a load of shit! "Put up floor
supports," they say, so I do that. "Do the flooring,"
they say, so I do the flooring. Now you want me to rip it
up? Is it my fault if you want a cement floor? Look,
production chief, if I'm not paid for this work I'll tell the
gang to down tools. You'll have to appoint a dispute
commission.

NEMOV: We're not responsible for your bosses' mistakes,
foreman; pay for them yourself.

DOROFEYEV: Who took my handbook on concrete? Come
on, who's got it? I can't work in conditions like . . .

MACHINE-SHOP FOREMAN (*who looks like a typical Young Communist*): What did you say? Lathe turning? Sixteen man-days? It's like something out of a comic magazine. I ask you . . .

1ST GANG LEADER: It was that day when there was no electricity. The bushes were urgent, so you made us turn the lathes by hand, didn't you? You didn't talk about comic magazines then.

MACHINE-SHOP FOREMAN: Well, you'll have to phrase it differently, do you understand? You can't leave nonsense like that in a historical record . . . (*He picks up the work order-forms and takes them into the work superintendent's room.*)

NEMOV: Yes or no? Are you going to pay for the floor supports, for removing them, and for two journeys carrying the boards?

1ST FOREMAN: Where do you expect me to find the money? *Enter* BRYLOV. *He saunters over and mixes with the others and then sits down next to* DOROFEYEV, *where he stays until he leaves the stage.*

GAI: What about carrying the stuff to the mixer? Why isn't that in?

DOROFEYEV: It's less than ten metres. We don't pay anything for that.

GAI: All right, it's eight metres, but it means two men all day on the barrow.

DOROFEYEV: There's nothing about it in the standard rates. Let me get on with my work.

CHMUTA: Give me that order! Give it back! (*He snatches the order-form out of the foreman's hands and tears it to pieces.*) You can go and jump in the lake! The plaster falls off, so who has to do the work all over again? Me? We built the stove and you've got to pay for it . . .

GAI: Comrade Fomin, I appeal to your conscience. The men are being pushed over the limit. All day long on the barrows, then back to camp, swallow down a mug of hot water with cabbage in it and it's time to go to bed. If we

309

could only give them some porridge in the evening.

FOMIN: I understand exactly, my dear boy. I'm exhausted myself. Look, my nose and my beard, they're all I have left in the world. They've told us to cut the orders, not to give the camp any money. I'd get the sack if I signed these puffed-up figures of yours . . .

A VOICE: That's a fine job you've done with the concrete; all the fittings have fallen out.

DOROFEYEV: Don't touch those books, don't touch them!

IST FOREMAN (*to* DOROFEYEV): Why did you let the gang leaders get their hands on these registers? Twenty was marked down here, and now someone's added a nought – two hundred!

3RD GANG LEADER: It looks like your handwriting.

DOROFEYEV: How can I stop them? They take the damn things themselves. This place is impossible to work in.

2ND GANG LEADER: Did I put floor supports in, or did I not?

IST FOREMAN: There's something been changed here too. And here.

YAKHIMCHUK: The smiths haven't been earning a penny on these figures, not even as they stand now.

SMITH FOREMAN: How much did you earn for the chains, then? Three norms a day, wasn't it?

CHMUTA (*shouting*): You can't even do your job properly!

NEMOV: So you are not going to pay?

2ND FOREMAN: That's right.

NEMOV (*to* 2ND GANG LEADER): O.K., tell your man, down tools! It's time this was put a stop to – treating everyone like slaves.

2ND GANG LEADER *moves towards the exit but he is stopped at the door by* KHOMICH *shouting in a voice of command.*

KHOMICH (*sitting on the table, motionless, with his back to the audience*): Just a minute! You, gang leader, where are you off to?

2ND GANG LEADER: To tell my men to down tools. What's it to do with you?

KHOMICH: Now calm down. What's all this, a sit-down strike? Who gave you permission?

2ND GANG LEADER: Production chief gave me permission. Who do you think you are?

KHOMICH: What production chief? I'm production chief. *Suddenly the noise stops and is replaced by complete silence and general immobility.* LYUBA *peers out from the kitchen wearing a white apron. She freezes in this pose.*

NEMOV: You mean . . . What do you mean?

KHOMICH: I mean what I say.

NEMOV: Excuse me but . . . who appointed you?

KHOMICH: The camp commandant.

NEMOV: But I was with him half an hour ago.

KHOMICH: I was with him ten minutes ago.

NEMOV: How could it happen? He never called me in, he never told me . . .

CHMUTA: It can happen! My dear Nemov, in the camps anything can happen.

NEMOV: But why? . . . People don't behave like that . . . Not even cannibals behave like that . . . I'll go and enquire . . . No one's told me anything . . .

KHOMICH: They won't let you past the check-point. You can join your gang and work with them for the rest of the day, do your bit for the quota. (*Raising his voice.*) Attention all gang leaders! I've had enough of this permanent racket over the rate-fixing. In future everyone entering this office without my permission will wish he'd never been born.

CHMUTA: Three cabinet ministers spent ten years trying to re-educate me. They got nowhere, and neither will you.

KHOMICH (*speaking in the same tone as before*): It's like a circus! Everyone yelling, going on strike, prisoners lounging around indoors hiding from the rain . . . Go and get them out to work, every single man!

The gang leaders silently and unhurriedly begin to disperse.

311

DOROFEYEV: Hmm, it's so quiet all of a sudden. (*Peering at* KHOMICH *out of the corner of his eyes.*) Now we'll be able to get some work done. There's going to be law and order, I can see that right away. (*To* BRYLOV.) I've been having such terrible headaches . . .

BRYLOV: So have I, my head's like a football.

DOROFEYEV (*pointedly*): My head aches because I'm ill.

BRYLOV: I had this dream, you see, I can't get over it, and it was days ago . . .

YAKHIMCHUK (*to* NEMOV): What about it, then? You'll join us in the foundry?

BRYLOV: What do you think you're playing at? I'm boss in the foundry. We've got enough mouths to feed. We're short of coke. What are we going to live on?

YAKHIMCHUK (*to* BRYLOV): Don't make so much noise. Who feeds who, that's what I want to know.

NEMOV: I'm very grateful to you comrade, but it depends on whether . . . (*Looks at* KHOMICH.)

KHOMICH: You see, I'm a gentleman. You never did *me* any harm personally. If Yakhimchuk wants you, that's all right by me.

BRYLOV: What do you mean "all right by you"? I don't want him, I'm boss in the foundry!

YAKHIMCHUK *leads* NEMOV *away. Now that the gang leaders have left, the foremen begin to leave as well.*
KHOMICH *jumps off the table and comes right to the front of the stage.*

KHOMICH: Dorofeyev . . . (DOROFEYEV *stands up hurriedly.*)

DOROFEYEV: Yes, sir, I'm listening. (*He walks up to him.*)

KHOMICH (*so that the others can't hear him*): The camp commandant has assigned you a task. It is your job to *double* the productivity of every single gang!

DOROFEYEV: S-sir, how can I do that? If it says one rouble in the book how can I make it two roubles?

KHOMICH: Stop trying to find someone stupider than yourself, Dorofeyev, and stop swinging the lead. All

312

right, it's thirty-two kopecks for a metre of plaster work, everyone knows that. But what about, say, a conic pinion? How long does it take to make one of those? Ten hours? Fifty hours? Who the hell knows?

DOROFEYEV: But that's a criminal offence. I don't want to get a second term. They're standard rates which the State has . . .

KHOMICH: What State? This isn't a State, this is Campland!

DOROFEYEV: Gurvich'll find out in no time. He'll give me the sack.

KHOMICH: If he does we'll fix you up inside the camp. We'll keep you warm. But if *we* kick you out, you'll drop dead under a tree. Do you understand? (*Enter* ZINA *from the right. She is all dolled up, carrying a sheaf of papers and walking towards* GURVICH's *office.*)

ZINA: Congratulations! (*She shakes* KHOMICH's *hand.*) I heard about it yesterday.

KHOMICH (*walking away from* DOROFEYEV): You couldn't have heard yesterday. I was only appointed today.

ZINA: My old man Pososhkov knew about it yesterday. He finds everything out, knows it all before the commandant does. Tonight we're having a party in your honour. You haven't got a wife yet, have you? You'd better get moving.

KHOMICH: Ah-hh, the sweet life . . . "My lovely, silly happiness with white windows looking out on to the orchard . . ." (*Exit right.* GURVICH, *a pack of work order-forms in his hand, comes smartly out of his room and runs into* ZINA. *The machine-shop foreman is with him.*)

GURVICH: Dorofeyev? (DOROFEYEV *jumps up.*) These metalworkers' figures – you cooked them, didn't you? (*He throws the order-forms at* DOROFEYEV *across the room.* DOROFEYEV *picks them up hurriedly.*) How much did you rate them per washer?

DOROFEYEV: Three kopecks, comrade Gurvich. Just like it says in the handbook . . .

GURVICH: Do you realise there are four thousand washers? You know how much they'll collect that way? Change it to three-tenths of a kopeck.

DOROFEYEV: But comrade Gurvich, they're standard State-approved rates . . .

GURVICH: That's enough about the State. Any more of this talk and I'll sling you out and have you laying bricks. I'll replace you with a non-prisoner. You and the camp boys are thick as thieves, aren't you? You've got gang leaders on your back the whole time, making you fix the order-forms. You'd better watch it, people end up in court for what you're doing. (*He flips through a document which* ZINA *has just handed him.*) Just a minute . . . "Prisoner Matveyev fell down the shaft because there was no proper fence round the . . ." What's this nonsense? Take it away and type it out again. Write: "In spite of the adequate fencing round the shaft, Prisoner Matveyev flung himself over the edge with the intention of committing . . ."

ZINA: But the safety inspector will . . .

GURVICH: He's not an inspector, he's a bloody fool, he'll agree to anything we say. Don't worry, I've fixed it. Do it out in four copies . . . (*Moves* ZINA *to one side. She leaves.*) Brylov, what about this bronze?

BRYLOV: Don't worry, it's in the bag. I know about these furnaces, I'll tell Munitsa how to do it. We'll get you the best bronze.

GURVICH: Yes, but when?

BRYLOV: Three days' time.

GURVICH: That's no good, I want it tomorrow. First smelting tomorrow.

LYUBA (*barring his way*): Dinner's ready, comrade Gurvich.

GURVICH: I haven't got time for dinner . . .

LYUBA: It'll dry up and boil away. What do we do, then?
GURVICH *waves his hands and leaves, accompanied by the machine-shop foreman.*

BRYLOV: "First smelting tomorrow" – huh! Quick as a flea,

314

isn't he? I'll complain about him to Head Office. "High-quality iron," he says. How the hell? One – there's no ambulatory, two – we have to charge the furnace by eye, three – the coating isn't right, four – there's no manganese. Shall I complain?

DOROFEYEV *sits there in silence, head in hands.*

KOLODEY *walks in slowly and looks around.*

KOLODEY: Well, how are things? Everything in order? No rules being broken? (*Silence.*) Dorofeyev, what do you use for sharpening pencils?

DOROFEYEV: A razor-blade, citizen commander. We've got a little bit of razor-blade.

KOLODEY: Don't you know cutting and stabbing objects are against the rules?

LYUBA: How can I peel Gurvich's potatoes, then?

KOLODEY: Use your teeth for all I care. But no knives! Have you got any knives in the kitchen?

LYUBA: No.

KOLODEY: I should think not. (*Sits down and lights a cigarette.*) All right, Lyuba, which girl in your barrack-room keeps sneaking off and spending every night in the men's quarters?

LYUBA: How should I know? I sleep during the night.

KOLODEY: I know, you lot are always asleep. Then I lift up the blanket and find it's a dummy, or else there's a man in with you. Then two seconds later you're dragged off to hospital to produce some squalling brat. Who does your work while you're in hospital?

LYUBA: I don't see how you can ban love-making. We're not made of wood. We're in here for ten years.

KOLODEY: If they ban it, they ban it, and that's that. You shouldn't have committed crimes, should you?

LYUBA: That's right. Just think how many children are born in the camps. They all ought to be strangled at birth.

KOLODEY (*startled*): What do you mean?

LYUBA: What else can we do with them? If the father's a

criminal and the mother's a criminal, what sort of a
child's it going to be? Another criminal. How's it going
to fill in those forms when it grows up?

KOLODEY: We-ell, yes. Perhaps you're right . . .

LYUBA: But then on the other hand I'm wrong. A son's not
responsible for what his father did, is he? Maybe we
ought to be glad there are children born in the camps. If
every woman had a child, that'd mean millions of extra
soldiers, right?

KOLODEY: That's true, very true . . . (*He sighs and stands
up.*) Oh well, you'll do what you're told, that's one thing
for sure. Poor Comrade Stalin – so many worries, so
many things to think about! All right, keep working.
(*Exit.*)

DOROFEYEV (*in despair to* BRYLOV): Who intended this
damn rate-fixing? Before the Revolution I worked as an
apprentice to a State-employed foreman. We had no rate-
fixing, no book-keeping, but we built a house that'll
stand for a hundred years without repair. Do you
remember the way it was?

BRYLOV: No ambulatory, no scales, sub-standard coating –
I'll have to complain . . . (*Exit.*)

LYUBA (*standing stock-still by the window*): Keep working,
keep working – poor wretched prisoners, rain or snow,
that's all there is to do. Then back to camp, off with the
wet things, dry them out – only where? In bed, that's
where. Bed's the only warm place in the camp. (*To*
DOROFEYEV.) Is your head still aching?

DOROFEYEV: You're a sweet girl, Lyuba. If only I could
take a spade and go out in the mud with the others.
Anything rather than torture myself in here. They're
squeezing me on both sides, I can't even breathe . . .

LYUBA (*sits down on the table at the front, facing the
audience*): No, Dorofeyev, you're wrong. Winter's
coming, we're better off here. When the snowstorms
start and they make you dig solid frozen earth without
even a pair of gloves . . . Oh no.

DOROFEYEV: I'll probably die soon. They say there's going to be another amnesty before Revolution Day. All the Article 58 prisoners will be released. They say it's there, lying on Stalin's desk, all he has to do is sign it . . .

LYUBA: Come off it, the only release we'll get is into the next world . . . (*Pause.*) I feel sorry for him . . .

DOROFEYEV: Who?

LYUBA: Him . . . you know . . . Nemov.

DOROFEYEV: Aren't you sorry for yourself?

LYUBA: Sorry for myself? No. Not any more.

The painted curtain falls.

During the interval the sentries on the towers are changed as before.

ACT III

Scene 1

The Bronze Has Got Stuck

The foundry, as in Act I Scene 2, except that this time the moulding earth has been shaped into a cone. In various places new moulding has been started. On the left and towards the back of the stage is a furnace for smelting bronze, a round brick structure with a tin hood and a flue which disappears into the ceiling. A constant tapping sound can be heard coming from the cupola-shaped furnace on the right, underneath which a pair of feet can be seen. Near the front of the stage MUNITSA *and* CHEGENYOV *are sitting on the floor.*

CHEGENYOV: You know what's happened? They've gone soft. Ten years? They ought to give idiots like you twenty-five! All right, I'm not going to touch it, you sort your own damn furnace out.

MUNITSA *sits there, silent and depressed. Enter* BRYLOV. *He sits down next to them on the floor.*

BRYLOV: You know, Munitsa, you're a stupid bugger. You are, you know. Do you think it's only your Rumania that's got furnaces? You think there aren't any in mother Russia? I've forgotten more about furnaces than you've ever clapped your eyes on, *but* . . . I keep my mouth shut. You know why I keep my mouth shut? Because life's easier without furnaces. No one pesters you. So long as there's coke, there's iron. Pour it in the moulds bit by bit, enough for you, enough for us. What more can a guy ask for, eh? What more can a guy ask?

CHEGENYOV: Well, for one thing, we ask for some butter. The stuff you brought was sour.

BRYLOV: You're crazy! How can butter be sour?

318

CHEGENYOV: Well, it is and that's that. It's all puffy and runny like cream cheese. Still on the make, aren't you? Only you'll never get rich the way you do it.

BRYLOV: Come on, boys, what's the matter? Something wrong? Well, maybe my old woman made a mistake. Maybe she had one too many and bought the wrong kind of butter.

CHEGENYOV: She drinks too, does she?

BRYLOV: My dear boy, who doesn't drink these days? My first wife kept herself in hand, but this one's pissed half the time. Mind you, she'd have to be a saint not to. I keep a crate of vodka under our bed. It's never empty. If it was, I'd never get a wink of sleep!

MUNITSA: So what Gurvich say?

BRYLOV: I have to carry the can, that's what. It's all my fault. "Brylov mucked up the bronze." "Brylov stopped the excavators." Did I make any promises? No, I did not. I always said that furnace of yours was a washout.

MUNITSA: But bronze must be! It must be!

BRYLOV: It'll pour down and make a hole in your head . . . You'll never make the big time, Munitsa. There are plenty of people cleverer than you in the world, but no one's ever thought up a furnace like yours. If it was that simple any fool could build a furnace. Now you'd better think up a way to break it open. You've ruined forty kilos of bronze, just burnt it up. All right, to hell with the bronze, it's not our money. But it'll be a problem to break open the furnace. The bronze has got stuck.

MUNITSA: We break it quick.

Enter YAKHIMCHUK *from the right.*

BRYLOV (*to* YAKHIMCHUK): He still wants to build his damn furnace.

YAKHIMCHUK: Well, why not? So long as he does it proper.

MUNITSA: How? How I do it proper?

YAKHIMCHUK: No ideas? You were the one who wanted to.

319

BRYLOV: I see, you're all against me, are you? All right, I'll throw the lot of you out and get my own men. It was bad enough when you brought your damn Marshal into the place. (*Nods in the direction of the cupola.*) Sponger! Why did you have to saddle me with him? The coke's running out, the iron's running out, what are we going to live on?

MUNITSA (*losing his temper*): This man no good. He son of a bitch, he can't do nothing!

CHEGENYOV (*reaches out for a spade*): You grits-eating jerk, I'll get you! You can't talk to a Don Cossack like that . . .

MUNITSA (*to* YAKHIMCHUK): But how? How to do it?

YAKHIMCHUK: I don't know. I'm not the one going for a bonus.

MUNITSA: So, you don't know. So don't say you know.

YAKHIMCHUK: But what if I do know?

MUNITSA: What if you don't know?

BRYLOV: I wish I'd never clapped eyes on the damn thing . . .

CHEGENYOV: Don't tell him, boss. Don't tell him. He'll collect a hundred thousand roubles . . .

YAKHIMCHUK: Cabbage-head! You need a narrower burner and smaller air-ducts. Those gaping holes aren't any good.

GURVICH *walks quickly in.*

GURVICH: O.K., what's this, a boy scouts' rally? First you make a mess of the bronze and now here you are holding meetings. You're a big-head, Munitsa, aren't you?

MUNITSA: You wait. Bronze in pipeline.

GURVICH: You lot have got everything in the pipeline – frying pans, irons, cooking pots. You're supplying the town with consumer goods better than a Moscow shop. I ought to post the lot of you, have you out cutting trees . . .

BRYLOV: My boys haven't done anything wrong. The furnace is impossible. Ask the engineers. I've been in foundries since I was so high, I don't like this sort of talk. You'd better send me to the Urals to organise those crucibles . . .

GURVICH: Send you to the Urals? I'd rather send you down the river. Look at this planing machine! You've got it turning out irons non-stop, haven't you? There's no time for the machine parts. (*He comes up to* YAKHIMCHUK *and puts his hands round his shoulder.*) Yakhimchuk, I appeal to you, as one human being to another, think of something, help me. The excavators are standing idle, they're not earning a penny. Can't we get a temporary furnace going, boys? Just for one smelting?

MUNITSA: O.K., Comrade Gurvich, we change burner, we change ducts, we get bronze. We get first-class bronze.

Enter MACHINE-SHOP FOREMAN

MACHINE-SHOP FOREMAN (*to* GURVICH): Cutting press has stopped, sir.

GURVICH (*as if bitten by a snake*): Oh no, not again! Yakhimchuk, you will help us? Munitsa, please, you'll get a bonus. Don't let me down, boys . . .

He and the foreman stride out.

BRYLOV (*to them all*): Don't do it! Just tell him you can't and that's that. I have to go now. Do what you can. If Gurvich wants to know where I am, say I'm at construction site number one . . . or number two . . . (*Exit.*)

CHEGENYOV: Who's been squealing to Gurvich about the irons? They're at us for things we don't even make. These damn squealers are making life impossible . . .

Exit.

YAKHIMCHUK: O.K., Munitsa, we'll go fifty-fifty on the bonus, right? (MUNITSA *does not answer.*) I was only joking. I'd never have said anything, only you're ruining all our work. It hurts me to see it. You and Gurvich have gone completely off beam. Where's the pencil? Come on, I'll draw it for you . . .

MUNITSA: We do brickwork together, right?

YAKHIMCHUK: All right, fine. (*They leave on the right. The stage is empty. The tapping sound inside the cupola stops. Enter* LYUBA *from the left.*)

LYUBA: Comrade Gurvich, telephone for you . . . Where is he? He must have dashed out. (*She looks into the room on the right, then comes back. Someone emerges from under the cupola.*) Oy, who's that?

It is NEMOV. *He straightens up. His canvas overalls are so torn that in places his skin can be seen through them. His face and his torn cap are covered with grey dust. He is wearing a pair of homemade celluloid spectacles and carrying a chisel and a hammer.*

NEMOV: It's me. Don't you recognise me?

LYUBA: No-oo, it can't be! You look a sight! (*She laughs buoyantly.* NEMOV *lifts his glasses, smiles and scratches his head with his hammer.*) How did you fit in there? There's not room.

NEMOV: Yes, it *was* a bit cramped. But I'm thinner these days. If only there wasn't so much dust . . . Lyuba, that's your name, isn't it?

LYUBA: You've remembered? Such a cold, efficient production chief. You never seemed to notice who anyone was.

NEMOV: Yes, you've got something there. I was still trying to get in with the authorities. A sudden crash and there I was still trying to pull myself back at the last step. In those days I preferred to bend others than to bend myself. But I feel freer now I'm an ordinary black-faced working man.

LYUBA: There's only one thing wrong with being a black-faced worker – they die.

NEMOV: Well, look at me – chiselling off the slag, singing songs . . .

LYUBA: That's because you're in the foundry. You get good rations in the foundry.

NEMOV: You know something – sometimes I think to

myself, are our lives so important? Are they the most valuable thing we have?

LYUBA (*with great attention*): What else is there?

NEMOV: It sounds funny talking about it here in the camp, but maybe . . . conscience . . .

LYUBA (*gazing at him intently*): Do you think so? (*Pause.*)

NEMOV: How are your hands? I remember you had trouble with them.

LYUBA: My hands? (*She holds them out.*)

NEMOV: But that's impossible! (*He drops the chisel and hammer and takes* LYUBA *by the hands.*) They're so beautiful and white. It's all gone?

LYUBA (*laughs out loud*): There was never anything there.

NEMOV: What do you mean? I saw it with my own eyes, black blisters all round here . . .

LYUBA: I was swinging the lead!

NEMOV: What does that mean?

LYUBA: I swung the lead, so as not to go on that transport. "Swinging the lead" is what they call it in the camp when you fix it to look ill – like a tumour or a blind eye or a fever.

NEMOV: Can you really do it?

LYUBA: He doesn't believe me! 'Course I can. I fooled you, didn't I?

NEMOV: It's fantastic. How did you fool the warder?

LYUBA: Oh, I think he guessed. But he took pity on me. Wouldn't you have taken pity on me?

NEMOV: . . . Probably not . . .

LYUBA: Have you finished examining my hands? Why don't you let go of them?

NEMOV: I need them . . .

LYUBA: What for? (NEMOV *kisses* LYUBA's *hands.*) You're not going to pretend you like me?

NEMOV: How can you say that?

LYUBA: When they brought us in – I mean the new transport – they made us sit on the ground. You came

up to the women, you looked us all over and you chose
. . . Granya. Do you remember?

NEMOV: Just a minute . . . what did you think when I
chose Granya?

LYUBA: I thought, why didn't he choose me?

NEMOV: It's simple, it was a different criterion.

LYUBA: But your eyes were open, weren't they? How could
you have chosen anyone else!

NEMOV: Lyuba, I was looking for a gang leader, someone
with drive . . .

LYUBA: I was terribly offended.

NEMOV: Of course I noticed immediately how . . . how
pretty you are.

LYUBA: So why did you try to send me out into the forests?

NEMOV: They needed a barber.

LYUBA: Why should I suffer because of that?

NEMOV: No, of course not, there's no reason why you
should suffer. A girl like you should wear a fine, white
dress, with lilies of the valley pinned here, across the
breast. Even in that uniform quilt jacket you look . . .
Give me your hands.

LYUBA: What for?

NEMOV: To kiss.

LYUBA: What sort of man kisses like that? On the hands?

NEMOV: It's all I dare.

LYUBA: You're funny. (NEMOV *kisses her hands.*) Your
hands are all cut.

NEMOV: The slag's sharp. I have to hammer it out with a
chisel. Sometimes I miss.

LYUBA: What a life! It's hard for you, isn't it?

NEMOV: It's almost a year now since I was arrested. Since
then it's been nothing but gloom and misery. Now for
the first time I feel happy.

LYUBA: Happy? On general duties?

NEMOV: Now that you're here . . .

LYUBA: I was here when you were one of the bosses.

NEMOV: It's wonderful not being one of the bosses. If I was

I'd think you were trying to get something out of me.
But now . . .

LYUBA: Now it's time I went. Let go of me.

NEMOV: Don't go.

LYUBA: Are we just going to stand here, like this? (NEMOV
mumbles something.) Come to the culture room this
evening. There's going to be a concert. Come backstage.
(*She moves slowly away from him, her back to the door.*)

NEMOV (*walking slowly after her*): Will I see you then,
Lyuba?

LYUBA *nods her head and leaves.* NEMOV *stops and stands
there gazing after her. The painted curtain falls.*

Scene 2

On the Roof

*This scene takes place on top of a building under construction,
with the sky as a background. It is not the roof but a partition
between two storeys. So far the outside wall at the back of the
stage has been built up a mere half-metre above floor level. Two
broad square pillars with descending staircases flank the wall,
rising another metre above it. From the left-hand pillar an inside
wall runs towards the audience. Two pairs of bricklayers are
standing on some scaffolding laying the wall. The wall comes
almost up to the curtain, and so forms a passage to the left there.
A similar right-angled inside wall has been begun from the right-
hand pillar but abandoned. To the right of the right-hand pillar,
invisible to the audience, stands a "pioneer"-type crane. The
only visible part of it is its turning carrier, which can be seen
lifting a platform and carrying it over the back wall. Each time
it does this the platform has two wheelbarrows on it.*

*Wooden planks are laid across the long beams of the flooring
to form tracks for the wheelbarrows, leading up from the crane
platform to the scaffolding by the left-hand wall.* GRANYA *and*

SHUROCHKA, *both in quilted trousers, are pushing the
wheelbarrows over to the wall, turning them over to pour the
mortar out for the four bricklayers, returning the wheelbarrows to
the crane platform and transferring the hook from the full
platform to the empty one.*

*A pair of "drudge" prisoners are pushing barrows of bricks
from the right over to the left-hand wall, about thirty bricks at a
time. As the curtain rises* GAI *is standing on a small raised
platform in the right-hand corner of the stage, watching the
others work, glumly and in silence. It is a warm sunny day, one
of the last good days of autumn. A crane is lifting a platform
with two wheelbarrows on it. A couple of professional crooks,*
GOLDTOOTH *and* GEORGIE, *appear from the right pushing a
barrow. They are naked to the waist, brawny and covered with
tattoo-marks. They don't walk, they dance across the stage, and
in their barrow there are only three bricks. They tip the bricks off
on to the scaffolding and leave the stage, dancing and humming
as usual, glancing from time to time at the gang leader.*

IST BRICKLAYER (*after the two professionals have
gone*): Comrade Gai, please get some more carriers, I've
no bricks to lay. Are they playing games or what?

GAI *says nothing. Meanwhile* GRANYA *and* SHUROCHKA
*have wheeled their barrows over to the left-hand wall and
returned to the right-hand pillar.*

SHUROCHKA (*hanging her head*): My God, it's hard work
. . . Roll on break-time . . .

GRANYA (*looking into the distance*): Over there I can see a
cart . . . It's got a load of straw.

SHUROCHKA: How can you see it's straw?

GRANYA: I can spot a hare at half a mile. You smell the
breeze? I can smell fallen leaves, it's from the forest, far
over there . . . (*She breathes air in.*)

SHUROCHKA: Can you really smell the leaves? If only we
could go outside, if only we could rest and forget it
all . . .

GRANYA: Not me, I'm better as I am.

SHUROCHKA: How can you say that?

GRANYA: I've had my fill of air in the camps, I've seen so much meanness and ghastliness. I'd never be able to rest, not even outside.

The crane brings over a new platform. GRANYA *transfers the hook and trundles the wheelbarrow noisily away to the left and off stage. There are tracks for the wheelbarrow laid there as well.* SHUROCHKA *follows her, pushing her wheelbarrow with an effort.*

2ND BRICKLAYER (*to* 1ST BRICKLAYER): I got a parcel notification. My family sent me a parcel, but the bastards here sent it back. No parcels till I up my figures to a hundred and twenty per cent, that's what they say. It's my own property too, my own food! Can they do that to me? I'll do my damnedest to see the commandant about it today.

1ST BRICKLAYER: 'Course they can do it to you. They can do anything. (*Reaction.*) Justice? It doesn't exist. Look at us drudges slaving away while the professionals take it easy. Do you think the gang leader will give them less rations than he gives you?

2ND BRICKLAYER: Our boss? Gai? You wait, he won't give in to them.

4TH BRICKLAYER, *an auxiliary worker who looks completely exhausted, collapses and sits down on the ground.*

3RD BRICKLAYER: Mishka! What's the matter?

4TH BRICKLAYER: My head's going round and round. Let me sit for a while. I just can't . . .

2ND BRICKLAYER: Let him sit down for a few minutes . . .

3RD BRICKLAYER: What do you mean, let him sit down? Why should I do double duty?

2ND BRICKLAYER: I'll give you a hand. The boy's a "goner". And no wonder, he won't drink hot water. How can he keep his strength up?

They carry on working. The "drudge" prisoners push their overloaded barrow to the wall almost at the double, empty it and push it back. GOLDTOOTH *and* GEORGIE *appear, walking as usual with their swinging dance-like gait. This time there is only one brick on their barrow. They throw* GAI *several glances as they go past him, then drop their barrow and sit down.* GRANYA *and* SHUROCHKA *carry on working.*

GEORGIE: O.K., that's the lot. Let's get some sun. (*He lies down to sun himself.* GOLDTOOTH *sits down and begins to sing a disgusting little song glorifying professional crooks. His body twitches as he sings, and he makes a face like a monkey.* GAI *remains motionless throughout the song. A wardress enters from the left, a mane of curls sticking out from under her military cap. Seeing the* 4TH BRICKLAYER *resting, she creeps up to him and strikes him a blow on the neck.*)

WARDRESS: Lazy son of a bitch! Get up and work! (4TH BRICKLAYER *gets up with difficulty and begins to pass bricks to the* 3RD BRICKLAYER. *The other bricklayers quicken their pace of work.* GOLDTOOTH *carries on singing and grimacing. The wardress walks over to the professional crooks and addresses* GEORGIE.) You, what are you showing everyone your belly for? You think it's beautiful?

GEORGIE (*lying there*): Hullo, darling, come over here. Lie down, we'll have a roll in the hay.

WARDRESS: Huh! Asking a bit much, aren't you? (*Exit right.*)

GOLDTOOTH: All right, let's have a smoke, O.K.? Give us a bit of paper, boss. (GAI *remains quite motionless.*)

FOMIN (*he walks straight across the stage*): Hurry up, Gai! This wall's taking much too long. (*Points at the left-hand wall.*) Look at it, it's holding us all up. (GAI *does not move.*)

GEORGIE (*sits up*): Hey, boss, come over here. Let's have a smoke. We'd better have a talk – about things in general. *Immediately* GAI *gets off his perch, strides across the stage and sits down next to them.*

GOLDTOOTH: Look here, boss, you've got to learn the rules. The likes of us aren't supposed to work. We've

only been working . . . out of respect. You'd better take
our barrows and give them to someone else. Let the
drudges sweat.

GEORGIE: In other words, we're "pros". Do you see?

GAI: "Professionals"?

GEORGIE: That's right.

GAI: What about rations?

GEORGIE: Oh, we get rations same as the rest. At least, we
take the bread ration. We don't like the soup, you can
give ours to the drudges. Most of our grub we get
straight from the kitchen. We've butter and lard up to
here. (*Hand under chin.*)

GAI: And who does the work?

GEORGIE: You mean, who gets yoked? The peasants, they
get yoked. The small fry. And the gentlemen fascists, the
Article fifty-eight boys.

GAI: How can we earn a proper ration? How can I feed my
men?

GOLDTOOTH: That's your headache. You'll have to settle
that one with the screws.

GEORGIE (*to* GOLDTOOTH, *indicating* GAI): He's got
something there, you know. Suck your cock and you
won't starve. That's the kind of camp this is. Don't be a
mug, then you can eat with us, with the best people.

GAI: Well if you're "pros" and you're not allowed to work,
why don't you stay in camp? Why push down the rest of
the gang's productivity?

GEORGIE: You know, boss, you want to grow up . . .

GOLDTOOTH: Looking for someone stupider than yourself?

GEORGIE: We're not shirkers. Cross my heart and hope to
rot in jail if we are. During the war they used to parade
everyone for work. Any shirkers – they'd just bump
them off.

GOLDTOOTH: We'd rather live a little longer.

GEORGIE: You die today, I'll die tomorrow.

GOLDTOOTH: You'll sort out the productivity. That's what
a gang leader's for.

GAI *gets to his feet and suddenly strikes one of the crooks full in the face, so hard that he falls over on to his back.* GAI *deals with the second crook likewise. They try to get up but* GAI *keeps pummelling them and prevents them from rising.*

GOLDTOOTH: What's the matter with him? Son of a bitch! Bitch!

GEORGIE: What are you doing? Stop it! You cheap bum! Bastard!

GAI: Who's a bastard? (*Hits him.*)

GOLDTOOTH: Fascist.

GAI: Who's a fascist? (*Hits him.*)

GEORGIE (*managing to get to one side*): Help! Fascists! The fascists are killing us!

Enter GURVICH *quickly, followed by* FOMIN *and* KHOMICH. *They pretend not to notice the fighting. In his hands* GURVICH *is holding an unrolled builder's plan.* KHOMICH *is playing with a slide rule.*

GURVICH: That's right, a brick and a half thick, that's what it says. You call this a brick and a half? You must be blind. Can't you read a plan? (*Points at the left-hand wall.*) Gai, I want that wall torn down. Do you hear? Tear it right down!

The professional crooks leave towards the right, mumbling threateningly. FOMIN *scratches the back of his head.*

KHOMICH: Sorry, my dear sir, no can do. You'll have to give us a chit for that.

GURVICH: A chit? For tearing down a wall? A summons to court, that's more like it. Half our foremen are drunk, the other half illiterate . . .

KHOMICH: That's your business. If you want, we can call it evacuation of rubbish.

GURVICH: I'll see it comes out of his wages. (*Points at* FOMIN, *who wipes his spectacles, lowers his head and buries himself in the builder's plan.*)

KHOMICH (*working something out on the slide rule*): . . . Manual transportation of rubbish to a distance of more

than a hundred metres, involving a lift of ten metres, the
total capacity in cubic metres being . . .

GURVICH: What lift? We've been through the orders for
the last three years. More rubbish has been removed
than the volume of the whole building . . .

KHOMICH: Then obviously the rubbish heap must be
enormous. That explains why it has to be lifted ten
metres.

GURVICH: I'll sign a chit for snow, for removal of snow.

KHOMICH: Snow's cheap. You'll have to sign for more than
a cubic kilometre to pay us back for that wall.

GURVICH: Snow's the best thing. One day it's here, the
next day it's melted. Control can't complain. All right,
Gai, break down the wall. Lay it again, this time two
bricks thick.

GAI (*gloomily, shouting towards the crane*): Zhenka, give them
a shout will you? We want crowbars and large hammers.
No more mortar for the moment.

Exit GURVICH *followed by* KHOMICH. ZHENKA *peers
out from the right wing and shouts down at the crane men,
his voice rumbling like thunder.*

ZHENKA: Hey! You clowns down there! Go to the tool-
shed, get two crowbars and two large hammers, and
bring them back to the crane! (*He vanishes.*)

FOMIN (*to* GAI): Try and break it down so that the bricks
stay in one piece, will you?

GAI: How the hell do you expect me to do that? Go on,
show me! (FOMIN *waves one arm and walks away.* GAI
addresses his workers.) Carry the bricks over here for the
moment. (*He points left.*) Shurochka, you go and help
move the bricks.

SHUROCHKA *leaves. The workers begin to carry the bricks
over to the left.* GAI *sits down.*

GRANYA (*to* GAI): What do I do?

GAI: Wait a second. I'll find you a job soon.

GRANYA: You're so brave taking on two men by yourself.
Especially two like that.

GAI: It's the only way to handle them. Ever since I was in
my first transit prison I've done my best to kick those
damn "pros". They're parasites, and I'll go on kicking
them till I'm in my last camp. You see we're "enemies of
the people" and they're "friends of the people". I reckon
the authorities keep them just to suck our blood. We
politicals are given to them to torment. They don't
separate us in the cells or in the transports. Everyone's
terrified of them.

*The crane brings over the crowbars and hammers. The
bricklayers take them and begin hammering at the wall. It
yields to the blows. Bricks, broken as well as in one piece,
begin to fall out of it.* GAI *just sits there gloomily.*

GRANYA: Why do you frown all the time? Wondering how
to feed the men?

GAI: It's a dog's life, being a gang leader. Why did I take it
on? If some poor drudge gets too weak to fulfil his norm,
what am I to do about it? Beat him up?

GRANYA: Someone's got to be gang leader. If it wasn't you
it'd be someone else, and he might be a bastard. It
would only make it worse for the drudges.

GAI: That's a dangerous argument . . . (*He is plunged into
thought. A long pause. The noise of people working on a
construction site.*) My division ended the war on the River
Elbe, and now look at me, stuck here. The deserters are
all released, the men from the front-line are kept inside.
What next? It's incomprehensible. But what can we do
about it?

GRANYA: You don't have to answer those questions. Your
brain can't deal with everything.

GAI: Who else is going to deal with it? (*He sighs.*) I had
some friends in my cell once. I was being questioned by
counter-espionage. But now we are scattered all over the
country. They sent some of us to Yenisei, some to
Jezkazgan, some God knows where . . .

GRANYA (*takes him by the shoulders*): You have a friend here
too.

GAI: You're a woman. And you're not a political.

GRANYA: I went through the war the same as you did. I stabbed a German scout to death with a bayonet. I ferried myself across the same rivers and bit the ground on the same bridgeheads.

GAI: They'll give you an amnesty. In a year you'll have forgotten the whole thing.

GRANYA: So will you.

GAI: Oh no, I won't forget. (KHOMICH *enters, but steps back as he notices them.*) I'll tell you something – there was a guy in our cell who used to say that if people didn't live in families, no tyrant would be able to stay on his throne. He'd be washed away as if by a flood. And that's the way it is. They break our necks and all we do is start families.

GRANYA: What are you talking about? There aren't any families in this place.

GAI: It's the same here as everywhere else. Our hands and feet are tied by "love". There's a new fashion just started in our culture room – dancing to the accordion. So what happens? Everyone dances! Idiots! Ten years for doing damn all, and they dance!

GRANYA: Just my luck, falling for a cold fish like you. You'll feel sorry for me too one day. Yes, even you . . .
From somewhere down below behind the building comes the sound of a rail being banged by an iron bar. The bricklayers stop work abruptly. Enter ZHENKA from the right.

ZHENKA: O.K., take it easy! Our gang's last for dinner. (*He lies down.*)

2ND BRICKLAYER: He's right, boys, let's take a nap. All that rummaging during the night, we're short on sleep.
The bricklayers find places for themselves and lie down on the scaffolding. GAI goes to the middle of the stage, lies down on his back and stays quite motionless. SHUROCHKA sits down where GAI had been sitting, next to GRANYA. She looks at herself in a pocket mirror.

SHUROCHKA: The years are passing, Granya . . . I think

we ought to get married while we're here in the camp.
Who'll want us later on when we're outside? (*Pause.*) Is
it true what they are saying? That Khomich offered to
put you in charge of the bread-cutting room, and you
refused?

GRANYA: He did.

SHUROCHKA: I don't believe it! You're turning into some
kind of wishy-washy intellectual. Turn down the bread-
cutting room? I've never heard of such a thing. Plenty to
eat, warm in winter, skirt and blouse, not these damn
quilted trousers all leaking at the seams, no need to
sweat your guts out . . .

GRANYA: What sort of a person cheats a drudge out of his
bread ration even by a gramme? I made my decision –
I'm not going to live like other people do in the camps.
There's only one important thing – I won't see myself
turned into a bastard. Live or die – what's the
difference?

KHOMICH *appears again and walks across the front of the
stage.*

KHOMICH: Hello, Granya. (*Pause.* GRANYA *gets up and goes
to meet him.*) Listen to me, my lady, there's something I
want to get straight: you and Mr Gai are like that, aren't
you? (*Lays one finger across the other.*)

GRANYA (*something occurs to her*): You're not planning to
have him posted?

KHOMICH: What do you mean? It's not my decision. (*He
tries to walk on, but she stops him.*)

GRANYA: There is something I'm longing to ask you . . .
You get extra pay . . . working for the security
department, don't you?

KHOMICH (*flinching*): How dare you! Let me go!

GRANYA (*holds him back*): You're preparing a file on him?
You're out to get him, is that right? (*She gives him a
shake.*) I'll tell you one thing: if they get him on some
security rap, or if they send him on a transport . . . I'll
kill you!

KHOMICH: You're out of your mind! What's it got to do with me?

GRANYA: Just watch it. I don't waste words. I killed a man once, he was worth a dozen of you. Killing you would be like squeezing a caterpillar, a green caterpillar . . . (*She pushes him away.*)

KHOMICH: You . . . You must be some kind of a witch. I've never met a woman like you before. You've no heart . . .

Unnoticed, GEORGIE *and* GOLDTOOTH *run noiselessly in from the right. They throw themselves upon* GAI, *who is asleep, throttling him and beating him.* KHOMICH *is the first to spot them. He rushes out left, stopping on the way only to look over his shoulder.* GRANYA *utters a short cry.* SHUROCHKA *screams, waking everybody up. The "drudge" prisoners get up, but no one dares come near enough to fight. Some of them pretend to fall asleep again.*

GRANYA: Don't just stand there! Save him! Save your gang leader! Lousy politicals, get up!

GRANYA *grabs one of the professional crooks. Wheezing, groaning and incoherent shouts as they fight. Slowly and with a painful effort* GAI *struggles up, whereupon all four of them fall in a disorderly heap towards the right, disappearing off stage. The rest just stay there, watching.* SHUROCHKA *screams again and again.*

A powerful blow sends GEORGIE *flying back on stage and sprawling on to the floor.* GOLDTOOTH *retreats, pursued by* GAI, *who keeps hitting him with a short thick wooden plank, until he falls down on the slag between the beams, trying unsuccessfully to rise.* GRANYA *follows* GAI *on to the stage, reeling as she walks.* GAI *stands between the two men, who are now lying on the ground. Exhausted and out of breath, he strikes first one and then the other lazily about the head. The board breaks and* GAI *tries to find another, but at that moment* LENNIE *rushes on stage from the left. He runs like a ballet dancer, jumps easily over a sitting "drudge" prisoner, turning the peak of his cap to the back as he flies*

through the air. GRANYA *just has time to shout* "Behind
you!" *And* GAI *just has time to turn as* LENNIE *runs into
him. They both roll on the ground. They jump up when they
are almost by the parapet on the back wall and each tries to
push the other off the roof. Stunned and covered with blood,*
GOLDTOOTH *sits on the ground.* GEORGIE *gets up with a
knife in his hand and takes aim to throw it at* GAI's *back.*
GRANYA *strikes him on the head with a board. She picks up
the knife which he has dropped, and runs up the ramp to the
left-hand pillar.* GEORGIE *pushes her in the back with a
long board from below.* GRANYA *almost falls down but then
grabs the board and they fight over it.*

LENNIE: Fascist bastard!

GAI: Who's a fascist? Who's a bastard?

*They fall to the ground and struggle by the parapet on the
wall. The cradle of the hoist-crane is hanging beside the
wall, indicating its edge.* GOLDTOOTH *gets up, picks up a
crowbar and walks towards them, but at that moment*
CHEGENYOV, *wearing torn overalls and cocked cap, rushes
on stage from the right. He sums up the situation at a glance,
overtakes* GOLDTOOTH *and grabs the crowbar out of his
hands as he swings to strike* GAI. *He hits* GOLDTOOTH
with the crowbar, who shrieks and falls to the ground.
GEORGIE *turns round, leaves* GRANYA *and throws himself
at* CHEGENYOV, *who swings the crowbar violently at him.*
GEORGIE *dodges the blow, they collide and roll on the floor.*
GAI *grabs* LENNIE *by the throat with both hands, pushes
him over the wall and holds him there is mid-air.*

GAI: Shall I drop you? How about that, bastard? Three
floors down, how about that? Who's a fascist? Come on,
who's a fascist? (*He pulls* LENNIE *by the throat up on to
the wall and leaves him on the parapet. Meanwhile*
GRANYA *has got down from the pillar and run along the
wall, which is in the process of being demolished. She throws*
GAI *the knife.*)

GRANYA: Pavel! Catch!

GAI (*catches the knife*): How about that for a toothpick?

GOLDTOOTH *gets up.* GRANYA *jumps down on him from
the wall and knocks him off his feet. Meanwhile,* GEORGIE
has overpowered CHEGENYOV *and is throttling him.* GAI
runs up to them, pushes GEORGIE *down, stands over him
and brandishes the knife over him.* All right, start praying
to your god, Mister "pro".

GEORGIE (*in a nasty voice*): Forgive me! Forgive me!

LENNIE (*sits down*): All right, Pavel, we'll be friends. We'll
make peace. Thieves' honour! Cross my heart and hope
to rot in jail.

GAI: (*Looks triumphantly down at the three of them.*) I see . . .
social allies, is that right? Your noble work of honour?
(*To* GEORGIE *and* GOLDTOOTH. *Pointing to the right.*)
Over there we have four hundred bricks. By the end of
dinner break they'll be on the site and ready for laying.
(*Points off stage to the left.*) Forward march!
GOLDTOOTH *and* GEORGIE *take their barrow and leave
the stage to the right.* CHEGENYOV *sits there trying to get
his breath back.*

GAI (*to* CHEGENYOV): Thanks, Cossack.

LENNIE (*feeling his neck*): You've got hands like pincers.

GAI: Attacking a man when he's asleep – how's that for
your code, your thieves' honour?

LENNIE: I wasn't here when they attacked you.

GAI: Lucky for you. Otherwise I would have dropped you
over the wall. You're their number one man, you'd
better give them a political lecture.

LENNIE: It's all over. We're friends, didn't you hear? (*To
the bricklayers, shaking his fist.*) All right, you peasants,
keep your mouths shut. Don't tell anyone what
happened! (*Exit right.*)

SHUROCHKA (*to* GAI, *reverently, as if praying*): You're a
hero, Mr Gai. A classical hero!

GAI: Bastards! If I hadn't been asleep I'd have beaten them
to pulp.
*He is still out of breath, one hand drooping at his side,
holding the knife.* GRANYA *comes up to him from behind,*

puts her arms around him and her head on his shoulder.
GEORGIE *and* GOLDTOOTH *emerge from the right pushing
a barrow with about fifty bricks in it. As they cross the stage
the painted curtain falls.*

Scene 3

The Concert

*A large spacious room with a temporary floor and walls which
have been made good but not yet plastered. In the back wall
there are two tall windows; outside the night is very dark. The
room is brightly lit. A few small steps by the left wall lead up to
the door, which leads on to the "stage". A small screen, part of
the set for a play, stands closer to the audience, screening off the
place where women change. Next to the screen, almost by the
proscenium, is a bench set against the wall. On the bench sit
NEMOV, in his black camp uniform, and LYUBA, dressed up to
take part in the performance. It is a busy room, full of bustle
and coming and going. People are changing clothes and
rehearsing and looking for things they need for the play. They
keep rushing out on to the "stage" and returning. Occasionally
the "stage" door is left open. When this happens one can hear
snatches of a farcical sketch. The characters are: a stupid
German officer, played by KOSTYA the work allocator; his idiot
of a batman; an old woman wearing a kerchief; her daughter, a
member of the underground, played by SHUROCHKA; her
grandson, a young pioneer, played by DIMKA; a frightening-
looking guerrilla figure in a black beard, who comes on to the
"stage" only towards the end of the play.*

*There is a small light-music band (ZHENKA among them)
huddled together on the right at the back of the stage. They are
trying to rehearse quietly, but the result is rather loud. VITKA,
the quick-moving red-haired compère of the show, is rushing
about more than anybody else.*

338

COMPÈRE (*to the group*): All right, boys, that's enough.

SOMEONE: What about supper, Vitka? Do the actors get supper?

COMPÈRE: I hear the cook's in the accounts department. (*He runs off. Enter* GONTOIR.)

GONTOIR (*in a tired voice*): Young man, take this gun.

DIMKA *walks off carrying the dummy gun.*

ZHENKA (*clears his throat and starts to sing*):
    Coming home on a prayer and a wing . . .

KOSTYA (*his voice audible from the "stage"*): Ich vill shoot you all, russische Schweine.

COMPÈRE (*rushing in*): Where's the bucket? Come on, we must have the bucket. (*A "prop" bucket is produced.*)

SOMEONE: Let's hear it again, Vitka. Who comes after who?

COMPÈRE: Zhenka, I've had a note from the lieutenant. The song of the American bomber pilot has to be cut.

ZHENKA: Why? They're our allies, aren't they?

COMPÈRE: Don't ask me. They *were* our allies, but don't ask questions. Just give them "The Blue Scarf" – loud as you can. (*Shouts.*) Can I have your attention! The "Stupid German" sketch is about to finish. The band will now play "Song of the Motherland". Then Lyuba, then Zhenka with his "Blue Scarf", then Dimka's Cossack dancing, then Lyuba again. Then the band plays the march and falls out. After that the play *Sheep and Wolves*.

Buzz of voices from the actors.

SHUROCHKA (*to* GONTOIR): Well, how is it going? (*Loud applause from the audience.*)

GONTOIR: You can hear for yourself . . . "Licensed for performance in corrective labour camps" – that's the sort of play it is.

COMPÈRE: I know nothing ahout it, nothing at all! (*Rushes out.*)

VOICE FROM THE STAGE: You think because I am an old woman that I am afraid of your tanks? Grandson,

339

translate into German for him – long live the collective
farms! (*Applause.*)

GONTOIR (*he speaks without the slightest foreign accent*): Is
this the kind of art we used to dream about? We were so
enthusiastic back in 1919. We came to young Russia to
create the neo-theatre, the first in the history of
mankind.

> Turn their rainbow to a yoke,
> Make harness of the Milky Way,
> Renew for us our earthly sphere
> So it may see a brighter day . . .

*He sits down and starts putting on his make-up to play a
part in* Sheep and Wolves. SHUROCHKA *walks out on to
the stage.*

ZHENKA (*sings sadly*): Coming home on a prayer and a
wing . . .

LYUBA: I was six. I remember a huge barge full of
dispossessed *kulak* farmers. There were no partitions in
the hold, no tiered bunks. People just lay on top of other
people. Maybe it was because I was small, but the walls
of the barge seemed to tower over me like cliffs. Guards
with guns walked round the top edge. Our whole family
was exiled, but our two elder brothers weren't living
with us, so they weren't touched. They came to the
transit camp. The boat had just left and they tried to
catch up with us. All the time they were on the look-out
for a chance to get their family out of trouble. They
didn't succeed. But they managed to buy me from the
escort commander. They gave him a shirt with a zip –
they were just coming into fashion. I don't remember
how they got me off the barge, but I remember we were
in a little boat, and the water shone brightly in the sun.

NEMOV: What about your parents?

LYUBA: They died up beyond the Arctic Circle. They
starved to death. They were dumped in the naked
tundra. How could they survive?

COMPÈRE: Pay attention, everyone! Official communiqué –

our supper has been approved. Contents will be clarified
later.

The band plays a muted flourish.

LYUBA: You can't imagine how we lived after that. I had no
room, so I lived five years in a bit of dark corridor.
There was no window and I couldn't do my homework
after school. I went to school every day hungry and
dressed like a beggar. I couldn't complain or ask for help
in case people found out we were *kulaks*. But I wanted
pretty dresses. I wanted to go to the cinema . . . My
brother married. He has his own children . . . They
married me off when I was fourteen . . .

NEMOV: Fourteen?

The sketch has finished. Noise and movement. SHUROCHKA
rushes behind the screen to change.

COMPÈRE: Musicians, on stage! Come on, Lyuba, get
ready.

VOICES: You missed out a whole passage.

I come back to it later.

Where's the vaseline?

Who's the pig who's been sitting on my dress?

Oh, it's so hot!

*The "old woman" from the sketch, her kerchief slipped to
one side, jumps on to the table, sits down on it and cheekily
lights up a cigarette. She says to the musicians* "Hi,
hooligans!"

DIMKA (*to* GONTOIR): Didn't I learn my part well, sir?

SOMEONE: Hey, what are you doing in the camps? You're
too young!

DIMKA: I escaped from trade school. They wouldn't give us
anything to eat.

SOMEONE: You're worse off here than you were there.

DIMKA: No! I get good rations now. I've learnt about life.

GONTOIR (*putting on his make-up*): What do you mean –
life?

DIMKA: Life's when you don't have to sweat your guts out.
Let the others sweat their guts out. (*He is changing into*

Cossack boy's dress for his dance. SHUROCHKA *comes out
from behind the screen dressed as a nineteenth-century
middle-class young lady. She is to play* GLAFIRA *in* Sheep
and Wolves.)

SHUROCHKA (*quoting from her part*): "What have you done
with me? I'm so nervous, I'm so nervous!"

NEMOV (*holding* LYUBA *back*): Wait another minute.

LYUBA (*indicating her dress*): Does it suit me?

NEMOV: Everything suits you.

LYUBA: I love acting and dressing up. It's wonderful
wearing a new outfit for every turn.

COMPÈRE: Lyuba, come on! How many more times?

LYUBA *runs off.* NEMOV *watches her go.*

SHUROCHKA (*putting on her make-up, to* NEMOV): Did you
hear the way Gontoir read Tolstoy?

NEMOV: What did you say?

SHUROCHKA: What are you smiling at?

NEMOV: Smiling?

SHUROCHKA: It made me sad. They chattered all the way
through, no one paid attention. There were only one or
two in the whole audience who appreciated how well he
did it. You didn't hear it either. It was from *War and
Peace*, the bit about the oak-tree.

NEMOV (*warming to the idea*): The bit about the black oak-
tree which turned green?

GONTOIR (*coming up to them*): You see, I'm incorrigible. I
insist on believing that beauty elevates human beings.
I keep wanting to cheer them up, to tell them there is
more to life than work parades, searches and prison soup.

COMPÈRE: All right, "Blue Scarf"! Get ready! Everyone
pay attention! The extra supper has been positively
confirmed – one jam-roll, two spoonfuls of boiled rice for
each person!

SHUROCHKA: Rice? You must be mad! Rice doesn't exist!

SOMEONE: What the hell's rice?

COMPÈRE *walks quickly off stage, leaving the door open.
We can hear* LYUBA *finishing her song.*

LYUBA: "For you I have but one request:
Do not put me to the test.
You may dance at my wedding, for sure,
But do not expect anything more."

Loud and prolonged applause, shouts of "Encore". LYUBA *appears in the doorway, but then goes back on to the "stage".*

SHUROCHKA: Monsieur Gontoir, have you heard the rumour? They say in a few days there's going to be a big transport, for the fifty-eighters.

GONTOIR: It's quite possible. They often do it before Revolution Day. But these rumours don't mean much. There's always rumours.

SHUROCHKA: I just don't have the strength. I couldn't stand a winter in a new place. Why do they torment us like this, moving us on all the time?

LYUBA *rushes in. She reaches the spot where* NEMOV *is sitting, then runs away again. Applause.*

GONTOIR: I heard something different. I heard that just before we arrived they arrested a young poet – I mean, they threw him in the cooler. One of the assistant doctors found some verses under his pillow. He's under investigation. They say he's dying. Have you heard anything about it?

Applause. LYUBA *comes back, her face shining, her movements quick and impetuous.*

SHUROCHKA: Congratulations, Lyuba. You sounded just like Shulzhenko.

LYUBA: Did I? You noticed, did you? Everyone says I'm like her. I was in key, wasn't I? I was frightened I wouldn't get it right. I have to change now. (*To* NEMOV.) Come on, you can help me. Quick! (*She runs behind the screen. Her naked arm appears from time to time from behind the screen to hand* NEMOV *a piece of clothing or to take one which* NEMOV *has selected from the pile of clothes on the bench.*

LYUBA (*from behind the screen*): Here, take this . . . put that

down . . . I want the one under the blue thing . . . Be
careful with it, remember none of it's mine. I borrowed
it from those women outside camp. Come on, you can
button me up. Come here.

NEMOV *goes around to the other side of the screen, so that
the audience cannot see him. The screen is then turned so that*
LYUBA *and* NEMOV *can be seen by the audience although
not by the other characters on stage.* LYUBA *is looking at
herself in a little mirror.* NEMOV *buttons up her dress from
behind, kisses her neck, embraces her and turns her round to
face him. A long kiss.*

NEMOV: Lyubonka, what's happening to me?

LYUBA: What indeed? (*They kiss.*)

NEMOV: Who taught you to kiss like that?

LYUBA: I learnt . . . (*They kiss.*)

NEMOV: Lyuba, you're . . . you're a desperate woman. You
seem to drink me in, swallow me. I won't be without
you now, do you hear me? I can't be without you . . .

LYUBA: We only got to know each other today, and you say
you can't live without me?

NEMOV: Ever since I was arrested I've felt as if I was living
in a cloud of black smoke. I haven't been able to smile.
But it's so wonderful now, now I'm with you. It's as if
you've released me, let me out into freedom.

LYUBA: Go on talking.

NEMOV: You told me about that barge and that dark
corridor where you lived. It made me feel you were my
little sister, and you'd been hurt. And now suddenly
those unbelievable kisses, and the way you tremble in my
arms. I've . . . I've fallen in love with you, Lyubonka.

LYUBA: How can you? You're married.

NEMOV: My wife's ten years away, a hundred fences of
barbed wire away. I can hardly imagine she exists.

LYUBA: You don't know much about me. My first husband
used to beat me and I left him. My second husband was
a complete waster. When I was arrested he renounced
me. Ever since then . . .

344

NEMOV: You poor girl . . .

LYUBA: I am not a poor girl at all. You see, I've had lovers
. . . More than one.

NEMOV (*starts*): How many?

LYUBA: More than one. You can't possibly love me.

NEMOV: But Lyuba, you had to do it, isn't that right? It
wasn't because you wanted it was it?

LYUBA: But what if I did want it? You think it has no
effect on a girl, getting married when she's fourteen?

NEMOV: Lyuba, it couldn't have been for that they saved
you from that prison barge?

LYUBA (*putting her arms around his neck*): You're so kind to
me. Why didn't I meet you earlier?

COMPÈRE: Lyuba, where are you? Get on stage!

LYUBA: (*Kisses* NEMOV *once more.*) I'm coming!
Slowly and unwillingly she walks away. NEMOV *sits down
on the bench and runs his fingers through the dress* LYUBA
*has just taken off. In a far corner someone is quietly playing
the guitar.*

SHUROCHKA (*aiming her words at* NEMOV, *very
distinctly*): "I have told you that love will bring you
nothing but suffering". (NEMOV *turns round and looks at
her.*) I am rehearsing my part, it's my part. Ostrovsky
wrote it. You look radiant, as if you'd been given the key
to heaven. I envy you, I do really.

NEMOV: I envy myself.

SHUROCHKA (*leaning towards him*): Do you know
everything about Lyuba?

NEMOV (*pronouncing every syllable separately*): I don't want
to know anything.
SHUROCHKA *moves away. We can hear* LYUBA *singing.*
KOSTYA *comes up to* NEMOV, *his make-up almost
completely removed. He is wearing his usual military
uniform.*

KOSTYA (*to* NEMOV): Well, how's life? I see you're not
missing any chances?

NEMOV: How's *your* life?

345

KOSTYA: Same as ever. A bit screwed up, though. I've had a row with the skivers. That bastard Rubyan keeps laying traps for me. Khomich is playing the great man. I got into a bit of a mess over you as well. I didn't think you'd get the push as soon as that. In fact, I reckon I've burnt my fingers. (*He moves away. Loud, stormy applause.* LYUBA *returns, but not immediately, only when the band starts playing a march. She sits down silently next to* NEMOV. *He takes her by the hand.*)

COMPÈRE: All right, Gontoir, *Sheep and Wolves.* Ready for the kick-off! Well done, Lyuba, superb! Even the commandant applauded! (*Runs off.*)

LYUBA: Why didn't you come out and hear me sing!

NEMOV: Where can we meet? I mean, on our own?

LYUBA: No, perhaps we'd better not.

NEMOV: We must, we must. I can't tear myself away from you now.

LYUBA (*sighs*): Look, wouldn't it be better if I stayed your sister? I'll be a good sister, you'll see.

NEMOV: No. (*He looks around, pulls* LYUBA *behind the screen and they kiss.*) When I kiss you I feel I want to die. Where did you learn to kiss like that?

LYUBA (*caressing him*): If only I could change back again, just for you. Become clean and pure.

NEMOV: Where can we meet? Where?

LYUBA: All right, I'll come to the foundry. To the attic where they store the coke. (*Pause.*) Do we really have to? Do we? (*They come and sit down on the bench.*) What do you think will happen? Have you thought about that? (*With sudden fervour.*) Darling, tell me one thing. Are you hungry? I mean now? Because I am. All my life I've been hungry. How will we be able to survive this camp? You'll never be able to fix things up for yourself, you haven't got a trade. By yourself you might be able to keep afloat, but with me round your neck you'll sink. In a little while you'll want to get rid of me.

NEMOV: No! Never!

LYUBA: The foreman will kick me out. I'll be on general
duties . . .

NEMOV (*in alarm*): Why did the foreman take you as a
runner?

LYUBA: It's what happens in the camps. Everyone does it.

NEMOV: So you and he have . . .

LYUBA: No, not yet. He doesn't have time. The telephone
keeps ringing.

NEMOV: But what if he finds time? Tomorrow, say?

LYUBA: Will you be able to find me another job, one as
good as that?

NEMOV: Lyuba, as from today . . .

LYUBA: What do you want of me? Don't you understand?
I'm what prisoners call a "love-girl". Do you know what
that means? I'm a "love-girl".
*The members of the band burst into the room. A din of
voices. They put down their instruments.* GONTOIR *and*
SHUROCHKA *walk on to the stage.* KOLODEY, KHOMICH
and MERESHCHUN *walk in from the opposite direction.*

KOLODEY (*to* GONTOIR): What a sight! You look like a
circus clown. Is it a funny play?

GONTOIR: Very funny.

KOLODEY: O.K., we'll laugh. Why shouldn't we laugh,
we're off duty? That stuff you did earlier all about the
oak-trees and the fir-trees, it went on and on. Everyone's
sick of timber-felling anyway. (GONTOIR *walks away.*
MERESHCHUN *laughs loudly.*) I mean it. What's in an
oak-tree? Four cubic metres, that's all. But he went on
and on . . .

KHOMICH: Where is she? Where is the seductress? Lyuba,
you sang brilliantly. You look like you're on your way to
a state banquet. You heard how they clapped, you might
have been a Hollywood star. Even the commandant had
to applaud. Congratulations. (*He shakes her hand.*)

KOLODEY (*walking round the room*): Well, how are you all
doing? Breaking any rules?

MERESHCHUN: Lyuba, you sang with such fire, such

347

expression! (*He shakes her hand and sits down on the bench next to her, on the other side from* NEMOV.) I once heard Shulzhenko sing. You're just as good as she is. I'd like to send a telegram to Sochi and order a bouquet of flowers for you – by special plane.

LYUBA (*flattered*): Thank you, thank you.

MERESHCHUN (*takes her by the elbow*): Why don't you ever come to the hospital? I could give you a couple of days sick leave before Revolution Day. Would you like that?

LYUBA: What for? I'm not ill.

MERESHCHUN: What do you mean, what for? Women always have things to do – washing their hair or their clothes. You come to the hospital tomorrow, I'll see you're let off work. Will you?

KHOMICH: Well, Nemov, how do you find work in the foundry? Not so good? You know, I spent days trying to think of some job we could give you. I couldn't think of anything.

NEMOV: Thank you, but I asked for nothing better.

KHOMICH: Maybe so, but educated men should behave like gentlemen. We should help each other out in time of trouble . . . (*He spots* ZHENKA.) Hey, mister, you sing like an angel. Why don't you ever sing classical music?

ZHENKA: I wrote a letter home. I asked them to send me Tchaikovsky . . .

KHOMICH: Why Tchaikovsky? Why not "The Gypsy Baron" or "The Blue Mazurka"?

COMPÈRE: All those who want to hear the play – it's time to join the audience. We're starting now.

KHOMICH *and most of the actors leave.*

KOLODEY: Don't start yet. Wait for me. (*To* NEMOV.) What are you doing here? Stand up when you're spoken to. (NEMOV *stands up*.) What are you on?

NEMOV: Nothing, citizen commander. I simply happen to be here.

KOLODEY: Nothing's ever simple with you prisoners.

You've always got ideas in the back of your heads. Get
out into the audience, you're not an actor.

NEMOV: What does it matter, sir? Can't I watch the play
from here?

KOLODEY: You're not allowed to watch from here. When
you're production chief, all right, fine, watch from
wherever you like. Only you're not production chief
now, you're a "drudge" prisoner, isn't that right? You've
had your sugar. Go on, get out there.

NEMOV: Please, sir, let me stay here.

KOLODEY (*becoming angry*): I said it's not allowed. We're on
the edge of the camp zone. How do I know you're not
planning to go over the fence? Go on, or I'll have you in
the cooler. (NEMOV *walks off, turning back to look at*
LYUBA.) Doctor!

MERESHCHUN (*without getting up*): What is it, boss?

KOLODEY (*quietly*): Do you have any alcohol in your
hospital?

MERESHCHUN: No, I don't. But for you – maybe! I'll see
what I can do.

KOLODEY: I just want a bit for myself. A hundred grammes
or so. I'll call in after the concert.

MERESHCHUN: Fine.

KOLODEY: All right, time to start, is it? Let's go in and
have a laugh. (*He leaves. The words of the play can only
faintly be heard. There are very few people left in the room.*)

MERESHCHUN: Lyuba, I was a colonel in the army, I was
divisional medical officer. Life inside was harder for me
to get used to than for the others. I had a taste of general
duties – thirty days. My feet swelled up so much I
couldn't take my boots off. So I gave in. Now you
wouldn't get me out of my hospital for all the gold in
Christendom. You see, Lyuba, in these camps hospital is
the key – the key to everything! I can fix you up in my
hospital as a food orderly.

LYUBA: I'm fixed up already.

MERESHCHUN: You're a runner, aren't you? Big deal! I

could fix you up so that you wouldn't need to leave camp until the end of your term. I'm not much of a talker, but I've really put down roots in this place. They're more likely to post the commandant than they are to post me. You think I want you just for one night? No, Lyuba, I don't. We'll live together properly – man and wife. (LYUBA *says nothing.*) I've just received a food parcel. (*He takes her hands in his.*) How many years has it been since you ate a cake, a real cake with chocolate icing? And real sausage! And American corned beef! It's like a dream, isn't it?

LYUBA (*taking her hands away from his*): I'm very happy for you, doctor. But eat it with someone else, not with me.

MERESHCHUN: Lyuba, I'd rather eat it with you. (*He embraces her.*)

LYUBA (*in a faint voice*): You see, doctor, you're irresistible. You can have any woman in the camp. I'm not the only woman in the world. It's so hard for me, listening to what you say . . .

She extricates herself from his arms and sits there gloomily. A single musician is producing sad sounds on a wind instrument. The painted curtain falls.

During the interval sentries are changed on the towers as before. The guards to be mounted march across the front of the stalls, moving on any members of the audience who happen to be there.

ACT IV

Scene I

The Bronze is Flowing

The foundry. The bronze furnace has been rebuilt. Occasionally a small flame can be seen in it through a chink. MUNITSA *and* YAKHIMCHUK *are standing next to the furnace.* MUNITSA *is fussing around. He keeps peering inside the furnace through the window.* YAKHIMCHUK *is reserved. There are a few prepared moulds standing next to the furnace.* NEMOV *is mixing the moulding earth with a spade. The door of the dryer is wide open.* CHEGENYOV *is sorting out some rubbish on the roof of the dryer.*

MUNITSA: She melt! The bastard, she melt! (*He dances up and down.*) Fifteen minutes more and bronze come, first-class bronze!

CHEGENYOV: Bronze'll come all right, now grandad's shown you how to do it.

MUNITSA: He don't know so much. (*Indicating* YAKHIMCHUK.) I build better than what he build. I know burner gotta be small.

YAKHIMCHUK: Then why are you such a fool, why couldn't you work it out for yourself? Why did your bronze burn away till nothing was left?

CHEGENYOV (*sorting out the rubbish*): Fittings, tubings, mouldings – look at it! God knows what we'd do if we didn't have holidays to sort it out. Well, I've had enough, I don't care if we need it or not, it's all going into the furnace. Then we'll have a bit of order.

Enter LYUBA *from the left wearing a buttoned-up quilt jacket. The door behind her slams noisily.*

LYUBA: Is Kuznetsov here? (*The foundry workers are busy*

351

and do not answer. LYUBA *makes a sign to* NEMOV *and walks slowly towards the dryer.* NEMOV *follows her. They stand in the doorway of the dryer, which gapes darkly, as wide as a cave. They talk quietly.*)

NEMOV: What is it?

LYUBA (*very upset*): Darling! (*She embraces him.*) I came just in case to say . . . to say goodbye!

NEMOV: A transport? Is that it?

LYUBA: Yes.

NEMOV: Wait a minute, maybe we can . . . Maybe they won't . . .

LYUBA: You think that doctor will put up with things the way they are? It had to be one of us – either you or me. (*Pause.*) Have you been happy this week . . . our week together?

NEMOV (*stroking her face*): It was so good . . . I was so happy . . .

LYUBA: I'm so grateful to you too. I'll keep this last week as long as I live, hidden deep inside me.

NEMOV: Is there nothing we can do?

LYUBA (*excitedly*): There is something! We can stay! We can even love one another – secretly, very secretly. Only you must promise . . . you must agree . . . to share me. You must share me with the doctor. I'll bring you things to eat.

NEMOV: Could you do that?

LYUBA: Yes, I could! Couldn't you? My dear little brother, couldn't you accept it? Why should you have to leave? At least I'd be able to see you from a distance maybe, but . . .

NEMOV (*hugging her*): Lyuba, I could never share you, not the smallest piece of you, with anyone.

LYUBA (*she frees herself from him and speaks very sadly*): Well, you must give me up, then. You'll lose all of me, all of me. (*She walks slowly back towards the main exit. The door slams and in runs* DIMKA, *in a happy mood.*)

DIMKA: Hurray! It's up in the main building. They've

turned the star on! Hurray! (*He runs round in a full circle, almost knocking* LYUBA *off her feet and then runs out. The door slams.* NEMOV *does not move.* LYUBA *opens the door and walks out. The door slams.*)

CHEGENYOV (*squatting on top of the dryer, he looks out through the top window in the direction indicated by* DIMKA. *From the top of the dryer he addresses the company in the manner of a public speaker*): Comrades, your attention! Today's anniversary will be celebrated in our camp with particular solemnity. Items on the agenda. Number one – the superb work and valiant exploits of Munitsa. Number two – the despatch of forty or fifty trouble-makers to the forests to chop down trees.

YAKHIMCHUK: You watch it with your forecasts. They'll come true.

CHEGENYOV: Number three – Old Igor has been transferred to the morgue after being stuck with a bayonet to make sure he was dead. Number four – there will be a general search in all barrack-rooms, mattresses turned over and floors taken up. Number five – there will be a personal search at the check-point. Underpants will be removed. Number six – there will be a Stakhanovite rally of the best "drudge" prisoners. Each Stakhanovite will be issued with one millet pasty, which means the rest of the camp have to take a cut in flour and millet next week. Number seven – there will be a free film-show, *Stalin in 1905*. Everyone will fight to get in and will end up sitting on everyone else, to make sure we don't feel we're at home. (*He jumps astride some suitable object.*) Mount your horses! Sabres at the ready! Charge! (*He makes a mock cavalry charge, waving an imaginary sabre. His elbows are sticking out of the holes in his sleeves.*)

YAKHIMCHUK: You bum, you'll get yourself into the glass-house.

CHEGENYOV: Stuff that, grandpa. Do you think I care about the damn foundry? If they'd given me *five* years,

all right, I wouldn't have minded slaving a bit. But
fifteen! Can you imagine – fifteen! I'll take the rest of my
term in travel rations from the Big Boss himself.

MUNITSA: What do you mean, travel rations?

CHEGENYOV (*indicating the end of his finger*): Nine
grammes. (*Pause.*) Lead injection. (*He points the finger at
his head, then lets his head droop as if he was dead.*)
Enter KAPLYUZHNIKOV, *a neatly dressed, portly fellow
wearing a fine fur coat, together with* GURVICH *and*
BRYLOV. *The wind, noisier than before, slams the door
behind them, They do not notice* CHEGENYOV, *who quietly
takes up a position as if he was working. He does some more
tidying up on the dryer and then jumps down.* NEMOV
*carries on with his spade, shovelling the moulding
earth.*

BRYLOV: You see, comrade chief engineer, Brylov always
keeps his word. I said you'd have bronze, and you have
bronze. I understand the situation. Your excavators are
at a standstill. So I have used my initiative.

GURVICH: Who's used his initiative? We'll soon see about
that. You've put so many spanners in my works . . .

BRYLOV: Comrade Gurvich, how could you say such a
thing? Strike a good horse with one hand, yes, but you
should wipe away its tears with the other. All you do is
hand orders while I rack my brains over your furnace.
Ask the boys, if you don't believe me.

MUNITSA (*roars with laughter and slaps his thigh*): Five
minutes more, then bronze come. I know about working
in foundry.

YAKHIMCHUK (*leaning aginst his slag-scrabber as if it was a
long sword*): Much better show the boss your trousers,
Munitsa. (MUNITSA *shows* GURVICH *his trousers. They are
in tatters.*)

KAPLYUZHNIKOV (*to* GURVICH): Why don't you issue
them with overalls? Seriously.

GURVICH: You must know why, comrade. Head Office
don't have funds.

KAPLYUZHNIKOV: No funds? Write to camp centre, then.
Maybe they'll find something.

YAKHIMCHUK: Why should they? And there's another
thing – ours is a high-temperature workshop. We're
workers like anyone else. Why don't they give us a milk
ration? Workers outside get it.

KAPLYUZHNIKOV (*quite astounded*): Milk? You want milk?
Whatever next? Tea and biscuits in bed, I suppose!
(*Reaction.*) You see, comrades – I mean citizens, not
comrades – you see, citizens, if we did that where would
it stop? I don't know . . . the milk situation's a bit
difficult at the moment. Do you see?

YAKHIMCHUK: Of course, citizen commander, we see. One
step to the right or left and the escort guard will open
fire.

KAPLYUZHNIKOV (*pretending he hasn't quite
heard*): Gurvich, when will the beams be ready? And the
plates?

GURVICH (*to* BRYLOV): What's happened to the cast-iron?
Why hasn't any been moulded?

BRYLOV: Yakhimchuk, what about this cast-iron? Has it
been hoisted?

YAKHIMCHUK: It's no problem hoisting it. That's just two
days' work. But who's going to mould it?

BRYLOV (*to* GURVICH): Chegenyov has been moulding the
simpler stuff. Munitsa's been busy with the bronze. He
hasn't got two pairs of hands.

GURVICH (*to* KAPLYUZHNIKOV): The iron's been held up
by the bronze.

KAPLYUZHNIKOV: Come, comrades, this won't do at all.
Our production line must deliver *all* the goods, the
bronze *and* the iron. If you succeed with the bronze, we
give you a pat on the back. But if you fail with the iron,
we put you on a charge. Any complaints?

GURVICH (*to* BRYLOV): We must have the iron in three
days, and that's that. What's the bronze got to do with
it? If Munitsa doesn't have enough time, all right, he can

do his mouldings in the evenings or on holidays. I'll see
he gets a special escort guard.

BRYLOV: Well, Munitsa, that's the score. You've got two
days. You'll spend your holiday here and do the
moulding. (*To* YAKHIMCHUK.) As for you, why aren't
you hoisting the iron? You're spoilt, that's what's wrong.

YAKHIMCHUK: Dimka! . . . Where is that devil of a boy?
(DIMKA *appears*.) You and Nemov go and deal with the
iron. Pull it up in the bucket. I'll do the bronze and join
you later. (*To* GURVICH.) You ought to have a
protective fence put there. (NEMOV *and* DIMKA *go out of
the back door*.)

GURVICH (*to* BRYLOV): Your foundrymen are a bit work-
shy these days. What's wrong? Rates too high? We can
easily lower them.

BRYLOV: Don't you touch the rates.

GURVICH: Why not? Because you live off them too, is that
it?

KAPLYUZHNIKOV: Of course we'll revise the rates. Making
bronze – that's a wonderful Revolution Day present. I'll
send a telegram to headquarters. (*Takes* GURVICH *to the
front of the stage.* BRYLOV *creeps up beside them, trying to
overhear what they are saying and to interrupt. From time to
time one can hear, from the room above, the sound of pieces
of iron being thrown on the sheet-iron ceiling of the
workshop*.) We must get the furnace documented, apply
for a patent. It's an invention! Yours and mine!
(GURVICH *tries to draw* KAPLYUZHNIKOV *away from*
BRYLOV, *but* BRYLOV *keeps following them*.) We'll have
to accept Brylov as co-owner.

GURVICH: But he didn't do a thing. He just got in the way.

KAPLYUZHNIKOV: You don't understand, he's got
connections in personnel. He'll denounce us all, he'll
make a real nuisance of himself. There's good money
here. I've had a word with the trade-union committee.
We'll arrange a bonus system – a few thousand roubles
each. Free holidays as well maybe. (*He nods to* BRYLOV

*to join them. The three heads are put together in a whispering
huddle. Meanwhile* YAKHIMCHUK *and* CHEGENYOV
*carry a bucket over to the furnace and fix it on a two-
pronged support.* MUNITSA *is fussing around the furnace,
peering in its window.*)

MUNITSA: Yes! One second! One second and she come!
BRYLOV *walks away from the two engineers and towards
the furnace.*

GURVICH: Yes, sir, I know it's against safety rules, I've got
common sense the same as the next man. But how can
we build a fence if the office won't let us have any
planks? They've already used more construction
materials than they're allowed.

KAPLYUZHNIKOV: You must find some, then. You must
find some.

GURVICH: You know the way I work: a hundred telephone
calls a day, instructors and inspectors calling on me three
times a week, every other day committee meetings at
Head Office. I'm supposed to prepare documents and
reports for them, and at the same time someone has to
take care of our production. The foremen are all drunk,
the rate-fixing office is full of prisoners I can't trust, I
have to check all the rates. The volume of work's always
being increased, and every minute I hear some job's been
bungled somewhere, or pipes laid in the wrong place,
which means that ditches have to be dug open. I'm
worse off than a prisoner. I come home in the evening, I
don't even want to look at my wife . . .

KAPLYUZHNIKOV: What can we do? I have five hundred
documents a week I'm supposed to sign. It's not easy for
me either. (*He leaves towards the right. Through the left-
hand door walks* KOSTYA *the work allocator, carrying a list
in his hand. He is followed by a group of prisoners already
dressed in winter clothes – quilted jackets and ear-flap hats.
The wind slams the door repeatedly, making banging sounds
like shots. There is anxious murmuring among those who
have just come in.*)

VOICE: Who's going? Who else has been posted?

VOICE: Kostya, where are they taking us?

KOSTYA: The Crimean riviera, of course!

VOICE: Am I in it or aren't I?

KOSTYA: Stop yelling, or someone will get it in the neck. Haven't any of you been on a transport before? There's a hell of a gale outside, I couldn't hold my list properly. (*To* CHEGENYOV, *who has just approached him.*) Where's Nemov?

CHEGENYOV: Is he posted?

KOSTYA: He was on the list, but the hospital crossed him out. Just a minute ago. (*He leaves, followed by a crowd of prisoners.*)

VOICE: If it's red wagons, they cut off all our buttons.

VOICE: If it's old goods wagons, they'll smash our suitcases.

VOICE: I hear they're taking us to Vorkuta.

VOICE: It's a lousy life, being a prisoner.

More threatening pistol-shots sound as the door slams.

GURVICH *and* KAPLYUZHNIKOV *return from the right.*

BRYLOV (*by the furnace*): All right, Munitsa, it's ready! Let it out!

MUNITSA: Right now! (*He strikes a hole. A stream of bronze pours down the shute into the bucket.*)

YAKHIMCHUK *and* BRYLOV (*together*): That's enough! Stop! Watch the slag! That's enough!

KAPLYUZHNIKOV: No, it's not enough! We want more!

YAKHIMCHUK (*in a commanding voice*): Close the hole! (MUNITSA *closes it.*)

GURVICH (*in a pleading voice, to* YAKHIMCHUK): Can't we get any more?

YAKHIMCHUK: No, we can't. The slag might spoil the bushes. Quality rather than quantity.

MUNITSA *cleans the surface of the bronze.* CHEGENYOV *and* YAKHIMCHUK *carry the bucket away and pour the metal into the moulds*

BRYLOV: Excellent! Well done! We'll soon have the excavators going!

MUNITSA (*standing by a mould he has just filled with metal*): So what I tell you? What Munitsa tell you? We have bronze!

YAKHIMCHUK: Wait till we get it on the lathe. We'll see what sort of bronze it is.

BRYLOV: Don't spoil our holiday. It's a victory for the whole foundry.

KAPLYUZHNIKOV: Well done! Well done! I'll go and send a telegram to Head Office. (*He leaves.*)

MUNITSA (*to* BRYLOV): So, we get bonus, yes?

BRYLOV (*sighs*): I don't really know, Munitsa. What's the bonus for? If it was a new type of furnace, maybe we would, but we didn't invent it. It looks better than it is, but only to those who don't understand. If you weren't a prisoner, well, maybe you could put a bit of pressure on, refer it to the trade unions, to the central committee . . .

GURVICH: O.K., Munitsa, O.K., let's see the bushes. Take off the moulds.

MUNITSA: No can do. They not set yet. They have to harden.
From the back room up above DIMKA *is heard to utter a loud yell. For the last time we hear a lump of iron falling on the ceiling.*

CHEGENYOV *rushes through the back door followed by* YAKHIMCHUK.

GURVICH: What's happened? (*He hurries after them, but bumps into* DIMKA *by the door.*)

DIMKA (*shouts*): A lump of iron fell on his head! (*Pause while they look at him.*) Nemov! Nemov's been killed! (*He rushes out, slamming the door with a noise like a pistol-shot.* CHEGENYOV *and* YAKHIMCHUK *carry* NEMOV *in, his head covered with blood. He is unconscious.* GURVICH *follows them, head bowed.*)

BRYLOV: What's the matter? How did it happen?

YAKHIMCHUK: You're no foundryman, you don't know your arse from your elbow. That's what's the matter! I

359

told you, didn't I? I said it was dangerous hoisting iron up in a bucket.

They carry NEMOV *out. The wind makes it difficult for them to open the door.*

MUNITSA (*running to catch up with* GURVICH): Sir! What about bonus? I get bonus? Yes?

GURVICH: Just look after the moulds. Take care of the iron.

The painted curtain falls.

Before the next scene begins the lanterns on top of the barbed wire round the orchestra pit are switched on. They stay alight until the end of the performance.

Scene 2

The Transport

The set as in Act I, Scene 1. The wind is whining, stirring up the powdery snow. It is dark. The inmates of the camp are crowding the work area behind the barbed wire. They stand motionless, staring towards the living area in the direction of the audience. About thirty other prisoners whose files have already been examined are sitting in the middle of the yard, right on the ground, their belongings with them, huddled together. A searchlight beam comes to rest on a newly hung placard with the slogan: "People are the most valuable capital – J. Stalin".
KOLODEY *is in charge of despatching the transport. He is assisted by the wardress, who has a mane of hair under her winter hat, the doctor's assistant* AGA-MIRZA, KOSTYA *and* POSOSHKOV. *The window of* MERESHCHUN's *cabin is lit up. He is standing at the steps, a white overcoat over his warm clothes.*

The high-sided lorry, the same one as in Act I, Scene 1, backs on to the stage from the right.
KOLODEY: All right, those who have been examined, single file, quick march!

The prisoners quickly begin to climb into the back of the lorry, pushing each other aside.

ESCORT-GUARD SERGEANT (*he is standing right in the back of the lorry behind a protective grill, armed with a sub-machine gun*): Sit down! Hurry up and sit down! On the floor, not on your bags! Don't turn round! Face the rear! No talking!

KOLODEY (*to* KOSTYA): Who's missing?

KOSTYA: Here are the last three. Hurry up, slowcoaches!

GONTOIR, GRANYA *and* SHUROCHKA *emerge from behind the hut on the left.*

ESCORT-GUARD SERGEANT: Gop . . . Gop . . .

GONTOIR: Gontoir, Camille Leopoldovich, born 1890, Article 58, paragraph one A stroke nineteen. Ten years.

ESCORT-GUARD SEGEANT: Take your hat off then! (GONTOIR *bares his silvery head. The sergeant compares him with the photograph on the cover of his file.*) You don't look much like your picture . . . All right, on you go. (GONTOIR *clambers into the lorry.*) Soykina!

SHUROCHKA (*fussing over her belongings*): Soykina, Alexandra Pavlovna, Article 58, paragraph twelve. Ten years. (*She is almost crying. Her things are too heavy for her. There is no one to help her. Finally* KOSTYA *heaves her luggage into the back of the lorry.*)

ESCORT-GUARD SERGEANT: Zybina!

GRANYA (*her voice clear and angry*): Agrafena Mikhailovna, born 1920, Article 136. Ten years.

GAI (*shouting from the work area*): Goodbye, Granya!

GRANYA (*shouts*): Goodbye, Pavel!

GAI: Write to me!

GRANYA: It's too late!

GAI: Don't give in, Granya!

GRANYA: I won't!

KOLODEY (*stepping in front of her*): Stop that! (*Taunting her.*) Don't want to leave your lover behind, is that what's the matter?

GRANYA (*shouting over his head*): Watch out for Khomich. He's a squealer! I'm sure he is!

WARDRESS: Shut your face, little bitch. You'll get a rifle butt in the teeth!

GRANYA *and* SHUROCHKA *disappear behind the side of the lorry.*

KOLODEY: Is that all?

KOSTYA: That's all.

KOLODEY: Let's have the list. (*He takes it from* KOSTYA. *To the* ESCORT-GUARD SERGEANT.) Now read out the name.

ESCORT-GUARD SERGEANT (*he has one file left in his hands*): Yevdokimov!

KOSTYA: Me? I've been posted?

ESCORT-GUARD SERGEANT (*shouts*): Alias . . .

KOLODEY: That's right, you've been posted. Hurry up, the escort's waiting.

ESCORT-GUARD SERGEANT: Alias . . .

KOSTYA (*stepping back*): Fuck you all! I won't let you take me.

POSOSHKOV (*stepping towards him*): Come on, Kostya, if you have to you have to.

KOSTYA: Go away, you cheap bastard! Traitor! Shit! Fuck off while you're still alive! (*He runs to one side, jumps up on the rubbish box, suddenly draws a knife and bares his stomach.*) Don't come any closer! You come a step nearer, I'll rip myself up the belly!

POSOSHKOV, AGA-MIRZA *and the wardress move towards him.*

KOSTYA: Get back! I'll carve myself up! You'll have to lug me to hospital with my guts hanging out. I'm not going!

POSOSHKOV: Kostya, please! We're your friends. It's an order – what can we do?

KOSTYA (*waving his knife*): You bloody son of a bitch, stinking shit-chewer, get back! So help me I'll cut your throat, then do myself in!

KOLODEY: Go on, grab him!

The attackers are undecided.

AGA-MIRZA: Kostya, you're making it worse for yourself.
They'll send you to a punishment camp.

KOSTYA: You lousy squealer, son of a bitch! I'm not
coming. I'll rip myself up the belly!

MERESHCHUN *creeps up to* KOSTYA *from behind and
strikes him a low blow under the knees.* KOSTYA *falls, they
throw themselves upon him, push him to the ground, take
away his knife and grip him by the throat.*

KOSTYA (*lying on the ground*): So you're with them too,
doctor? You bum! We'll meet again and then I'll fix you!

MERESHCHUN: What do you expect? Bloody fool! If you
rip your guts out, I'm the one who has to sew them
back.

KOLODEY (*to* POSOSHKOV): Get some rope.

POSOSHKOV (*takes some out of his pocket*): Here, I've got
some, sir. Nice bit of rope, specially for the occasion,
citizen commander. (*They bind* KOSTYA *hand and foot.*)

KOLODEY (*to someone*): Get his things out of the stores.

POSOSHKOV: Angel! Get his things! They're all packed and
ready, sir. (ANGEL *brings in* KOSTYA's *belongings and
heaves them into the back of the lorry. They push* KOSTYA
in as well, bound as he is.)

KOSTYA: Undo that bag! They're not all here! There's some
missing! The bastards have stolen some of my things!
My calf-skin boots! Scavengers! My leather overcoat!

KOLODEY: There's no time, the escort's waiting.

The back flap of the lorry is slammed shut.

ESCORT-GUARD SERGEANT (*in the back of the lorry*): All
prisoners pay attention! Any prisoner who rises to his
feet will be deemed to have attempted escape, in which
case I shall open fire without warning.

A second machine-gunner climbs in, the lorry starts off.

KOSTYA (*he is invisible inside the lorry, but his shouts can be
heard*): We'll meet again! I'll fix you all! You bastards,
you're not through with the camps yet! I'll fix you!

363

AGA-MIRZA: All right, you'll fix us. We're terrified. (*The lorry departs.*)

KOLODEY (*to* POSOSHKOV): Did you take his boots?

POSOSHKOV: I've got half a suitcase full, citizen commander. There's enough for you too. It's all other people's anyway. He even pinched his officer's uniform.

KOLODEY: You're quite a boy, doctor, aren't you?

MERESHCHUN: Cheap crook! Expecting me to sew up his belly! As if I've nothing better to do. (*Walks on into his hut.*)

KOLODEY (*to the* WARDRESS *and* POSOSHKOV): Now let's frisk the prisoners. Do it properly and take your time. Watch out particularly for knives, files, vodka, letters, photos, papers with notes, any money over one hundred roubles, ink pencils . . . (*Shouts over to the check-point.*) Let them in, ten at a time!

All four of them move to the back of the stage. ANGEL *runs up to the post and strikes the metal rail rhythmically a few times. Two check-point guards come out of their hut and stand on both sides of the parade, lanterns raised to light it. The first two files of five prisoners march in formation through the wide, opening gates.*

KOLODEY (*shouts*): Untie all boots and shoes! Loosen belts!

The prisoners carry out his order. The search begins. The wind is whining. ANGEL *walks over to the left in front of the barrack hut.* LYUBA *enters from the left, her head and body wrapped in a warm scarf. She walks past* ANGEL, *head bowed, looking at the ground.*

ANGEL (*calling her back*): Lyuba! You've been to the hospital? How is he? Nemov?

LYUBA: He's alive.

ANGEL: Hard nut to crack, isn't he? They won't crack that man's nut.

He leaves. In the background the prisoners are being searched. The lanterns in the guards' hands are flickering. The fine snow is whirling. For a moment LYUBA *does not move, then head bowed, she walks up the steps to*

MERESHCHUN's *cabin and knocks at the door. The door
opens to let her in. One can see her shadow in the window as
she takes off her scarf. The painted curtain falls.
It remains dark in the auditorium. The only light comes from
the lanterns on the barbed wire round the orchestra pit. The
sentries on the watch-towers do not move. The loudspeaker
plays a tune.
The overhead lights in the auditorium are not switched on. The
ordinary curtain is not lowered.*

DUE DATE

Printed
in USA